Men's Garments 1830-1900

A Guide to Pattern Cutting and Tailoring

Costumes Parisiens.

Journal Des Dames et des Modes
1836

PLATE 1. 1836. (Left) Typical Tail Coat of the period with flap pockets on the waist seam and the "M" design where the collar meets the revers. The vest fabric has a sloping stripe and the cream trousers are narrow fitting at the thigh, knee and bottom. (Center) Double-breasted Frock Coat with wide collar and revers. The cream patterned Vest can be seen above the opening of the coat. The short coat shows to advantage the slim trousers in a plaid (check) fabric. (Right) From Top hat to narrow trousers, the youth is dressed in similar attire to the adults. The exceptions are that his coat is without tails and for neckwear he has a "stock" (stiffened neck band) with a frilled fabric at the top edge.

R. I. Davis

Men's Garments 1830-1900
A Guide to Pattern Cutting and Tailoring
Revised, Second Edition

PLAYERS PRESS, Inc.
P.O. Box 1132
Studio City, CA 91614-0132

MEN'S GARMENTS 1830-1900

ISBN 0-88734-648-0
Library of Congress Catalog Number: 94-22441

Acknowledgement:
I am indebted to William-Alan Landes for his research and selection of
photographs and illustrations.

Typeset and Layout for Revised materials by Sharon Gorrell.

PLAYERS PRESS, Inc.
P.O. Box 1132
Studio City CA 91614-0132

Library of Congress Cataloging-in-Publication Data

Davis, R. I. (Ronald I.)
        Men's garments, 1830-1900 : a guide to pattern cutting / R. I.
Davis.
                    p.   cm.
        Includes bibliographical references and index.
        ISBN 0-88734-648-0
        1.   Tailoring--Pattern design.   2.   Costume--History--19th
century.   I.   Title.
        TT590.D38   1994
        646.4'072--dc20   94-22441
                                                            CIP

Simultaneously Published
U.S.A., Canada, U.K., Australia

Printed in the U.S.A.

Dedication:

    To the memory of my dear wife.

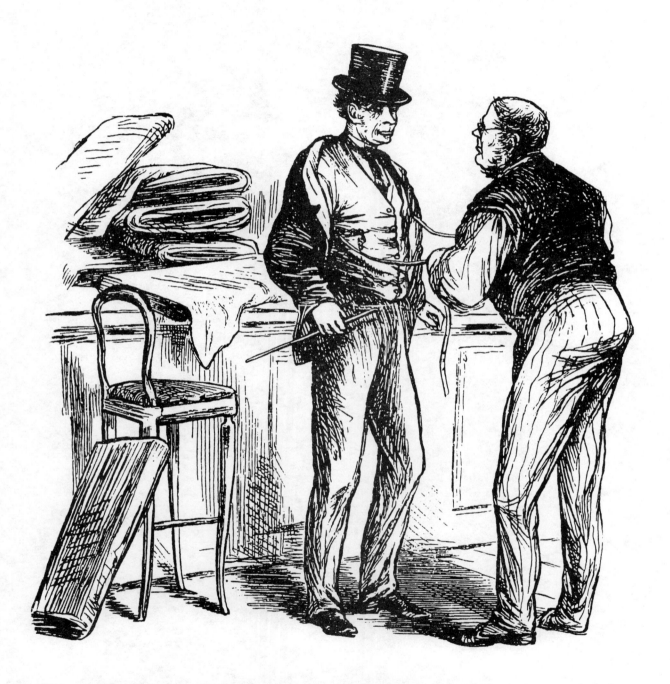

PLATE 2. c.1870's. *The customer is wearing a short Jacket which he has pushed off the shoulders to enable the Tailor to take the measurements over the Single-breasted Vest. This illustration features the tape measure, which was an invention of the 19th century (exact date not known). By the second half of the century it was in common use in the tailoring Industry. The customer's trousers are narrow all through the legs whereas the Tailor's trousers are only narrow from the knee to the bottom.*

CONTENTS

PLATE 3. 1890's. Dressed in the height of fashion this very large man wears the Frock coat with part silk facings. A patterned Vest with two bottom pockets for the watch chain to spread across his ample girth. Seen here, the tailor is measuring over the coat but in practice this measurement would be taken over the Vest. The trouser bottoms have been turned up and display the fashionable spats.

PREFACE

TAILORING NOTES - 1830 to 1900

Tailoring is regarded as one of the oldest among the various crafts. Throughout the centuries the tailor has applied his skills to making garments for both men and women.

Often poorly paid, the tailor could work at this craft in two different ways; either by working in an establishment for a master tailor or becoming a travelling craftsman known as a Journeyman tailor. As a journeyman he would visit various towns and villages throughout the country attending to his clients there and after a short period he would then move on. When one considers the workmanship involved in the padded doublets of the 16th and 17th centuries and the elaborate braiding of the 18th century coat, it becomes apparent that the standard of craftsmanship was very high.

To appreciate the high quality of the tailor's skill, the approach to this period's elegance, and to develop a feeling for the overall style and changes that took place, we have prepared a brief Gallery. Reviewing this Costume Gallery before working with the particular garments will give you a better feeling for the visual details for each garment.

The tailoring techniques that developed during the 19th century were brought about by several important factors. During the previous century there had been an increased demand for woollen cloth and consequently an upsurge in the making of this material. Then, in the second half of the 18th century, there appeared the Tail Coat which was a style based on the English riding coat. This coat was made of wool cloth and became the fashionable garment for men in the leading countries of Europe and in America. Tailoring skills were now directed towards the production of clothes made from woollen material. From the tailor's point of view, wool cloth could be

PLATE 4. *1824. Printed for Sir Richard Phillips & Co. 12th edition from* The Book of English Trades and Library of the Useful Arts.

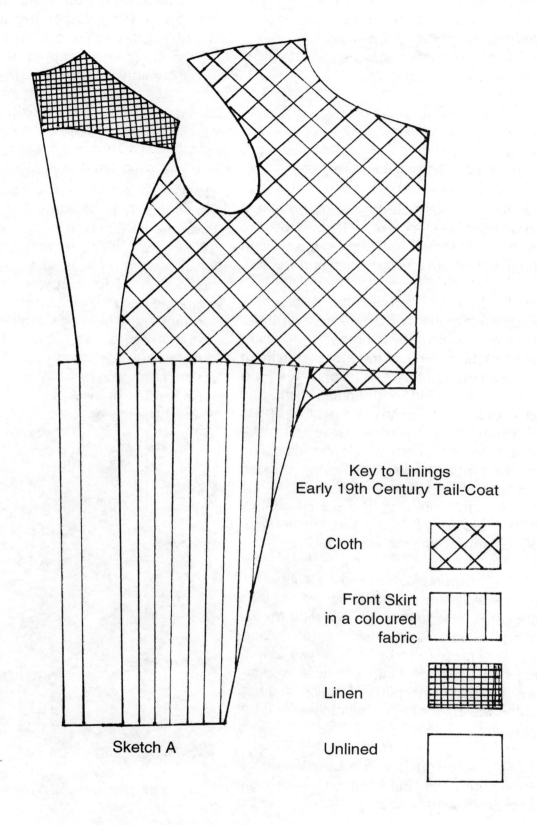

Key to Linings
Early 19th Century Tail-Coat

Cloth

Front Skirt
in a coloured
fabric

Linen

Unlined

Sketch A

manipulated by stitching and pressing to mould the fabric to the body shape. In addition, cutting techniques were improving and it was now possible to produce form-fitting and elegant garments.

The Tail Coat of the early 19th century was only partly lined. The front of the body was lined with the same cloth as the coat and the front skirts had a lining often in a different colour to the coat. The back and the back skirt were unlined except for a piece of linen across the back shoulders (Sketch A). The fronts and the collar had an interlining of canvas, and Dia. 1(g), page 19, shows the canvas stitched to the undercollar to give it firmness and flexibility. The sleeves were usually lined with a white cotton fabric. The use of padding was limited to the chest area with the shoulders remaining unpadded.

Another feature of the early Tail Coat was the use of unfinished or raw edges instead of sewing a seam to complete the edge. At that time the cloth was of a tightly woven texture with heavy milled finish which prevented the cut edge of the cloth from fraying or unraveling. To hold the edges of the collar together and the edges of the front to the facing, a row of stitching (sometimes two rows) was placed outside the coat and slightly away from the edge (Sketch B). The bottom edges of the tails (the hem) were cut to the exact length without any turn-in.

In the second half of the 19th century the making of men's garments began to follow a standard procedure. There was a wide range of different types of woolen fabrics which required seams in place of raw edges and turn-ins along the bottom edges. However Top-coats that were made from heavier fabric still had raw edges, a practice that continued after 1900.

Coats were now lined all through except for a narrow cloth facing at the front. Our present day coats are constructed in the same manner. A popular lining of the late 19th century was a heavy glazed cotton called 'Italian' and used for jackets and morning coats etc. For evening dress and frock coats a richer type of lining might be used such as a satin or silk serge. Sleeves continued to be lined with white or cream cotton.

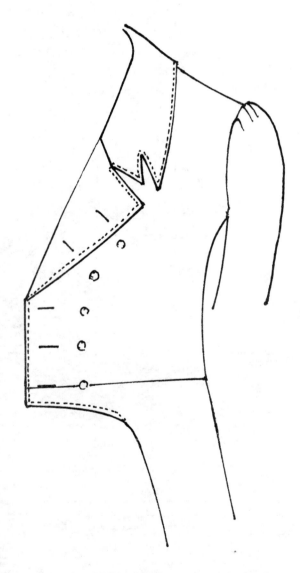

SKETCH B. *Early 19th Century Tail Coat with raw edges and narrow hand stitching.*

The canvas interlining that gave firm foundation to the coat fronts was given much more attention than it had previously warranted. In addition to the canvas through the fronts extra canvas was placed in the chest and front shoulder and these layers of canvas were stitched together with a herring bone stitch (Sketch C).

Padding was no longer placed in the chest but had now moved to the shoulder where it extended from the front of the armhole over the shoulder to the back. Toward the end of the century a strip of wadding was placed in the top of the sleeve which filled out the sleeve fullness and gave the sleevehead a smooth appearance.

The introduction of the sewing machine (1840's) took much of the tedium out of the tailoring procedure and also helped to speed up the process of making garments. The tailor's "tools of his trade" remained much the same as in previous centuries. These tools were comprised of cutting shears, scissors, pressing iron, needles of various sizes and a block or board for pressing seams and different parts of the garment. Not forgetting the essential tailor's thimble with it's open top, and a tape measure.

The tailoring methods developed during the second half of the 19th century became the basis for garment making by Bespoke and Custom tailors into the next century.

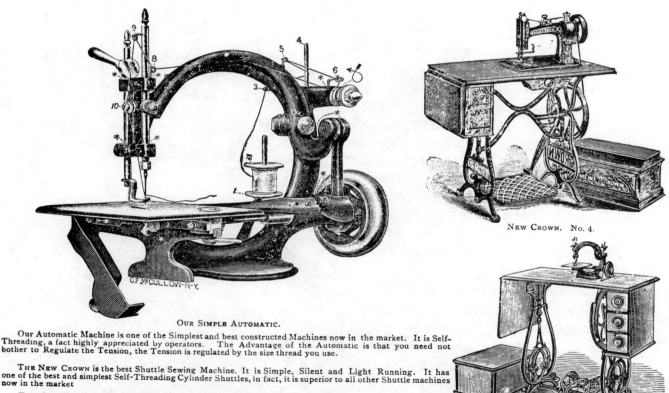

OUR SIMPLE AUTOMATIC.

NEW CROWN. NO. 4.

OUR OLD TENSION.

Our Automatic Machine is one of the Simplest and best constructed Machines now in the market. It is Self-Threading, a fact highly appreciated by operators. The Advantage of the Automatic is that you need not bother to Regulate the Tension, the Tension is regulated by the size thread you use.

THE NEW CROWN is the best Shuttle Sewing Machine. It is Simple, Silent and Light Running. It has one of the best and simplest Self-Threading Cylinder Shuttles, in fact, it is superior to all other Shuttle machines now in the market

THE OLD TENSION.—The demand for this class of machines has grown largely during the last 5 years. Its great elasticity of stitch has been proven by its adoption in Dress Making Establishments, Ladies Suits, Underwear, Collars, Cuffs, Lace Goods, and also by Manufacturers of Hosiery, Umbrellas and Parasols.

Please Call and Examine, or Send for Illustrated Catalogue to
KRUSE MANUFACTURING CO., 124 East 14th Street, N. Y.

PLATE 5.   1886.   An advertisement for sewing machines that appeared in several American catalogues.

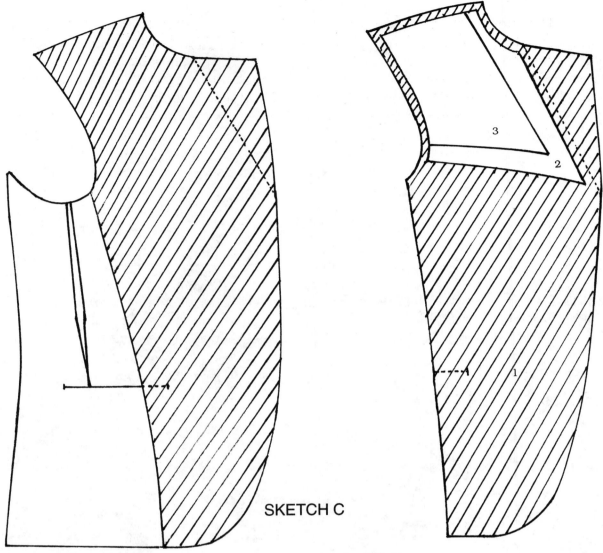

SKETCH C

Lounge Jacket — Late 19th Century
— Position of canvas interlining.

1. Interlining
2. Shoulder canvas
3. Extra layer of canvas or cloth

The three layers of fabric on the
shoulder are sewn together with
a herringbone stitch.

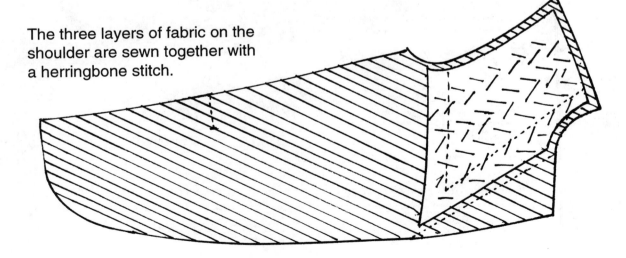

Be sure your tailor is a man of sense;
But add a little care, a decent pride,
And always err upon the sober side.

OLIVER WENDELL HOLMES
(1809–1894)

PLATE 6. *Late 19th Century. The young boys are sewing garments under the watchful eye of the tailor. A further inducement to attend to the work in hand is provided by the notice: "The eyes of the Lord are everywhere." The tailor wears the traditional Vest as also seen in PLATE 2.*

THE GALLERY

The style of men's garments, over any period, change gradually. It is only when we look back and compare one period in time to another that we see the differences in *period of style.*

Within any period there are variations upon the predominate or major style. These variations are because of individual craftsmen, individual taste, individual physical differences, and regional or economic needs. Some of these variations will, for one reason or another, become *popular* and become the primary variation or start the development of a new garment. In order to better understand the growth and relationship of various styles; the fact that some variations are earlier or later; and that a particular garment may have preceded the primary or famous garment of a period, we have included this Gallery and selected illustrations throughout the text to accompany the primary figures. The illustration selections used within the text are an extension of the Gallery and many times the notes will refer you back to the Gallery. The importance of these references is so that you can decide if a variation of the particular pattern might be more suitable for the need of a particular costume; either for time reference to signify slightly earlier or later, or for character, personality or style reference, to set apart a particular garment in a group or cast.

In addition, this particular selection of photos, plates, sketches and illustrations within the Gallery was chosen to visually give the reader an overall view of changes that took place in the years from 1830 to 1900. Again, it must be emphasized that the Gallery is but part of the entire collection herein and it should be used with the other illustrations and, most importantly, with the

G1. 1835. (L) Cloth Frock Coat with wide collar in silk or velvet. Holes in the revers (lapels) are put to practical use with flower displayed in the left rever. Vest is Double-breasted with wide collar and revers. Trousers are slim at the thighs and cut wider from the knee to the bottom. (R) Double-breasted Frock Coat has a full skirt cut back from the fronts. Note seam down centre of the front of the coat. Trousers are moderately narrow all though the legs. On both costumes the sleeves are tapered from elbow to a very small cuff, and trousers have a fly front fastening.

G2. 1860-65. High buttoning Single-breasted jacket, loose fitting. This style of garment is also referred to as a "Sack" or "Sac" jacket. Single-breasted Vest with long points. The narrow trousers are cut long to fall onto the shoe. The hat is of a distinctive shape and was called a "Bollinger."

primary figures.

In addition to this selection it is recommended that you build a library of pictures and illustrations to expand your primary sources. Consider early photographs, postcards, paintings, magazines, and reprints of the above. The larger your Gallery, or reference collection, the more precise you can be in individualizing a particular garment.

As a designer, if you intend to vary from a particular period for a production or design reason your *Gallery* will help you select the type of variations that will be within reasonable or, if the case may be, even unreasonable parameters.

Throughout this text the most accurate and accepted dates for each garment have been selected. Be careful when you collect other source material that you compare your dates; many dates are selected from photos or paintings, or news references which can be grossly inaccurate in relation to the dating of a particular garment. It is not unusual for a garment to be worn years after it was actually purchased and certainly not unheard of for an artist to take

a little license with his painted garment. Even newspapers have a tendency to run a photograph that may have been taken years earlier. In some garments, there may be differences in dates from one country to another; the closer we are to the mass media world the more accurate and less difference because of regionality.

As you work with this book, take the time to follow the notes and references and compare variations; you will find it most helpful in understanding each garment. Frequent reference to the *Gallery* so that you follow the general changes in style will also set the feeling of overall trends for you.

This *Gallery* was chosen also for the styles of illustrations, photos, etc. so that they reflect the particular period.

The illustrations within the Gallery have been numbered G1— G50. This will help to save time when referring back to an illustration. You will know which illustrations are within the Gallery (G) and which are within the text (Ill.).

William-Alan Landes

G3 1895. Front and back view, Single-breasted Morning Coat — three button fastening, welted outbreast pocket, narrow stitching on the coat edges. Single breasted Vest. Moderate width trousers, creases pressed into the centre of the leg, front and back. Homburg hat (L), Bowler hat (R). Montgomery Ward Catalogue.

G4. 1830. Short flared frock coat, trousers without straps and carrying a top hat.

G5. 1830. Rear view of the coat without cape, shaped at the waist and full skirted. The side-edges in back pleats are a feature of this type of coat. Front view, caped coat with wide silk revers (lapels). The points of the vest echo the shape of Tail-Coat at bottom edge. Close fitting Pantaloons terminate above ankles and are fastened at sides with buttons and holes.

G6. 1832. A Tail-Coat with small cuffs. The vest is single-breasted and has a shawl collar. The trousers legs are strapped at the bottom.

G7. 1830-40. Tail-Coat and waistcoat for day wear. Loose fitting trousers but narrow at the bottoms.

G8. 1831. (L) Single-breasted Top-Coat with velvet collar. (R) Tail Coat with deep velvet collar and flap pockets on the waist seam. Both figures are wearing trousers that are shaped at the bottom and secured under the shoe with a strap and buckle.

G9. 1835. Single-Breasted Frock coat with a turned down collar. The trousers are "straight" in design, i.e. the legs are of a similar width at the knee and the bottom.

G10. 1837. Tail coat with "M" shaped collar. Vest has shawl collar and is straight across at the bottom edge, with either 6 or 7 buttons at the front. Trousers, fairly close fitting at the thigh and knee, then becoming wider at the bottom.

G11. 1837. Two styles of cloaks, both are cut very full with the hem finishing between the knee and the calf. The trousers are narrow at the bottoms and strapped under the shoe.

G12. 1838. Tail Coat with wide collar and revers (lapels). The vest has a stand collar and the fronts are embroidered. Trousers are very narrow, similar to pantaloons except that these are longer. This outfit would be worn for Evening wear.

G13. 1839. Tail coat with narrow Double-breasted front fastening. The points of the vest are showing below the front of the coat and a second darker vest can be seem at the vest opening and at the edge. The fashion of wearing more than one vest was in vogue c1820 to c1840. The Trousers are strapped at the bottom. To complete the outfit there is a calf-length cloak with a silk collar.

Gl4. 1839. (L) Top Coat with large collar and deep cuffs. (R) Tail Coat, Double-breasted waistcoat with shawl collar, fly front trousers.

G15. 1839. Frock coat with a full skirt and worn with moderately loose trousers which are strapped at the bottom. This outfit, of a tweed material, would be for wearing during the day, usually in the morning.

G16 1840

G17 1842

G18 1840-50

G19 1844

G 20 1845

G21 1845-50

G16. 1840. Top Coat in Frock coat style with shoulder cape. Shawl collar of vest can be seen with second vest showing above. Close fitting trousers are strapped at bottom.

G17. 1842. Frock coat with narrow sleeves, worn over shawl collar vest, straight across at bottom edge. Trousers, narrow all through the legs, strapped at bottom.

G18. 1840-50. (L) Single-breasted coat with the front in line with cut-away skirt; an example of a Morning coat. Stripe of vest fabric is cut on the "cross" or bias to form interesting chevron design. Trousers show decoratively braided sideseams. (C) Single-breasted Frock coat; vest has low opening and long points. Trousers are braided at sideseam. (R) Informal Robe of patterned silk with tasseled cap; usually worn at breakfast time, later developed into the Dressing Gown.

G19. 1844. Doublebreasted knee-length Frock coat, decorative holes in revers. Vest has short stand collar, open to top button. A third pocket is at top on left side. Trousers, moderately loose at thigh and knee.

G20. 1845. Tail coat worn unfastened, usually had velvet collar. Note seam between holes and buttons. Vest has "step" at top and small points at bottom front. Trouser legs are fairly loose, strapped at bottom.

G21. 1845-50. (L) Short Frock coat, well shaped waist, full skirt. Vest can be seen. Trousers, for all three figures, moderately loose, slightly "flared" at bottom laying over shoe. (C) Tail coat with wide collar and revers. Long vest is well below coat. (R) Loose coat worn over double-breasted Tail coat, note seam down center front). Points of vest can be seen below front of Tail coat.

G22. 1850. (L) Frock coat with full skirt, wide revers and collar, worn for hunting or shooting. Vest can be seen above coat. Breeches, covered with knee-length gaiters, side-fastened with straps and buckles. Broad-brimmed hat with rounded crown is forerunner of Bowler hat. (C) Double-breasted top coat with wide collar and revers. Side pockets and top pocket (outbreast). Moderate width striped trousers, slightly flared at bottom, fit over shoes. (R) Frock coat undone, shows shawl collar vest with low opening and short points at bottom front. Trousers, similar to Center figure.

G23. 1850. Early form of single-breasted loose fitting jacket, with braided edges. Bottom pockets are "piped," without flaps, top pocket (outbreast) is a narrow "welt." Slim fitting Trousers, slightly wider at knee than bottom. Vest covered by jacket.

G24. 1853-56. Double-breasted Frock coat with four front buttons and four for show, used for outdoor wear. Note panel seam at front. Vest beneath coat can be seen above coat opening. Trousers, wider at knee than at bottom.

G25. 1854. (L) Short cape over Evening Tail coat. Shawl collar vest, fastened with five buttons. Narrow Trousers, knee and bottom width are similar. (R) Short semi-circular cape over loose coat. Narrow Trousers.

G26. 1855. Tail coat with wide collar and decorative holes in revers. Shawl collar vest fastens with five buttons and has small points at bottom front. Trousers are shaped over foot and fastened under shoe with strap and buckle.

G27. 1857. Tail coat with "M" shaped collar, reflecting 1830's style. Seam around sleeve above cuff is False or "formed." Five button Shawl collar vest has straight bottom edge. Long Trousers "break" in a fold onto the shoe.

G28. 1859-63. (L) Four button front Morning coat, only top button is fastened; moderate collar and revers, pockets with flaps at sides. Vest is straight across bottom edge, high at opening. Trousers are wide at knee and bottom with braid down sideseam. (C) Shapely Top coat over single-breasted Frock-coat. Vest is visible above opening of Frock coat. Trousers similar to figure on Left. (R) "Tweedside" jacket with narrow turned-down collar and wide braid at edges and cuffs. Low-crown hat was often worn with this style. Matching trousers in same style as (L) & (C). Vest, probably single-breasted.

G29. 1860's. Typical Frock coat of the 1860's. The sleeves have wide elbow and narrow cuff. Trousers are wide and falling in folds onto shoes. William H. Seward, Lincoln's Secretary of state, by Matthew Brady.

G30. 1862. Tail-coat with braided edges. Single-breasted vest with three buttons and second vest can be seen underneath. '60's sleeve is wide at elbow, narrow at cuff. The line is echoed in shape of trousers, wide at thigh and knee but narrow at bottom.

G31. 1863. Figures at extreme left and right are wearing double-breasted frock coats. Two central figures wear Tail coats with decorative buttonholes on revers. Trousers are generally narrow in legs with bottom width same as knee (L, seated) or slightly wider than knee (C and R, seated). Harper Brothers, publishers, James, John, Wesley and Fletcher. New York. Beards include mutton chops, Dundrearies and stucco. By Matthew Brady.

G32. 1864. Thigh-length Frock coat with moderate width collar and revers. Single-breasted vest has seven buttons with bottom two left undone. Trousers are slim with knee and bottom width the same.

G33
1870

G34
1870

G35
1871

G36 1871

G37
1877

G33. 1870. Dark blue Walking Suit. Double-breasted vest, drab trousers, and carrying a grey beaver top hat.

G34. 1870. Fashion plate with famous faces of the period. (L) Mr. Dickens wearing short double-breasted Frock coat, single-breasted vest with revers and light trousers. (R) Mr. Disraeli in single-breasted jacket, known as Oxonian, four buttons at front with top one fastened. Matching trousers with bottoms sloping down toward back. Vest is straight across at bottom edge.

G35. 1871. Single-breasted High Button Morning coat suit. Note outbreast pocket, and flap pockets on waist seam. Bottom edge of vest is level with waist seam of coat. Trousers are moderate width and straight across at bottoms. Bowler hat would be black although brown was worn with country outfits.

Gazette of Fashion. Re-drawn by William-Alan Landes.

G36. 1871. A mixture of styles within the period. (L, seated) expresses his individuality among the more sober Frock coats and Tail coats. He wears a jacket with braid on edges and sleeves, braid on side of trousers. Vests of all figures are single-breasted. Two central figures wear black dress vests with low openings. Six beard styles: full, saucer, Dundrearie, stucco, mutton chops, patrician. By Matthew Brady.

G37. 1877. Silk top hat, monocle and pointed moustache were hallmarks of fashionable wealthy men known as "Swells," Single-breasted Chesterfield is narrow at waist and flared at hem which ends just below knee. Straight style checkered trousers are part of the image.

G38. 1880-1890. Single-breasted, high-buttoning Morning coat with co-ordinated trousers.

G39. 1880-1890. Single-breasted Button 4 suit.

G40. 1880-1890. Single-breasted, three-piece suit. Jacket has two front buttons and long rolling revers. Vest has very high opening and is straight across at bottom edge. Trousers are on a "straight" style being same width at knee and bottom.

G41. 1880-1890. Single-breasted Morning coat, high-buttoning waistcoat and trousers. Coat, waistcoat and trousers were now mainly of the same fabric.

G42. 1880-1890. Single-breasted Top coat with a fly front and four outside flap pockets. Striped trousers have shaped bottoms that slope down toward the back.

G43. 1880-1890. Evening Dress Tail coat and trousers in the same material. White single-breasted dress vest. The figure carries a collapsible top hat called a "Gibus" after the designer.

G44. 1880-1890. Single-breasted fly-front Overcoat worn over a Double-breasted Frock coat. Conventional striped trousers similar to G42.

G45. 1886-1890. Single-breasted Jacket with outbreast welt on right side. Moderate width trousers which are cut long and fall in folds onto the shoe. Hats were an important part of the male attire and this hat is one of a variety of styles of that period.

G46 1891

G47
1895-1900

G48 1896

G49
1898

G50
1899

G46. 1891. Pullman Brothers, of the railroad sleeping car industry. The three figures in background wear high-button single-breasted jackets. Two figures in foreground have long rolling revers. Seated figure on left wears single-breasted vest with top button now much lower than previous decade. Right-hand seated figure has revers on his single-breasted vest. In general, trousers are narrow with knee and bottom being same width. The two standing figures are a fine testimony to the tailor's skill, note how well the jackets fit at the front of these men.

G47. 1895-1900. Single-breasted overcoat with a three-button front. Coat is very long and loose-fitting in waist. Figure wears short spats which can be seen below bottom of trousers.

G48. 1896. (L) Back view of loose "Sac" top coat, with velvet collar and wide stitching on seams. (C) Long Double-breasted Top coat in a Frock coat style, with flaps on side pockets and separate cuffs on sleeves. (R) Double-breasted loose Top coat with velvet collar. The four outside pockets have deep flaps. Figure wears a Trilby hat which was coming into fashion at this time.

G49. 1898. Single-breasted Overcoat with concealed front fastening (Fly front). Trousers have cuffs or turn-ups which came into fashion in the late 1890's. Figure wears a Bowler hat with curled brim.

G50. 1899. Norfolk Jacket with patch pockets and a hole and button for fastening on waist belt. Knicker Breeches. Soft country cap with the crown cut into segments, there is a button at the center. Re-drawn from original.

Men's Garments
1830 — 1900

R. I. Davis is the head
pattern-cutter for the
leading theatrical
costumiers, Angels of
Shaftsbury Avenue,
London. He has been
making costumes for
theatre, film and television
for over 40 years, and for
39 years has lectured at
the London College of
Fashion.

PLATE 7. 1899. "The Education of Mr. Pip", Charles Dana Gibson. In this illustration the difference in age between the two figures is further emphasised by their mode of dress. The young man on the right wears a fashionable Single-breasted jacket with a three button fastening. The jacket is quite short giving an appearance of length to the narrow trousers. The Bowler hat is appropriate with the lounge suit. His older companion is more formally dressed in a black Frock Coat, striped trousers (also narrow) and a light coloured Vest. The Top hat with the curved brim completes the outfit. Both figures have shirts with stiff collars.

INTRODUCTION

The nineteenth century was an age of exploration, of industrial and commercial expansion and of scientific discoveries. The Great Exhibition of 1851 gave further momentum to all this activity – with the emphasis on a 'scientific' approach to all human endeavour. The tailor's craft was at first unaffected by this upsurge in technology, although changes due to mechanization were occurring in other crafts. Even the invention of the sewing machine in the 1840s made very little difference to the traditional methods of producing men's garments. Where, however, large quantities of the same item (such as uniforms, ready-made clothing and shirts) were required, the sewing machine was exploited to the full and the design of machines for those particular sections of the clothing industry become an industry in itself.

To the craftsman making individual garments, the sewing machine was used only for 'long' seams such as the back and front sleeve seams or the trousers side seams. Every other part of the garment would be hand sewn.

The tailor took pride in his skill of moulding and manipulating the cloth to the desired effect, and using the iron to shrink and stretch into shape.

Although tailoring methods remained fairly constant, the approach to the cutting of men's garments was undergoing considerable change. It was realized in the early part of the century that in order to reach a higher standard of fit and style, new and more reliable methods of pattern construction were required. From 1820 there had been improvements in design such as the placing of a waist seam in the tail coat and later (in the 1830s) the forming of a sidebody as a separate panel. 'Systems' of pattern cutting continued to be published throughout the nineteenth century and many discussions on the subject were held by the Cutters' Societies that were established in different parts of the country.

It is greatly to the credit of those engaged in the trade that they were willing to devote so much time and enthusiasm to improving cutting techniques. Among the better-known writers of the period are W.D.F. Vincent and J.P. Thornton, who produced excellent works, with editions reprinted well into the twentieth century. Although the discussions on the best 'system' to use were never resolved, a great deal of work was done to establish the basic principles of pattern cutting, which have formed the stepping stones for cutters and pattern designers of our own times.

As such a wealth of literature on the cutting of men's garments of the nineteenth century is available, why is it not possible to refer to those books and produce the required garments? The answer is that the patterns produced at that time were designed with a view to the tailoring methods that existed then, and that they were based on the accepted idea of the average male figure of that period. Bearing this in mind, the patterns presented in this book have a three-fold purpose:

1. They should correspond to modern methods of making garments.

2. They are based on the present-day concept of the average male figure.

3. The finished result should have the characteristics of the period garment.

Whenever we draft a pattern for the individual we are using a 'system' of some kind. It must be realized that all 'systems' have their limitations and cannot take into consideration all the variations of the human figure. It is only by careful and patient use of the information available that one can obtain the desired result.

For those involved in the making of period costume, it is hoped that the methods presented in the following pages will assist and guide the reader in becoming proficient in this absorbing and satisfying subject.

Taking the measurements (figs. A, B, C)

It must be emphasized that the greatest care should be observed when taking the measurements of the body. After all, the basis of the pattern and the fit of the garment will initially depend on how accurately these measurements have been taken.

Ideally, one should measure over a waistcoat or shirt and not over a very loose or thick garment such as a woollen sweater, etc.

By placing a narrow tape or cord around the waist level and securing it in position, this gives a fixed point for taking various measurements, e.g. nape to waist, side waist to heel seam.

The measurements should always be taken in the same sequence and the following list is the generally accepted order:

1   Nape to back waist
2   Nape to jacket length
3   Nape to back of knee
4   Nape to ground
5   Half across back
6   Sleeve length
7   Chest girth
8   Waistcoat opening
9   Waistcoat front length
10 Trousers side seam
11 Inside leg
12 Waist girth
13 Seat girth

1 Nape to back waist

The 'nape' refers to the seventh cervical vertebrae, located at the back neck where the bone slightly protrudes. Do not measure from the shirt collar seam or similar, as this could be quite inaccurate. From the nape, measure to the waist-level tape, which should be 'settled' into the back waist hollow.

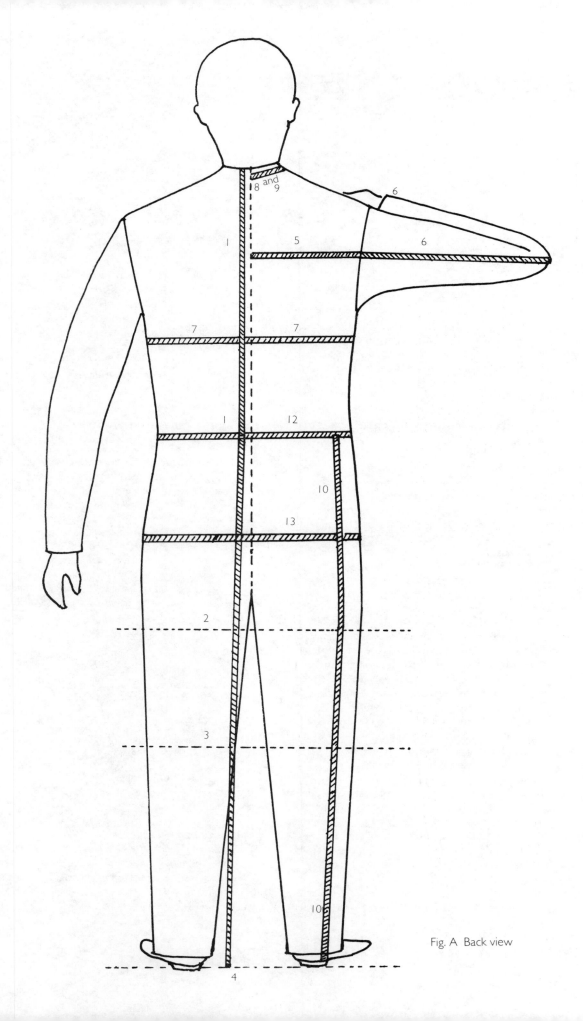

Fig. A Back view

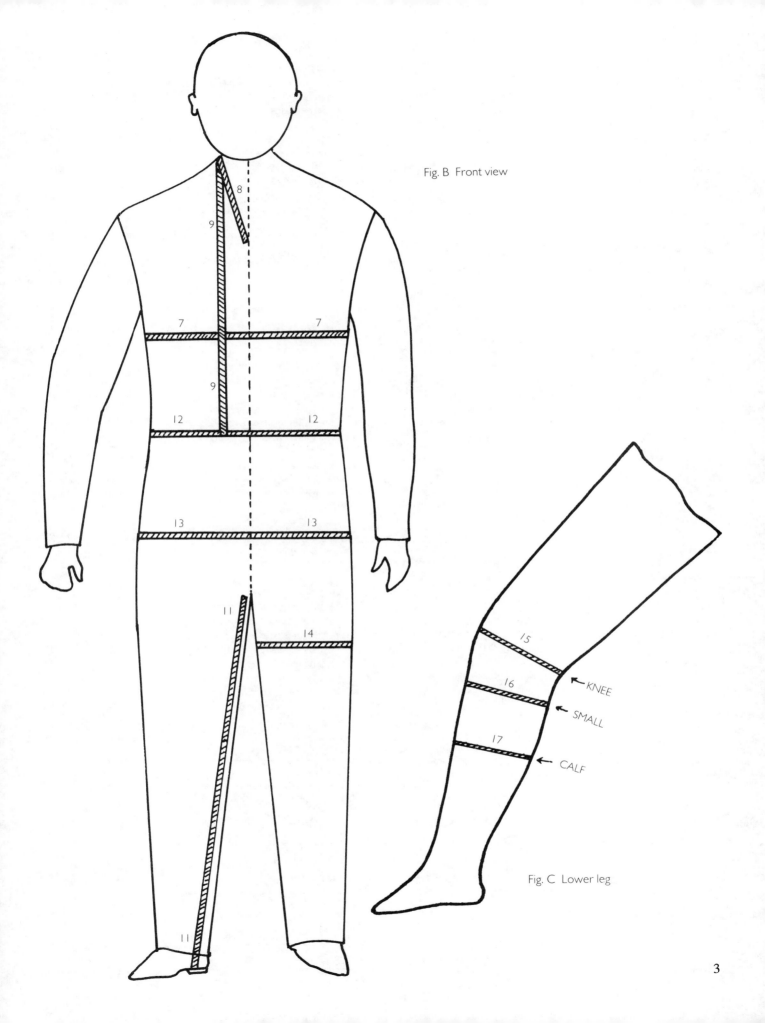

Fig. B Front view

Fig. C Lower leg

KNEE

SMALL

CALF

3

2 Nape to jacket length

This is difficult to assess, as it will depend on the style of jacket required. For an average length add 30.5cm (12in) to the 'nape' to back waist measurement (no. 1 above).

3 Nape to back of knee

A useful measurement for obtaining the length of tail coats. The tail coat length can be above or below the knee or at the knee position according to style and design.

4 Nape to ground

This measurement applies to overcoats and cloaks; the length of these garments is reckoned as being so many centimetres or inches 'from the ground' depending on the design requirements.

5 Half across back

From about 12.5cm (5in) down from the nape, measure from the spinal column to the side of the body.

6 Sleeve length

The right arm is raised to the level of the shoulder and bent forward from the elbow. Measure in the same way as 5 (half across back) by starting at the spinal column to the side of the body but continue to the elbow point and further along the arm to the wristbone. This is the tailor's method of measuring the sleeve, the advantage being that the sleeve length is being measured from a fixed point (centre of the back) which is an accurate way of taking the measurement.

7 Chest girth

Place the tape measure around the most prominent part of the chest and make sure that the tape is well up at the back and does not slip down under the shoulder blades. The tape should be fairly close to the body but not pulled too tight.

8 Waistcoat opening

Starting at the nape, the tape measure is brought round the neck to the centre front of the chest to a point approx. 11.5cm (4½in) below the front neck. This gives a fairly high opening but can be adjusted to design requirements.

9 Waistcoat front length

Start at the nape as in no. 8 above, but bring the tape measure round the neck and down the front to the waist level. To calculate the waistcoat length add to this measurement 6.5cm (2½in) for a dress waistcoat or 12.5cm (5in) for a lounge waistcoat.

10 Trousers side seam

Take the measure at the right side of the body, from the waist level to the heel seam of the shoe. Add to the side seam measurement 2.5cm (1in) (to increase the 'rise' for trousers worn with braces) *plus* 4cm (1½in) (the width of waistband), i.e. a total of 6.5cm (2½in).

11 Inside leg

To be taken from the crotch to the heel seam of the shoe. Keep the tape measure close to the leg.

12 Trouser waist

This measurement is to be taken *close* over the existing trousers at the waist level. For trousers worn with braces (as presented in this book) 2.5cm (1in) must be added to the waist measurement.

13 Seat girth

The tape measure is placed around the body over the most prominent part of the seat. In taking this measurement, the tape should be held close to the body but not tight.

For pantaloons and knickerbreeches, additional leg measurements are required:

14 Thigh girth

Approximately 5cm (2in) down from the crotch take the measurement quite close but not tight.

With the leg slightly bent, the following measurements are taken under the trouser and against the leg:

15 Knee

16 'Small' (the hollow below the knee)

17 Calf

It is essential to master the technique of taking measurements – and this can only be achieved by continual practice. It is suggested that those who are not yet experienced should at first keep the above list by them when taking measurements. Eventually, through constant repetition they will become familiar with the order of measuring.

Having taken the measurements, make a note of any physical features such as sloping or square shoulders, full chest, etc. The *height* could be added to the above list of measurements, as this helps to give a 'picture' of the figure involved and could affect the depth of armhole and general styling.

Depth of armhole

(See point C from A on dia. 1(a), p. 14).

An armhole that is too shallow or too deep for the figure concerned can lead to acute discomfort in wear, and furthermore it is difficult to correct once the garment is completed.

The patterns presented throughout this book are of standard measurements and are based on a height of 176cm (5ft 9in) and a chest girth of 96cm (38in). The measurement chart on the following page shows the armhole depths for different chest sizes but at the standard height of 176cm (5ft 9in).

The following formula is useful for calculating the armhole depth when there is a variation above or below the standard height:
⅛ height plus ⅛ chest minus a constant figure of 10cm (3⅞in).

So, for example, the depth of armhole for a man of height 188cm (74in) and chest 96cm (38in) is calculated thus:

		cm	in.
⅛ height	=	23.50	9¼
⅛ chest	=	12.00	4¾
	Total	35.50	14
Minus the constant		10.00	3⅞
Armhole depth	=	25.50	10⅛

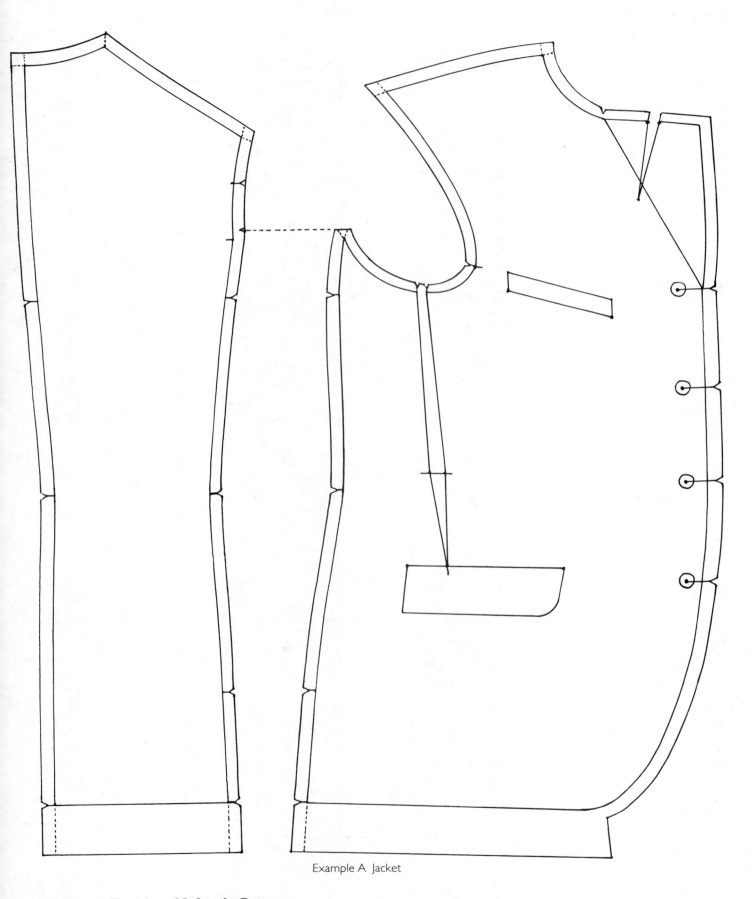

Example A Jacket

Seams and Turn-ins added to the Patterns.

5

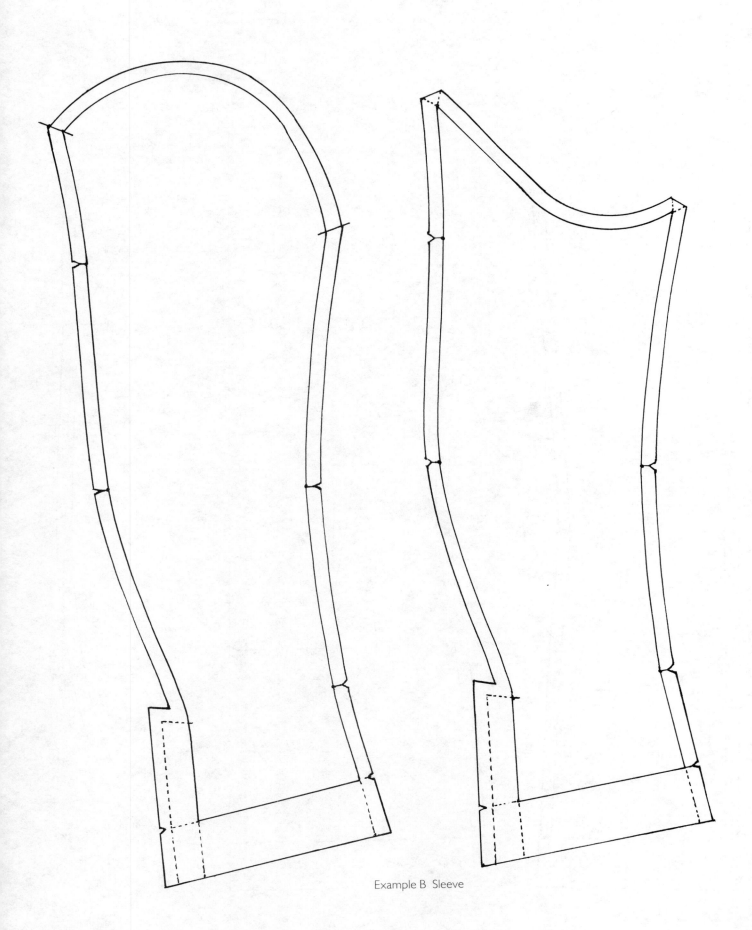

Example B Sleeve

6

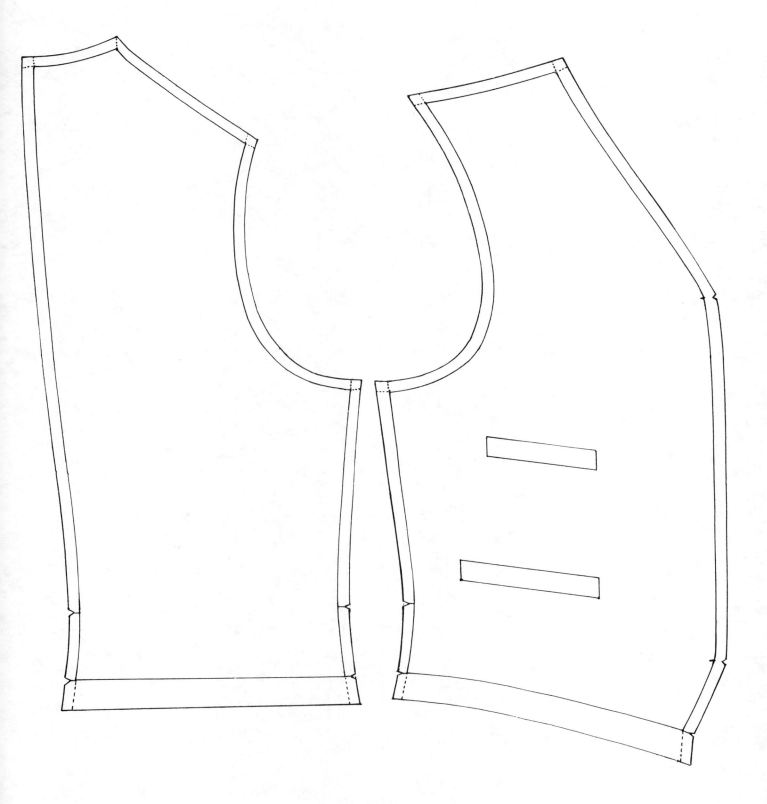

Example C Waistcoat

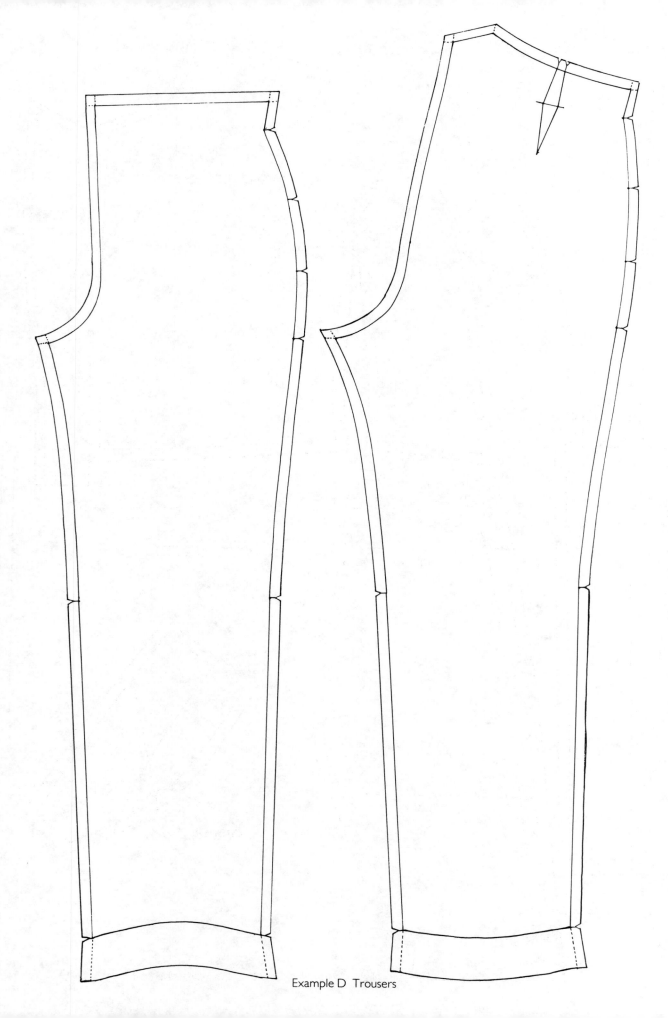

8

Example D Trousers

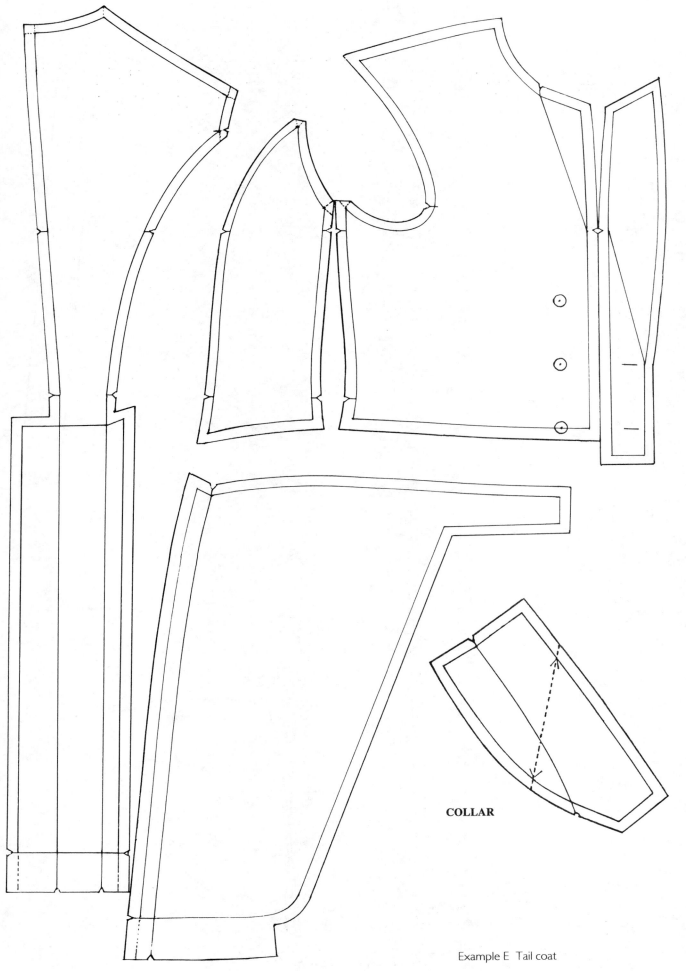

COLLAR

Example E Tail coat

9

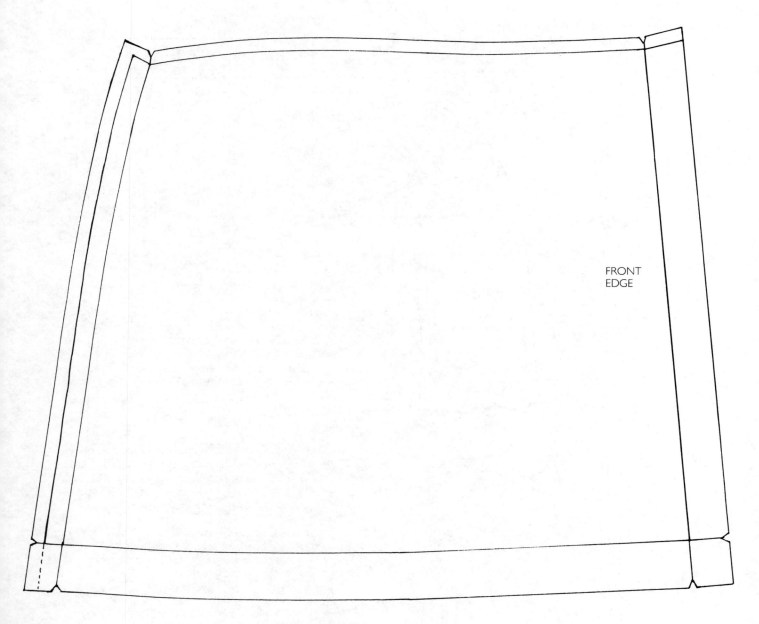

FRONT
EDGE

Example F Frock coat skirt

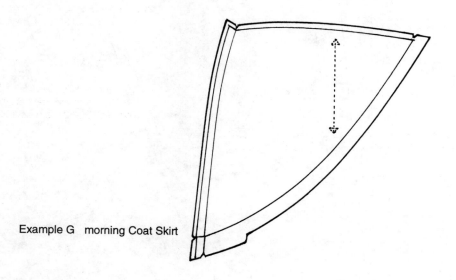

Example G   morning Coat Skirt

10

Size chart of proportionate measurements

	Centimetres Height – 176cm					Inches Height – 69in (5ft 9in)				
Chest	88	92	96	100	104	34	36	38	40	42
Trousers waist (increased 2.5cm/1in)	78	82	86	90	94	30	32	34	36	38
Seat	94	98	102	106	110	36	38	40	42	44
Nape to back waist	43.5	44	44.5	45	45.5	17	17¼	17½	17¾	18
Half across back	19.5	20	20.5	21	21.5	7½	7¾	8⅛	8½	8¾
Sleeve length from centre back	82.5	82.5	82.5	82.5	82.5	32½	32½	32½	32½	32½
Nape to armhole depth	23	23.5	24	24.5	25	9	9¼	9½	9¾	10
Trousers 'rise'	31	31.5	32	32.5	33	12	12¼	12½	12¾	13
Trousers inside leg	80	80	80	80	80	31½	31½	31½	31½	31½

Notes on pattern cutting

To 'square'

When constructing the pattern, certain lines are placed at right angles (90 degrees) to each other and are referred to as being squared. It is essential that the right angles are accurate, otherwise the balance of the garment could be affected.

Scale

The scale is calculated as half the chest for coats and waistcoats, and half the seat for trousers and breeches. Fractions of the scale are applied to various parts of the pattern, i.e. back neck, width of armhole, etc.

Seam and turn-in allowances

It is important to note that all the patterns presented in this book are nett and must have seams and turn-ins added.

The drawn examples **A-G** (see pp. 5–10) show seams of 1cm (⅜in) with a turn-in along the bottom edge of 5cm (2in). On all the examples notches are indicated at turn-ins and balance points.

Example **F** shows the skirt pattern of the frock coat. Note that the front edge has a turn-in of 4cm (1½in).

"The method of presenting the pattern drafts has been arranged so that seams can be added before cutting out the pattern. The only exceptions are the Topcoat patterns on pages 114, 120, 123, where the sideseams overlap. To separate the back from the front, trace the back pattern on to another sheet of paper."

Checking the pattern

Having added the seams etc. and cut out the pattern, it is important to check that the various parts that are to be sewn together will be compatible with each other.

Coat

1. Lay the back and front shoulders together. The back shoulder will be 1cm (3/8 in) longer than the front.
2. Place the sideseams together, they should be the same length.
3. Check that the top and undersleeve patterns are similar in length both at the back and the front seams.

Waistcoat

Same as 1. and 2. above.

Trousers

Lay the front and back patterns together and check the sideseams and the inside leg seams.

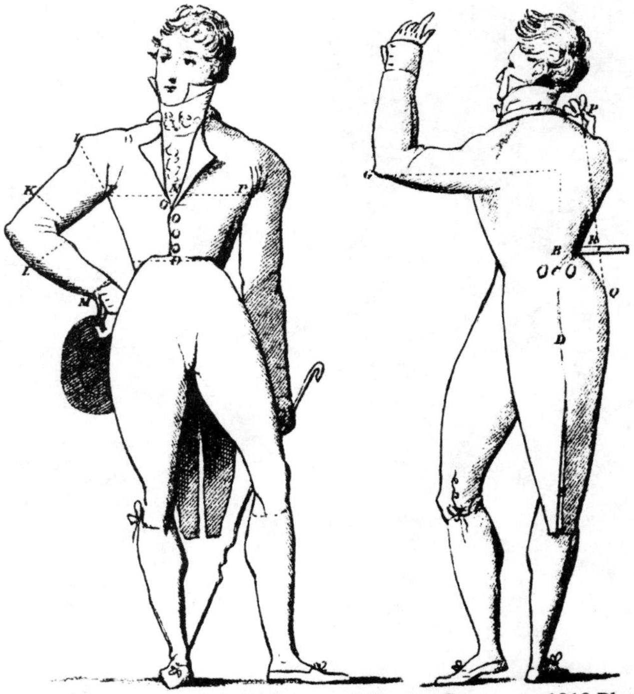

PLATE 8. From Hearn's *Rudiments of Cutting Coats, etc.*, 1819 Plate 1: on Measuring.

PLATE 9. 1830's. (R) Evening Dress Coat, 'M' shaped collar, with the coat length finishing at knee level. Double-breasted Vest with Shawl Collar, the bottom edge level is even with the front of the Tail Coat. The Pantaloons fit close to the legs and finish just above the ankles. The bottoms are fastened at the sides with three buttons. The hat is a Chapeau-bras, usually carried as part of evening wear and occsionally worn. (L) Back view of the Tail Coat showing the pockets and flaps on the waist seam. In this instance the figure wears narrow trousers strapped under the shoes. The Top hat is slightly narrower at the crown and has a curled brim. Petit Courrier des Dames, 1830.

PLATE 10. 1851. (L) *The short outer garment is a loose coat known as a Paletot and worn here over the shoulders like a cloak. The shortness of the Single-breasted coat worn beneath the Paletot complements the narrow style of the trousers. (C) Double-breasted Tailcoat with a moderate width of rever and collar. The trousers have a broad stripe down the sideseams which was a popular feature of the 1850's. (R) Thigh-length Frock coat worn over a Double-breasted Vest, narrow trousers with the bottoms fastening under the shoes. The Gentleman's Magazine, October 1851.*

I DRESS COATS

The term dress coat refers to a style of tail coat where the fronts are cut back at the waist position to a point where the tails begin (fig. I). In the early part of the nineteenth century the dress coat was fashionable for both day and evening wear and could be in either single- or double-breasted style. By the 1820s, the style for evening wear was mainly single-breasted with the fronts left undone to reveal the waistcoat. Around the middle of the century the dress coat was discontinued for day wear, in favour of the increasingly popular frock coat, and was only worn for formal evening occasions.

Between 1820 and 1840 important changes occurred in the cut of these styles. Before the 1820s the only seams on the tail coat were at the centre back and the sides, with the front pattern and skirt being cut in one piece. In the early 1820s, to improve the fit of the garment, a seam was introduced across the waist of the fronts so that the skirts were cut as a separate part (dia. I(c)).

During the late 1830s a further development was a seam dividing the armhole to form a side panel known as a sidebody (dia. 2(a)). In addition to the waist seam and sidebody, the front panel (dia. 2(a)) became part of the conventional design of the dress coat. In its final form, which continued up to 1900, the dress coat pattern comprised the following parts:

1 back
2 sidebody
3 front
4 front panel
5 skirt
6 sleeve (topsleeve and undersleeve)
7 collar

Evening dress coat, 1830
(fig. I; dia. I(a)–(g))

Measurements

	Height	Nape to waist	Full length	Half back	Sleeve length	Chest	Waist	Seat
cm	176	44.5	100	20.5	82.5	96	86	102
in	69	17½	39½	8⅛	32½	38	34	40

Scale is half the chest = 48cm (19in) : ⅛ scale = 6cm (2⅜in)
¼ scale = 12cm (4¾in)

Back pattern (dia. I(a))

A = starting point.
Square across and down from A.
B from A = 10cm (4in).
C from A = 24cm (9½in) (armhole depth).
D from A is the nape to waist plus 1cm = 45.5cm or 17½in plus ½in = 18in.
Square a short line across from B.
Square a long line across from C and D.
Note: The line from C is the chest line.
The line from D is the waist line.

At the top:
1 from A = 20.5cm (8⅛in) (half back measure).
Square down from 1.
2 is located on the line from B.
3 is on the chest line from C.
4 from C = 1.5cm (⅝in).
5 from D = 3cm (1⅛in).
Join A – 4 – 5.
Square a line down from 5.
6 from A = 100cm (39½in) (full length).
Square a line across at 6.
The centre back is A – 4 – 5 – 6.
From the basic lines of dia. I(a) continue as in dia. I(b).

Dia. I(b) At the top line:
7 from A is ⅛ scale plus 1.5cm (⅝in) = 7.5cm (3in).
8 squared up from 7 = 1.5cm (⅝in).
Curve 8 to A for the back neck.
Join 8 to 2 with a straight line.
Slightly hollow between 8 and 2 to complete the back shoulder.
9 above 3 is ¼ scale minus 2cm (¾in) = 10cm (4in).
Join 2 to 9 with a moderate curve, as in diagram.
10 from 3 is ¼ scale = 12cm (4¾in). 10 is the back balance point for the sleeve and is half-way between 2 and 9.
11 from 4 is ¼ scale = 12cm (4¾in).
12 from 5 is ⅛ scale minus 1cm (⅜in) = 5cm (2in).
Join 11 to 12 with a straight line.
E is half-way between 11 and 12.
F squared from E = 1cm (⅜in).
Curve 9 – 11 – F – 12.
13 on the line from 6 is the same as 12 from 5 i.e. 5cm (2in).
Join 12 to 13 to complete the back side seam.
G from 5 = 4.5cm (1¾in).
H from 6 = 4.5cm (1¾in).
Join G to H. This is the allowance for the back opening (back vent) and must be included when cutting out the pattern.

Fig. 1. (i.) Front view of Evening Dress Coat, Dress Vest and Pantaloons. Note the seam round the cuff of the coat just above the cuff opening. This is a 'Formed' cuff which is explained on page 34, Diagram 4C. (ii.) Back view of Evening Dress Coat.

(ii) back

Ill. 51. 1830-1840. Evening Tail Coat with the collar rolling high at the back of the neck, narrow sleeves flaring out at the cuffs and gathered at the sleevehead to give a puffed effect, brass buttons. Single-breasted Vest with shawl collar, note the special pocket for a watch. The narrow pantaloons have an instep strap at the bottoms to fit under the shoe and are a sign of smartness in dress. The frill at the wrist is still the mark of the dandy, but cravats are becoming very simple.

(i) front

15

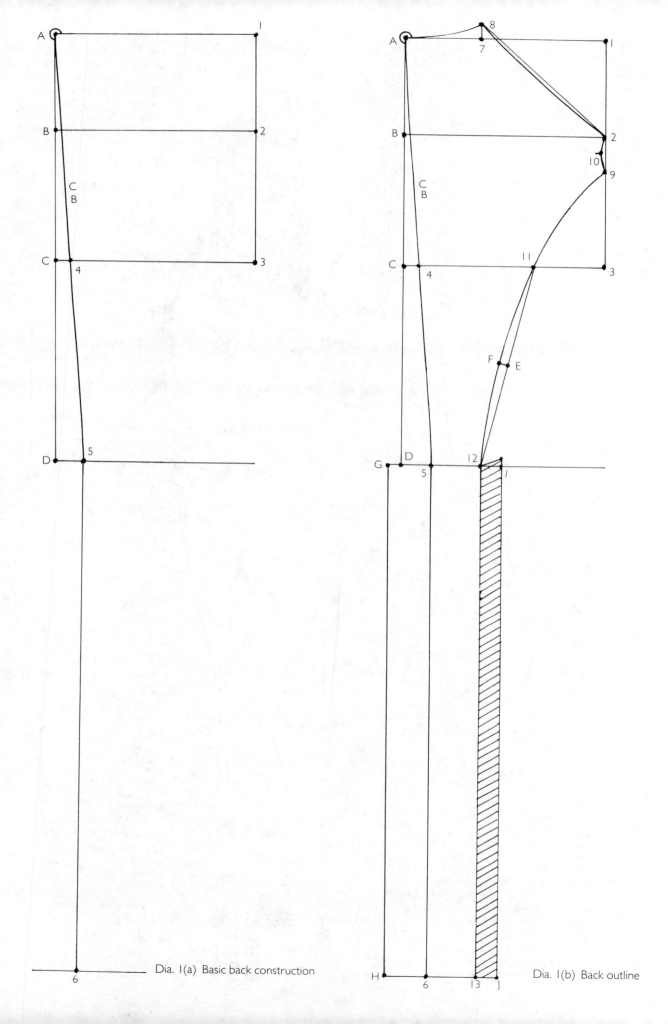

Dia. 1(a) Basic back construction

Dia. 1(b) Back outline

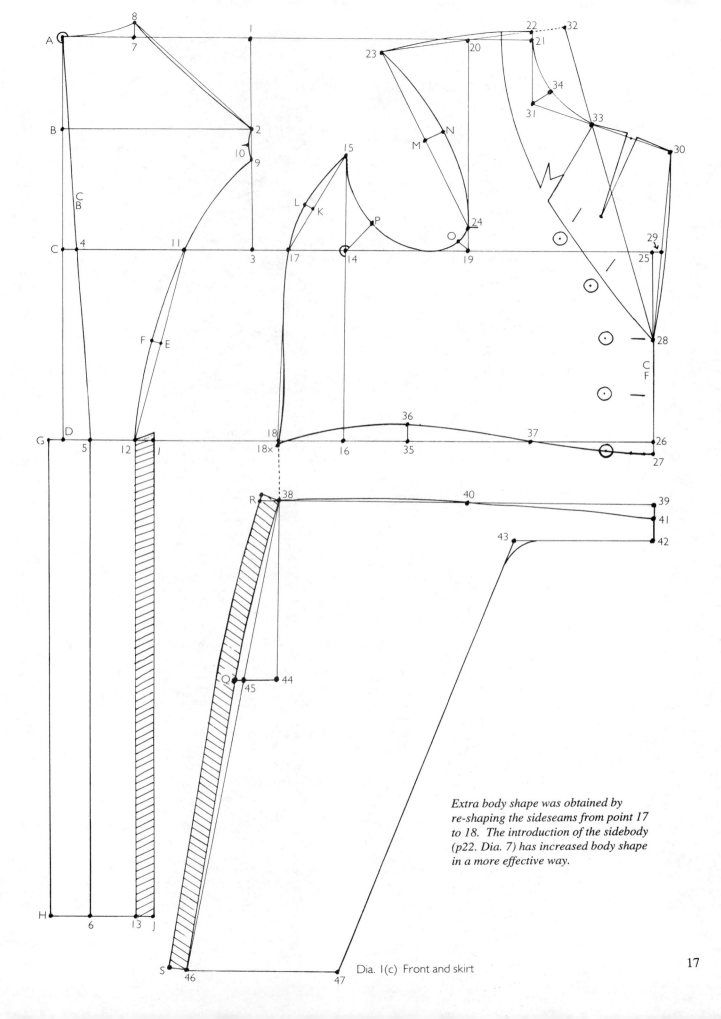

Extra body shape was obtained by re-shaping the sideseams from point 17 to 18. The introduction of the sidebody (p22. Dia. 7) has increased body shape in a more effective way.

Dia. 1(c) Front and skirt

17

I from 12 = 2cm (¾in).

J from 13 = 2cm (¾in).

Join I to J for half the skirt pleat (shaded section) which is in the form of a knife pleat. Spring up 1cm (⅜in) above I and join to 12.

Note: The back width from centre back to 10 is narrower than the measurement 20.5cm (8⅛in). This narrow back is a feature of the 1830s and 1840s tail coat and is compensated for by the large sleeveheads of those periods (Fig. 1).

The outline of the back pattern is now completed.
Continue the lines across from A, C and D.

Front pattern (dia. 1(c))

14 from 3 = 10cm (4in).

Square up from 14.

15 above 14 is the same as 9 from 3 plus 0.5cm (¼in), i.e. 10.5cm (4¼in).

Square down from 14 to the waist line and mark 16.

17 from 14 = 5.5cm (2¼in).

18 from 16 = 7cm (2¾in).

Join 15 to 17 with a straight line.

K is centre of 15 and 17.

L squared from K = 1cm (⅜in).

Join 17 to 18 with a straight line.

Curve 15 – L – 17 – 18.

18x continued from 18 = 0.5cm (¼in).

19 from 14 is ¼ scale plus 2cm (¾in), = 14cm (5½in).

Square up from 19 and mark 20 on the top line.

21 from 20 is ⅛ scale plus 1cm (⅜in), = 7cm (2¾in).

Square up a short line from 21.

22 above 21 = 1cm (⅜in).

Join 22 to 20 and continue the line.

For 23 from 22, measure the back shoulder 8 to 2 and subtract 1cm (⅜in) = 17cm (6⅝in). Therefore, the front shoulder 23 from 22 = 17cm (6⅝in).

Curve from 22 to 23 to complete front shoulder.

24 above 19 = 2.5cm (1in).

24 is the front balance point for the sleeve.

Join 23 to 24 with a straight line.

M is centre of 23 to 24.

N squared from M = 2.5cm (1in).

O at an angle to 19 = 2cm (¾in).

P at an angle to 14 = 4.5cm (1¾in).

Curve the armhole 23 – N – 24 – O down to the chest line, then continue up through P to 15.

25 from 19 is ½ scale minus 3.5cm (1½in) = 20.5cm (8in).

Square down from 25 and mark 26 on the waist line.

27 continued from 26 = 1.5cm (⅝in).

The centre front is 25 to 27.

28 above 26 = 11.5cm (4½in).

29 from 25 = 1cm (⅜in).

Join 28 to 29 and continue the line.

30 from 29 = 11.5cm (4½in).

31 squared down from 21 = 7cm (2¾in).

Join 30 to 31.

Join 30 to 28 with a moderate curve.

32 opposite 22 = 3.5cm (1⅜in).

Join 32 to 28 for the fold or 'crease' line of the lapel.

Mark 33 at the neck line.

34 from 31 = 2.5cm (1in).

Curve the neck 22 – 34 – 33.

The neck dart is placed half-way between 30 and 33.

Mark 1.3cm (½in) to be sewn out at the top and make the dart 9cm (3½in) long.

To complete the waist seam of the front:

35 from 16 = 7cm (2¾in).

36 squared up from 35 = 2.5cm (1in).

37 is half-way between 26 and 35.

Curve 18x – 36 – 37 – 27 as in the diagram.

Note: The evening dress coat is not fastened at the front, but left open to show the waistcoat. Because of this, the centre front is also the front edge, and the buttonholes and buttons are for decorative effect only.

Skirt pattern

Square down from 18x.

38 from 18x = 6.5cm (2½in).

Square across from 38.

Measure the waist curve of the front 18x – 36 – 37 – 27 = 42cm (16½in).

Apply this measure from 38 to 39.

40 is the centre of 38 to 39.

Square down from 39.

41 from 39 = 1.5cm (⅝in).

Curve 38 to 40 then join 40 to 41.

42 from 41 = 2.5cm (1in).

43 squared from 42 = 15cm (6in).

44 from 38 = 20cm (8in).

45 squared from = 4cm (1½in).

Join 38 to 45 and continue the line.

46 from 38 is the same as 13 to 12 on the back, i.e. 54.5cm (21½in).

Q from 45 = 1cm (⅜in).

Curve the back skirt 38 to Q and join Q to 46.

R from 38 and S from 46 = 2cm (¾in).

Join R to S parallel with 38 to 46.

Spring up 1cm (⅜in) above R and join to 38.

This represents half the skirt pleat as shown by the shaded section.

Draw a horizontal line across from 46.

47 from 46 = 16.5cm (6½in).

Join 43 to 47 and curve in front of 43 as in the diagram.

Sleeve pattern, 1830

Top sleeve (dia. 1(d))

1 = Starting point.

Square across and down from 1.

2 from 1 is ⅛ scale = 6cm (2⅜in).

3 from 2 is the same as 10 from 3 on the back pattern (dia. 1(b)) = 12cm (4¾in).

4 from 3 = 20cm (8in).

For 5 from 2, measure the back pattern from centre back to 10 = 19.5cm (7¾in). Deduct this amount from the sleeve measure of 82.5cm (32.½in). Therefore, 5 from 2 = 63cm (24¾in).

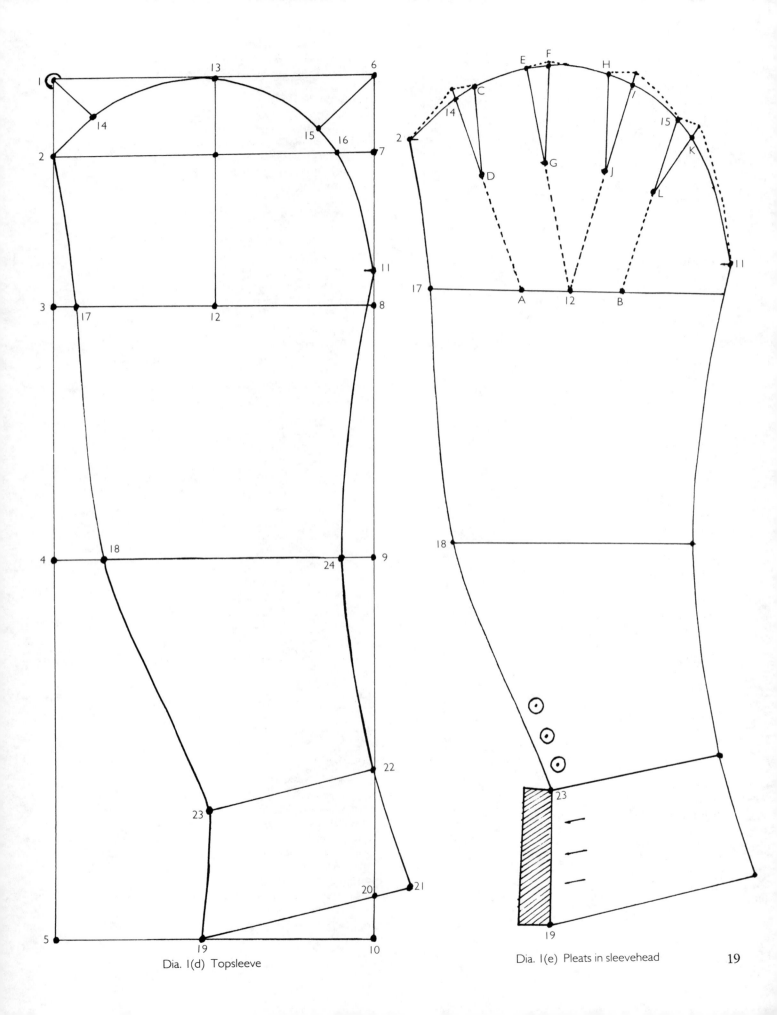

Dia. I(d) Topsleeve

Dia. I(e) Pleats in sleevehead

19

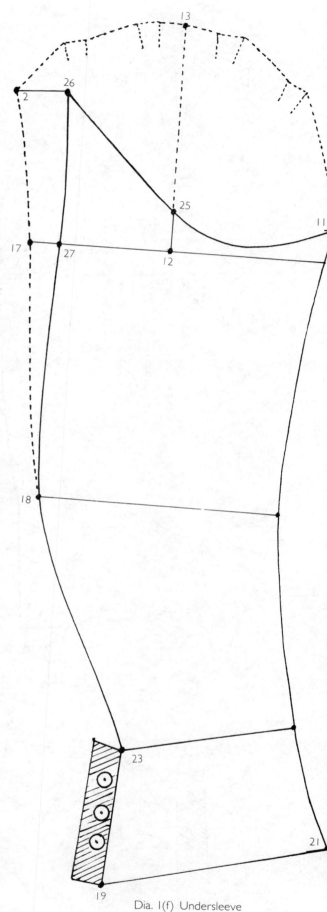

At the top:

6 from 1 is ½ scale plus 0.5cm = 24.5cm (or 9½in plus ¼in = 9¾in).

Square a long line down from 6.

Square across from 2 and mark 7.

Square across from 3 and mark 8.

Square across from 4 and mark 9, forming elbow line.

Square across from 5 and mark 10.

11 above 8 is the same as 24 above 19 on the front pattern (dia. 1(c)) = 2.5cm (1in).

12 is the centre of 3 and 8.

Square up from 12 and mark 13 on the top line.

14 at an angle from 1 = 4cm (1½in).

15 at an angle from 6 = 5.5cm (2¼in).

16 from 7 = 2cm (¾in).

Curve the sleevehead 2 – 14 – 13 – 15 – 16 – 11.

17 inside 3 = 2.5cm (1in).

18 inside 4 = 4cm (1½in).

19 from 5 = 11.5cm (4½in).

20 above 10 = 3cm (1¼in).

Join 19 to 20 and continue the line.

21 from 20 = 2.5cm (1in).

22 above 20 = 10cm (4in).

Draw a line from 22 that is parallel with the cuff 19 to 21.

23 from 22 = 12.5cm (5in).

To complete the back seam:

From 2 hollow the line to 17, then curve to 18 and 23.

Join 23 to 19 with a straight line.

24 inside 9 = 2.5cm (1in).

Curve the front seam 11 – 24 – 22 and join 22 to 21 with a straight line.

Dia. 1(e) There are four pleats to be folded over in the sleevehead before it is sewn into the armhole. Their position is as follows:

A from 12 = 4cm (1½in).

B from 12 = 4cm (1½in).

Join 14 to A.

C from 14 = 2cm (¾in).

D from 14 = 6.5cm (2½in).

Join C to D (pleat 1).

E from C = 4.5cm (1¾in).

Join E to 12.

F from E = 2cm (¾in).

G from E = 7.5cm (3in).

Join F to G (pleat 2).

H from F = 4.5cm (1¾in).

I from H = 2cm (¾in).

Join I to 12.

J from I = 7.5cm (3in).

Join H to J (pleat 3).

Join 15 to B.

K from 15 = 2cm (¾in).

L from 15 = 6.5cm (2½in).

Join K to L (pleat 4).

The diagram shows how one side of each pleat is raised a small amount at points K – I – E – 14. This is to avoid any distortion of the sleevehead curve after the pleats are folded over.

Undersleeve (dia. 1(f))

Using the topsleeve as a basis, proceed as follows:

25 above 12 = 2.5cm (1in).

Dia. 1(f) Undersleeve

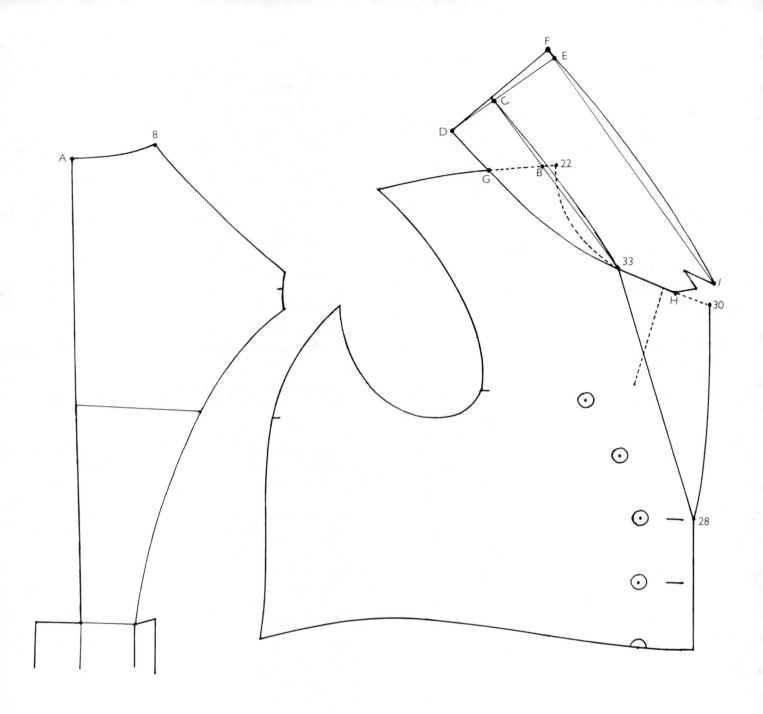

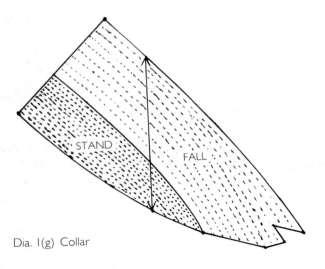

STAND

FALL

Dia. I(g) Collar

21

26 from 2 = 4cm (1½in).
Curve down from 11 then up through 25 to 26.
27 from 17 = 2cm (¾in).
Curve 26 to 27 and continue the curve into 18.
The undersleeve is exactly the same as the topsleeve from
    18 – 23 – 19 – 21 and the front seam 11 to 21.

The sleeve is left open from 23 to 19 and there is a fastening of three
holes and buttons. The three buttons above 23 do not fasten and are
purely decorative. The shaded sections are added to the pattern
and are 2.5cm (1in) wide. On the topsleeve this addition to the
pattern is turned in along the edge of the opening and on the
undersleeve it serves as a button stand.

Collar, 1830s (dia. 1(g))

Use the outline of the front pattern of dia. 1(c) and close up the neck
    dart.
Transfer the relevant points which are 22 – 28 – 30 – 33.
B from 22 = 1.3cm (½in).
Join 33 to B and continue the line.
C from B is found by measuring the back neck A to 8 = 8cm (3⅛in).
Curve the 'crease' line from C to 33.
Square a line across from C.
D from C = 5cm (2in).
E from C = 7cm (2¾in).
F squared from E = 1cm (⅜in).
Join F to D.
G from B = 5cm (2in).
Join D to G and gradually curve from G to 33.
H from 30 = 4cm (1½in).
I above 30 = 2cm (¾in).
Join F to I with a curve for the outside edge.
Follow the diagram from I to H to complete the 'M' design of the
    collar.

The pattern represents the undercollar which is cut on the 'cross' or
bias of the material. A firm canvas or similar type of interlining should
be stitched to the undercollar as shown in the separate diagram.
Use narrow rows of stitches on the 'stand' for extra stiffness, and
wider rows on the the 'fall'. The finished effect is of a collar rolling
high at the back and 'standing away' from the neck. This type of collar
has been aptly described as a 'horse's collar'.

NOTE:

*An example of the 'horse's collar' described above. Illustration
G4 (1830).*

Gent's shirt.   All sizes; 50 cents each.

Double-breasted dress coat, 1840

(fig. 2; dia. 2(a)–(e))

Measurements

	Height	Nape to waist	Full length	Half back	Sleeve length	Chest	Waist	Seat
cm	176	44.5	96	20.5	82.5	96	86	102
in	69	17½	38	8⅛	32½	38	34	40

Scale is half the chest = 48cm (19in) : ⅛ scale = 6cm (2⅜in)
¼ scale = 12cm (4¾in)

Back pattern (dia. 2(a))

A = starting point.
Square across and down from A.
B from A = 10cm (4in).
C from A = 24cm (9½in).
D from A = 44.5cm (17½in) (nape to waist).
E from D = 3.5cm (1½in) for the fashionable dropped waistline of
    the period.
Square a short line across from B and E.
Square a long line across from C and D.

At the top:
1 from A = 20.5cm (8⅛in) (half back).
Square down from 1.
2 is located on the line from B.
3 is on the line from C (chest line).
4 from C = 1.5cm (⅝in).
5 from D = 3cm (1⅛in).
6 from E = 3cm (1⅛in).
Join A – 4 – 5 – 6.
Square down from 6.
7 from A = 96cm (38in) (full length).
Square a line across at 7.
The centre back is A – 4 – 5 – 6 – 7.
At the top:
8 from A is ⅛ scale plus 1.5cm (⅝in) = 7.5cm (3in).
9 squared up from 8 = 1.5cm (⅝in).
Curve 9 to A for the back neck.
Join 9 to 2 with a straight line.
Slightly hollow between 9 and 2 to complete the back shoulder.
10 above 3 is ¼ scale minus 2cm (¾in), i.e. 10cm (4in).
Join 2 to 10 with a moderate curve.
11 from 3 is ¼ scale = 12cm (4¾in) and is the back balance point
    for the sleeve.
12 from 4 is ¼ scale minus 1cm (⅜in), i.e. 11cm (4⅜in).
13 from 5 is ⅛ scale minus 1cm (⅜in) = 5cm (2in).
Join 12 to 13 with a straight line.
F is centre of 12 and 13.
G squared from F = 1.3cm (½in).
Curve 10 – 12 – G – 13.
14 from 6 is the same as 13 from 5 = 5cm (2in).
Join 13 to 14 and square down from 14.
Mark 15 on the line from 7.

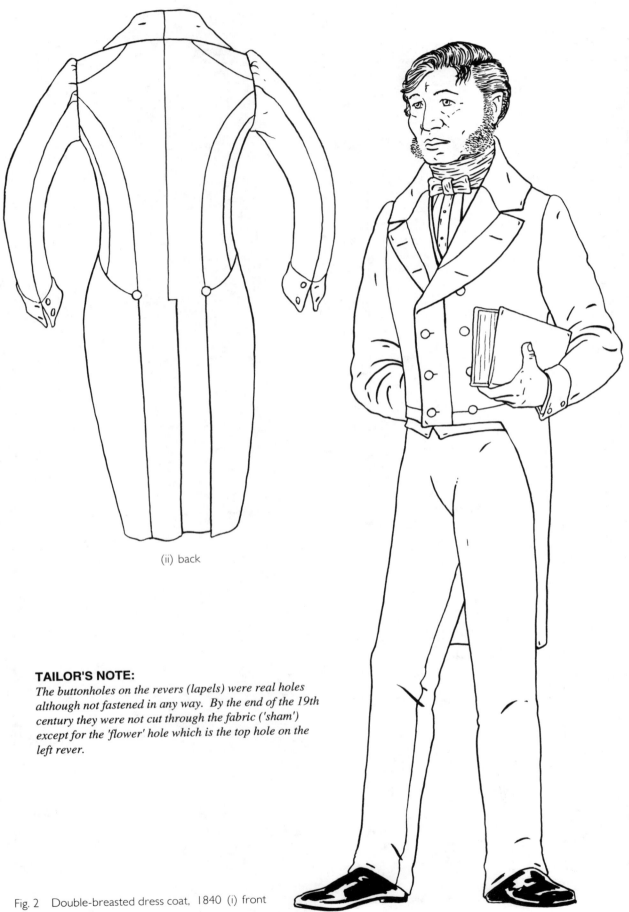

(ii) back

TAILOR'S NOTE:
The buttonholes on the revers (lapels) were real holes although not fastened in any way. By the end of the 19th century they were not cut through the fabric ('sham') except for the 'flower' hole which is the top hole on the left rever.

Fig. 2 Double-breasted dress coat, 1840 (i) front

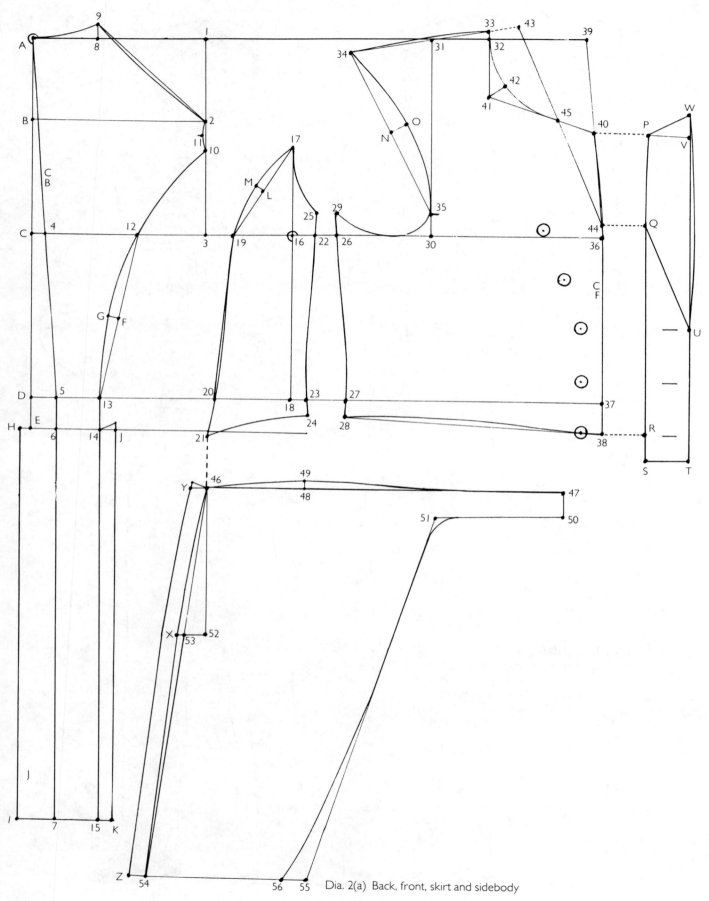

Dia. 2(a) Back, front, skirt and sidebody

H from 6 = 4.5cm (1¾in).
I from 7 = 4.5cm (1¾in).
Join H to I.
J from 14 and K from 15 = 2cm (¾in).
Join J to K.
Spring up 1cm (⅜in) above J and join to 14.

Sidebody and front

On the chest line:
16 from 3 = 10cm (4in).
Square up from 16.
17 above 16 is the same as 10 from 3 plus 0.5cm (¼in), = 10.5cm
    (4¼in).
Square down from 16 to the waist line and mark 18.
19 from 16 = ⅛ scale plus 1cm (⅜in) i.e. 7cm (2¾in).
20 from 18 = same as 19 from 16 plus 2cm (¾in) = 9cm (3½in).
Join 17 to 19 with a straight line.
L is centre of 17 and 19.
M squared from L = 1cm (⅜in).
Join 19 to 20 with a straight line.
Curve 17 – M – 19. Continue with a moderate curve from 19 – 20.
At 20 spring out to the lower waist line and mark 21 just below the
    line.
22 from 16 = 3cm (1⅛in).
23 from 18 = 2cm (¾in).
Join 22 to 23 and spring out below 23.
24 from 23 = 2cm (¾in).
Curve 24 to 21 to complete the bottom edge.
25 continued above 22 = 2.5cm (1in).
Curve 25 to 17 to complete the sidebody panel.
26 from 22 = 2.5cm (1in).
27 from 23 = 4.5cm (1¾in).
Join 26 to 27 and spring out below 27.
28 from 27 = 2cm (¾in).
29 continued above 26 = 2.5cm (1in).
30 from 26 is ⅛ scale plus 5cm (2in), = 11cm (4⅜in).
Square up from 30 and mark 31 on the top line.
32 from 31 is ⅛ scale plus 1cm (⅜in) = 7cm (2¾in).
33 squared up from 32 = 1cm (⅜in).
Join 33 to 31 and continue the line.
For 34 from 33, measure the back shoulder 2 to 9, subtract
    1cm (⅜in) = 17cm (6⅝in).
Curve 33 to 34 to complete the front shoulder.
35 above 30 = 2.5cm (1in). 35 is the front balance point for the
    sleeve.
Join 34 to 35 with a straight line and mark N half-way.
O squared from N = 2.5cm (1in).
Curve 34 – O – 35 and from 35 curve down to the chest line, then
    up to 29 to complete the armhole.
36 from 30 is ½ scale minus 3.5cm , i.e. 20.5cm or 9½in minus
    1½in, i.e. 8in.
Square down from 36 and mark 37 on the waist line.
38 continued from 37 = 4cm (1½in).
36 – 37 – 38 is the centre front (CF).
To complete the waist seam, curve 28 to 38.
39 from 32 on the top line = 11.5cm (4½in).
Join 39 to 36.

40 from 39 = 11.5cm (4½in). Slight curve from 40 to 36.
41 squared down from 32 = 7cm (2¾in).
Join 40 to 41.
42 at an angle to 41 = 2.5cm (1in).
43 opposite 33 = 3.5cm (1⅜in).
44 above 36 = 1.5cm (⅝in).
Join 43 to 44 and mark 45 on the neck line.
Curve 33 – 32 – 42 – 45 to complete the front neck.

Front panel

Draw a line across from 40.
P from 40 = 6.5cm (2½in).
Q squared up from 44 = 5cm (2in).
Join P to Q with a moderate curve and square down from Q.
R is marked opposite 38.
S below R = 3cm (1¼in).
T squared from S = 5cm (2in).
U squared up from T = 16cm (6¼in).
Join U to Q.
V from P = 4.5cm (1¾in).
Curve V to U.
W continued from V = 2cm (¾in).
Join W to P.

The top buttonhole is at U and the bottom hole opposite R.
The holes are placed 1.5cm (⅝in) from the front edge.
The buttons are 3.5cm (1⅜in) back from the centre front.
The top two buttons are decorative and referred to as 'show'
buttons. These are placed at an angle so that they are not hidden
when the lapel is turned back.

Skirt pattern

46 squared down from 21 = 6.5cm (2½in).
Square across and down from 46.
For 47 from 46, measure 21 to 24 plus 28 to 38 and add
    1cm (⅜in) = 43cm (17in) approx.
48 from 46 = 11.5cm (4½in).
49 squared up from 48 = 1.3 (½in).
Curve 46 to 49 – then join 49 to 47 as in the diagram.
50 squared down from 47 = 3cm (1¼in).
51 squared across from 50 = 15cm (6in).
52 squared down from 46 = 18cm (7in).
53 from 52 = 2.5cm (1in).
Join 46 to 53 and continue the line.
54 from 46 is the same as 15 from 14 on the back, =
    48cm (19in).
Draw a horizontal line across at 54.
X from 53 = 1cm (⅜in). Curve 46 – X – 54.
Y from 46 and Z from 54 = 2cm (¾in) for half the skirt pleat.
Join Y to Z to run parallel with 46 – X – 54.
Spring up 1cm (⅜in) above Y and join to 46.
55 from 54 = 19cm (7½in).
Join 55 to 51.
56 from 55 = 2.5cm (1in).
From 51, gradually curve to 56.
Where the lines meet at 51, fill in the corner with a small curve.

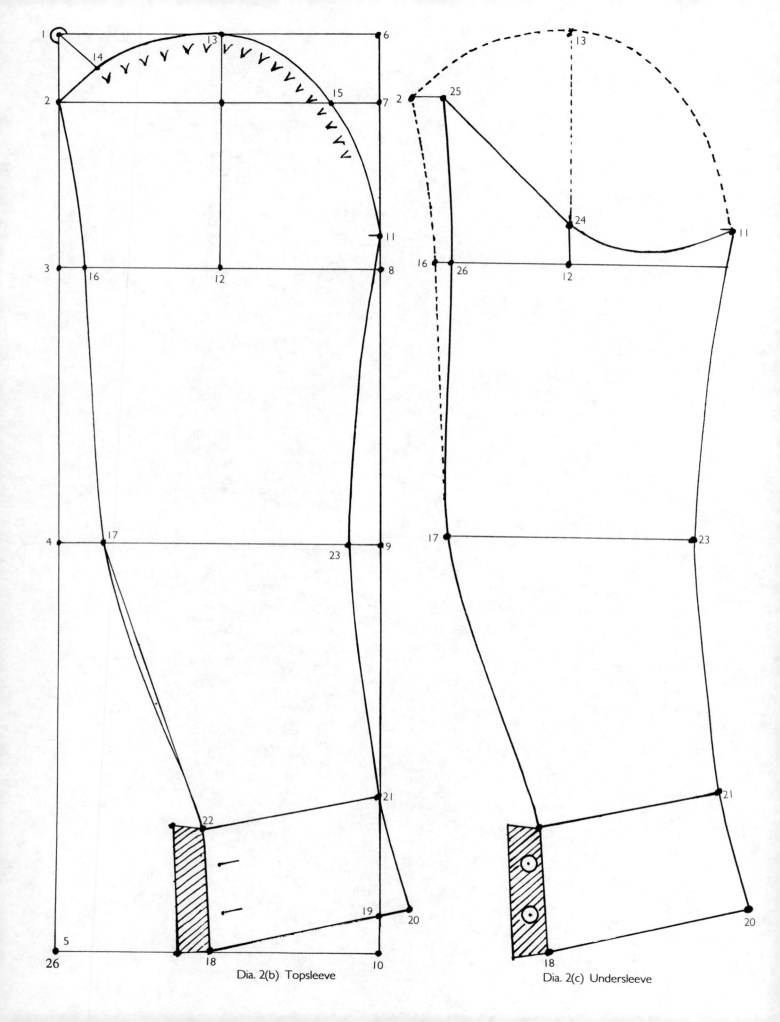

Dia. 2(b) Topsleeve

Dia. 2(c) Undersleeve

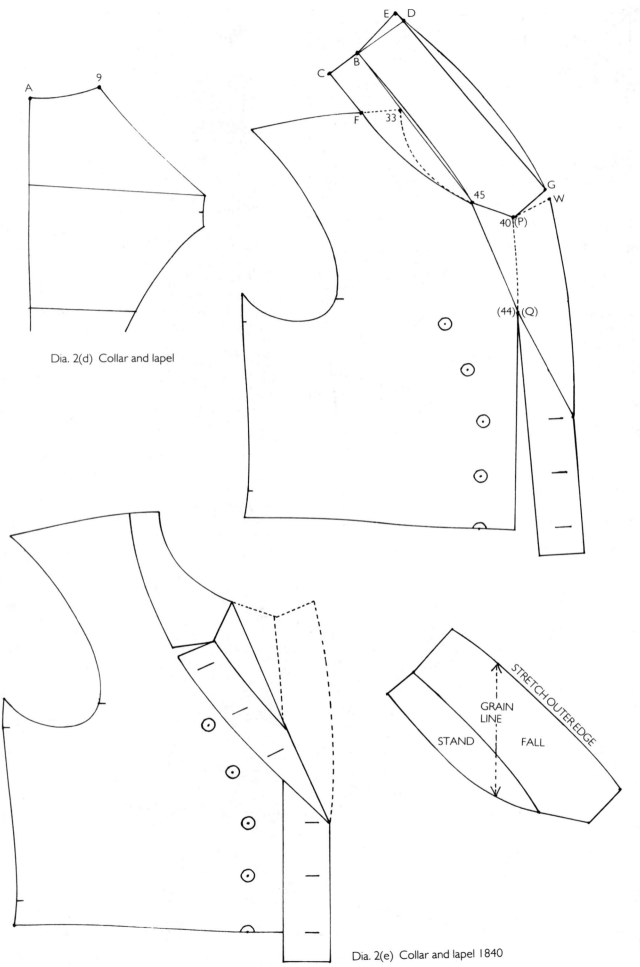

Dia. 2(d) Collar and lapel

Dia. 2(e) Collar and lapel 1840

STRETCH OUTER EDGE

GRAIN LINE

STAND   FALL

27

Sleeve pattern, 1840

Topsleeve (dia. 2(b))

1 = starting point.

Square across and down from 1.

2 from 1 is ⅛ scale minus 1cm (⅜in) = 5cm (2in).

3 from 2 is the same as 11 from 3 on the back pattern = 12cm (4¾in).

4 from 3 = 20cm (8in).

For 5 from 2, measure the back pattern from centre back to 11 = 19.5cm (7¾in). Deduct this amount from the sleeve measure 82.5cm (32½in). Therefore 5 from 2 = 63cm (24¾).

At the top:

6 from 1 is ½ scale minus 1cm = 23cm or 9½in minus ½in, i.e. 9in.

Square a long line down from 6.

Square across from 2, 3, 4 and 5, and mark 7, 8, 9 and 10.

11 above 8 = 2.5cm (1in), same as 35 from 30 on front pattern.

12 is the centre of 3 and 8.

Square up from 12 and mark 13 on the top line.

14 at an angle to 1 = 4cm (1½in).

15 from 7 = 3cm (1¼in).

Curve 2 – 14 – 13 – 15 – 11 for the sleevehead.

Note: The sleeve is gathered into the armhole as shown by the 'V' symbols. Sleeve point 2 joins to 11 on the back pattern and sleeve point 11 joins to 35 on the front pattern.

16 from 3 = 2cm (¾in).

17 from 4 = 3cm (1¼in).

18 from 5 = 11cm (4¼in).

19 above 10 = 3cm (1¼in).

Join 18 to 19 and continue the line.

20 from 19 = 2.5cm (1in).

21 from 19 = 9cm (3½in).

Draw a line from 21 to 22, parallel with the cuff 18 – 20.

22 from 21 = 13cm (5in).

To complete the back seam:

From 2, hollow the line to 16, then curve to 17 and 22.

Join 22 to 18 with a straight line.

23 from 9 = 2cm (¾in).

Curve the front seam 11 – 23 – 21 – 20.

Join 21 to 20 with a straight line.

Undersleeve (dia. 2(c))

Using the topsleeve as a basis, proceed as follows:

24 above 12 = 2.5cm (1in).

25 from 2 = 2cm (¾in).

Curve down from 11 then up through 24 to 25.

26 inside 16 = 1cm (⅜in).

Join 25 to 26 and continue to 17.

The front seam, cuff and from 17 to 18 are exactly the same as the topsleeve.

The sleeve is left open from 22 to 18 with a fastening of two holes and buttons. The shaded sections are added to the pattern as explained in the previous sleeve pattern.

Collar, 1840

Dia. 2(d) Join the front panel of dia. 2(a) to the front pattern as P to 40 and Q to 44.

Mark the points 33, 45, 40 and W.

Join 45 to 33 and continue the line.

B from 33 is the same measurement as A to 9 on the back pattern, = 8 cm (3⅛in).

Curve the 'crease' line from B to 45.

Square a line across from B.

C from B = 4cm (1½in).

D from B = 6.5cm (2½in).

E squared from D = 1.3cm (½in).

Join E to B.

F from 33 = 4.5cm (1¾in).

Join C to F and gradually curve to 45, then a straight line to 40.

G from W = 1 cm (⅜in).

Join G to 40.

To complete the outer edge of the collar, join E to G with a straight line, then with a moderate curve as in the diagram.

Dia. 2(e) The undercollar is cut on the 'cross' (or bias) of the material and stitched to a firm interlining. The effect should be of a collar that is flexible but not as stiff as the 1830s style. The collar fits closer to the neck and is not as high at the back of the neck. The outer edge should be stretched to lay over the back shoulders.

The left-hand diagram illustrates the collar shape and the effect of the lapel turned back. The seam of the centre front is reproduced on the facing and false holes are placed on each lapel.

Evening dress coat, 1860–1900
(fig. 3; dia. 3(a)-(c) and 4(a)-(e))

By the second half of the nineteenth century, the style of the evening dress coat had become standardized, but minor changes in the cutting of this garment (and tail coats generally) can be noted.

1 The shoulder seam which had previously been placed in a low position on the back was now raised to a higher level.

2 The half back measurement as applied to the pattern was increased.

3 The back seam of the sleeve coincided with the seam of the back, instead of being placed above it (see Fig. 3).

4 The collar became narrower and fitted more closely to the neck.

5 Sleeve styles changed from being very narrow to the wide elbow of the 1860–70s. From 1880 to 1900 the sleeve became more moderate, with the width at the elbow only slightly wider than the cuff width (see Fig. 4).

NOTE:

The sewing machine had been invented some 15 years earlier and was gradually, but not extensively, being used in craft tailoring.

(ii) back

TAILOR'S NOTE:
The arrangement of the silk on the revers (lapels) is called a 'half' silk facing. The buttonholes on the edge of the revers are only for decoration.

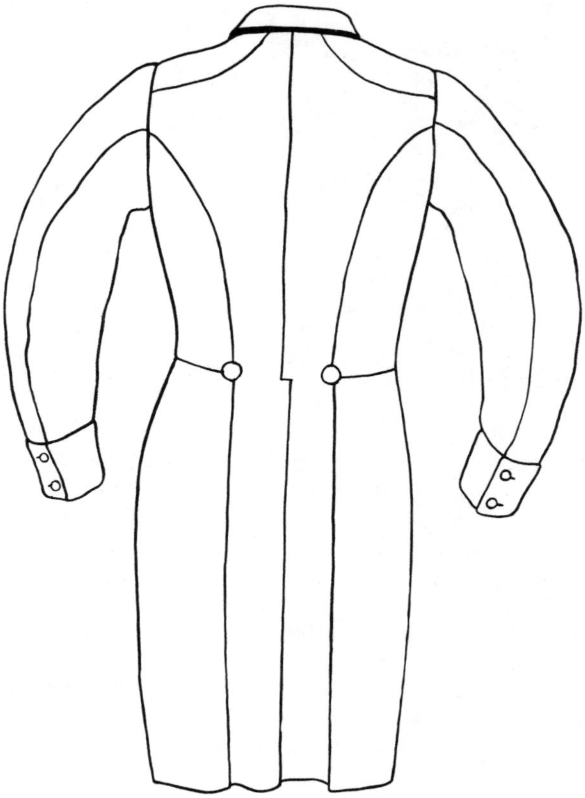

Ill. 52. Evening Dress Coat - 1870. Half silk facings and braided edges. Note the wide sleeve and narrow cuff of the period.

Fig. 3   Evening dress coat, 1860–70s (i) front

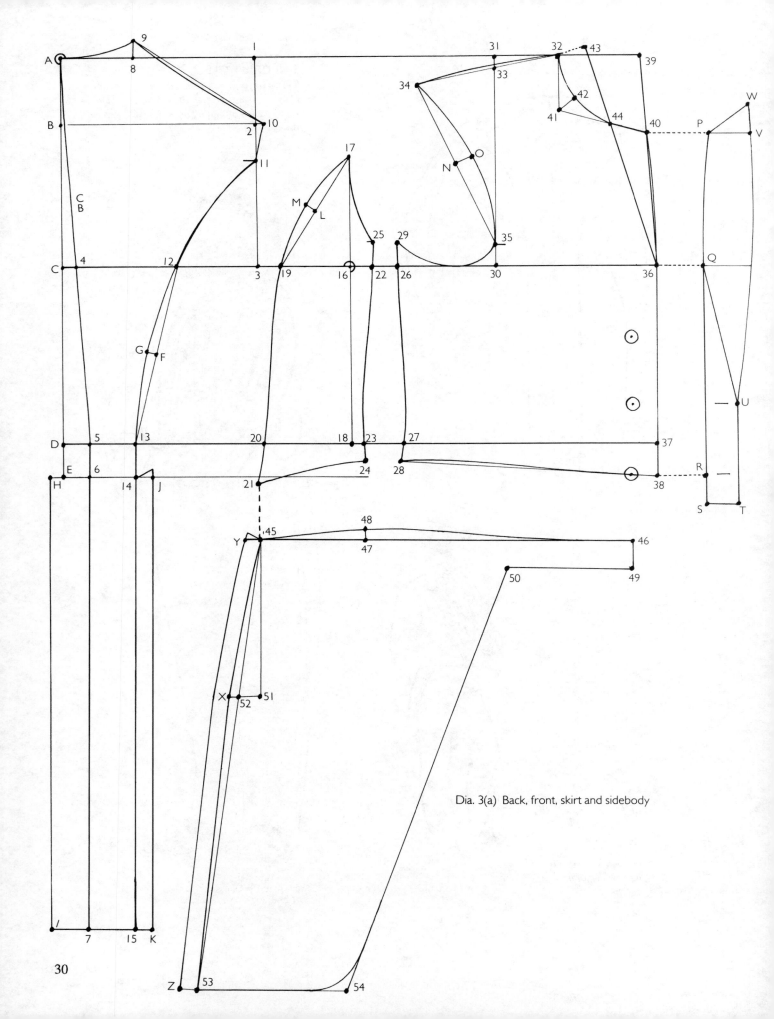

Dia. 3(a) Back, front, skirt and sidebody

30

Evening dress coat, 1860–1900
(fig. 4; dia. 3(a) and 4(a)–(c))

Measurements

	Height	Nape to waist	Full length	Half back	Sleeve length	Chest	Waist	Seat
cm	176	44.5	100	20.5	82.5	96	86	102
in	69	17½	39½	8⅛	32½	38	34	40

Scale is half the chest = 48cm (19in) : ⅛ scale = 6cm (2⅜in)
¼ scale = 12cm (4¾in)

Back pattern (dia. 3(a))

A = starting point.
Square across and down from A.
B from A = 7.5cm (3in).
C from A = 24cm (9½in).
D from A = 44.5cm (17½in).
E from D = 3.5cm (1½in).
Square a short line across from B and E.
Square a long line across from C and D.

At the top:
1 from A is half back (20.5cm or 8⅛in) plus 1cm (⅜in) = 21.5cm (8½in).
Square down from 1.
2 is located on the line from B.
3 is on the chest line from C.
4 from C = 1.5cm (⅝in).
5 from D = 3cm (1⅛in).
6 from E = 3cm (1⅛in).
Join A – 4 – 5 – 6.
Square down from 6.
7 from A = 100cm (39½in) (full length).
Square a line across at 7.
The centre back is A – 4 – 5 – 6 – 7.

At the top:
8 from A is ⅛ scale plus 2cm (¾in) = 8cm (3⅛in).
9 squared up from 8 = 2cm (¾in).
Curve 9 to A for the back neck.
10 squared from 2 = 1cm (⅜in).
Join 9 to 10 and slightly hollow the back shoulder.
11 from 3 is ¼ scale = 12cm (4¾in).
Join 10 to 11 with a moderate curve. 11 is the balance point for the sleeve.
12 from 4 is ¼ scale minus 1cm (⅜in) = 11cm (4⅜in).
13 from 5 is ⅛ scale minus 1cm (⅜in) = 5cm (2in).
Join 12 to 13 with a straight line.
F is centre of 12 and 13.
G squared from F = 1cm (⅜in).
Curve 11 – 12 – G – 13.
14 from 6 is the same as 13 from 5 = 5cm (2in).
Join 13 to 14 and square down from 14.
Mark 15 on the line from 7.
H from 6 = 4.5cm (1¾in).
I from 7 = 4.5cm (1¾in).

Join H to I.
J from 14 and K from 15 = 2cm (¾in).
Join J to K.
Spring up 1cm (⅜in) above J and join to 14.

Sidebody

On the chest line:
16 from 3 = 10cm (4in).
Square up from 16.
17 above 16 is the same as 10 from 3 plus 0.5cm (¼in) = 12.5cm (5in).
Square down from 16 and mark 18 on the waist line.
19 from 16 = ⅛ scale plus 1.5cm (⅝in) = 7.5cm (3in).
20 from 18 = 19 to 16 plus 2cm (¾in) = 9.5cm (3¾in).
Join 17 to 19 with a straight line.
L is centre of 17 and 19.
M squared from L = 1.3cm (½in).
Curve 17 – M – 19 and continue with a moderate curve to 20.
From 20 spring out to the lower waist line and mark 21 just below the line.
22 from 16 = 3cm (1⅛in).
23 from 18 = 2cm (¾in).
Join 22 to 23 and spring out from 23.
24 from 23 = 2cm (¾in).
Curve 24 to 21 for the bottom edge.
25 continued above 22 = 2.5cm (1in).
Curve 25 to 17 to complete the sidebody panel.

Front

26 from 22 = 2.5cm (1in).
27 from 23 = 4.5cm (1¾in).
Join 26 to 27 and spring out below 27.
28 from 27 = 2cm (¾in).
29 continued above 26 = 2.5cm (1in).
30 from 26 is ⅛ scale plus 4.5cm (1¾in), = 10.5cm (4⅛in).
Square up from 30 and mark 31 on the top line.
32 from 31 is ⅛ scale plus 1cm (⅜in) = 7cm (2¾in).
33 below 31 = 1.5cm (⅝in).
Join 32 to 33 and continue the line.
For 34 from 32: Measure the back shoulder 9 to 10 minus 1cm (⅜in) = 16.5cm (6½in).
Curve 32 to 34 to complete the front shoulder.

35 above 30 = 2.5cm (1in). 35 is front balance point for the sleeve.
Join 34 to 35 with a straight line and mark mid-point N.
O squared from N = 2cm (¾in).
Curve 34 – O – 35 and from 35 curve down to the chest line and up to 29 for completion of armhole.
36 from 30 is ½ scale minus 7cm (2¾in) = 17cm (6¾in).
Square down from 36. (Note: This is not the centre front.)
Mark 37 on the waist line.
38 continued from 37 = 4cm (1½in).
Complete the waist seam by joining 28 to 38.

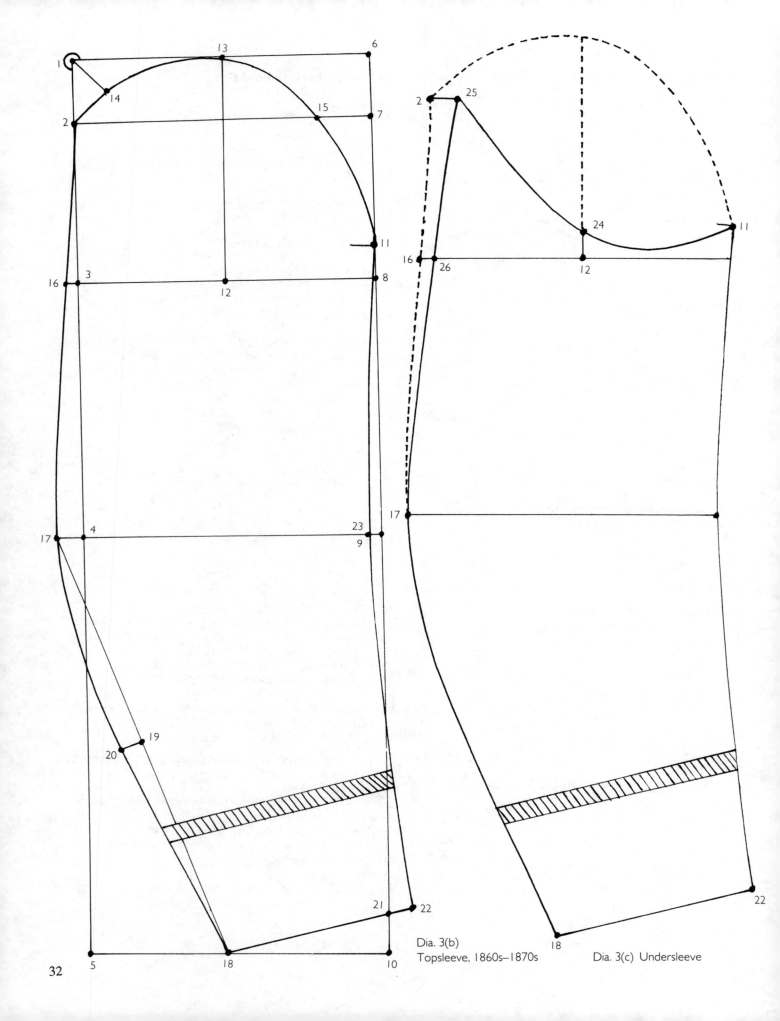

32

Dia. 3(b)
Topsleeve, 1860s–1870s   Dia. 3(c) Undersleeve

On the top line, 39 from 32 = 8.5cm (3¼in).
Join 39 to 36.
40 from 39 = 9cm (3½in).
Curve out from 40 to 36.
41 squared down from 32 = 6.5cm (2½in).
Join 40 to 41.
42 at an angle to 41 = 2.5cm (1in).
43 from 32 = 3cm (1¼in).
Join 43 to 36 and mark 44 at the neck line.
Curve 32 – 42 – 44 to complete the front neck.

Front panel

Draw a line across from 40.
P from 40 = 6.5cm (2½in).
Q from 36 on chest line = 5cm (2in).
Join P to Q with a moderate curve.
Square down from Q and mark R opposite 38.
S below R = 3cm (1¼in).
T squared from S = 3.5cm (1⅜in).
U squared up from T = 11.5cm (4½in). Join U to Q.
T to U = front edge.
V from P = 4.5cm (1¾in).
Curve front edge of lapel from U to V.
W is continued 3cm (1¼in) from V.
Join W to P.

The top buttonhole is placed at U and the bottom hole is on a level
with R. The buttons are placed 3cm (1¼in) back from the front
seam. The fronts are left open and never fastened, the holes and
buttons being only for decoration.

Skirt pattern

45 squared down from 21 = 6.5cm (2½in).
Square across and down from 45.
For 46 from 45, measure 21 to 24 plus 28 to 38 and add 1cm (⅜in)
    = 41cm (16¼in).
47 from 45 = 11.5cm (4½in).
48 squared from 47 = 1.3cm (½in).
Curve 45 to 48 and join 48 to 46 as in the diagram.
49 squared down from 46 = 3cm (1¼in).
50 squared across from 49 = 14cm (5½in).
51 squared down from 45 = 19cm (7½in).
52 from 51 = 2.5cm (1in).
Join 45 to 52 and continue the line.
53 from 45 is the same as 14 to 15 on the back – 52cm (20½in).
Draw a line across at 53.
X from 52 = 1cm (⅜in).
Curve 45 – X – 53.
Y from 45 and Z from 53 = 2cm (¾in).
Join Y to Z to run parallel with 45 and 53.
Spring up 1cm (⅜in) above Y and join to 45.
54 from 53 = 16.5cm (6½in).
Join 50 to 54.
Curve the corner at 54.

Sleeve pattern, 1860s–1870s

Topsleeve (dia. 3(b))
1 = starting point.
Square across and down from 1.
2 from 1 is ⅛ scale minus 1.5cm (⅝in) = 4.5cm (1¾in).
3 from 2 is the same as 11 from 3 on the back pattern (dia. 3(a) =
    12cm (4¾in).
4 from 3 = 19cm (7½in).
5 from 2 is the sleeve length 82.5cm (32½in) minus the half back
    20.5cm (8⅛in) = 62cm (24⅜in).

At the top:
6 from 1 is ½ scale minus 2.5cm (1in) = 21.5cm (8½in).
Square a long line down from 6.
7 is squared across from 2.
8 is squared across from 3.
9 is squared across from 4 and is the elbow line.
10 is squared across from 5.
11 above 8 is the same as 35 from 30 on the front pattern (dia. 3(a))
    = 2.5cm (1in).
12 is the centre of 3 and 8.
Square up from 12 and mark 13 on the top line.
14 at an angle from 1 = 4cm (1½in).
15 from 7 = 4cm (1½in).
Curve the sleevehead 2–14–13–15–11.
16 from 3 = 1cm (⅜in).
17 from 4 = 2cm (¾in).
18 from 5 = 10cm (4in).
Join 17 to 18 with a straight line.
19 is the centre of 17 and 18.
20 squared from 19 = 1.5cm (⅝in).
Join 2 to 16 and from 16 curve to 17–20–18 to complete the back
    seam.
21 above 10 = 2.5cm (1in).
Join 18 to 21 and continue the line.
22 from 21 = 2cm (¾in).
23 inside 9 = 1cm (⅜in).
Join 11 – 23 – 22 for the front seam.
When sewing in the sleeve, point 11 joins to 35 on the front pattern
    (see dia. 3(a)).

Undersleeve (dia. 3(c))
Using the topsleeve as a basis, proceed as follows:
24 above 12 = 2cm (¾in).
25 on a level with 2 = 2cm (¾in).
Curve down from 11, then up to 24 and 25 as in the diagram.
26 inside 16 = 1cm (⅜in).
Join 25–26–17.
17 to 18 and 18 to 22, and the front seam are exactly the same as
    the topsleeve.

Note: If the edges of the coat are braided (as was fashionable in the
period 1860s–70s) then a narrow braid is sewn round the sleeve
approx. 9cm (3½in) up from the cuff.

NOTE:

Although the same basic dress coat pattern is used from 1860 to 1900, Fig. 4 shows the changes that occurred from 1880. The revers became narrower and the sleeves more moderate in width. The cuffs, however, were slightly wider than previously.

G43 page xxiii, is another example of a dress coat of this period.

Fig. 4   Evening dress coat, 1880–1900

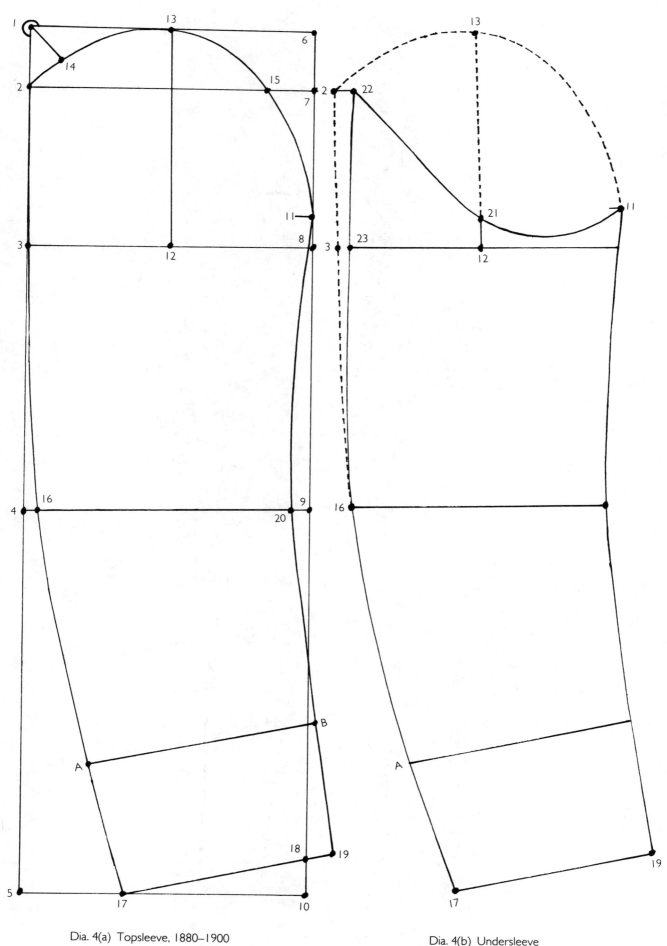

Dia. 4(a) Topsleeve, 1880–1900

Dia. 4(b) Undersleeve

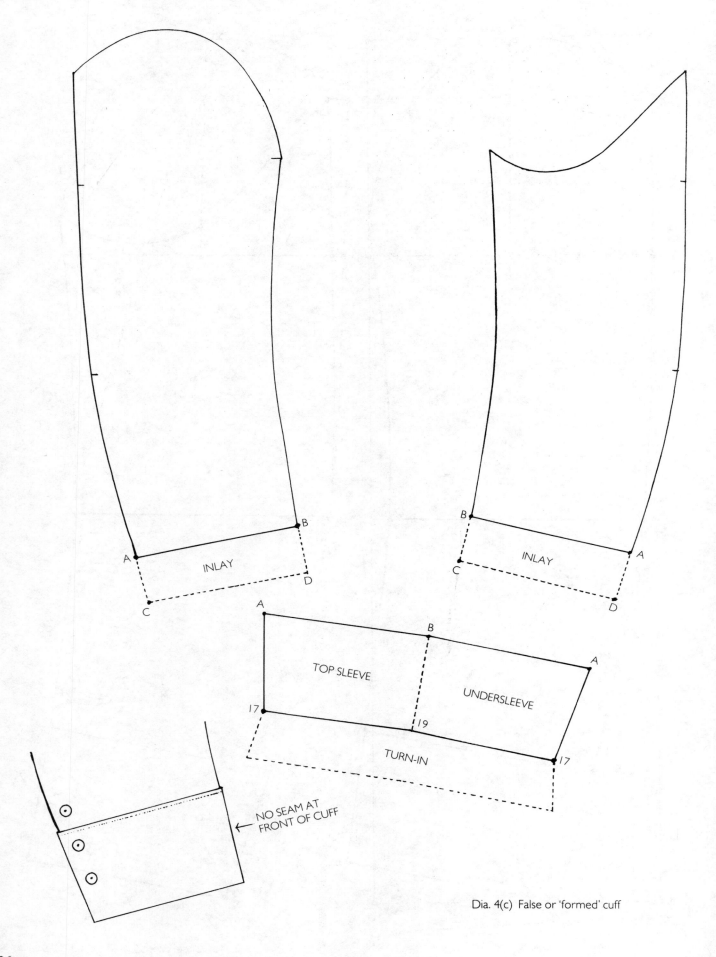

INLAY

INLAY

A

B

C

D

B

A

C

D

A

B

TOP SLEEVE

A

UNDERSLEEVE

17

19

17

TURN-IN

NO SEAM AT
FRONT OF CUFF

Dia. 4(c) False or 'formed' cuff

36

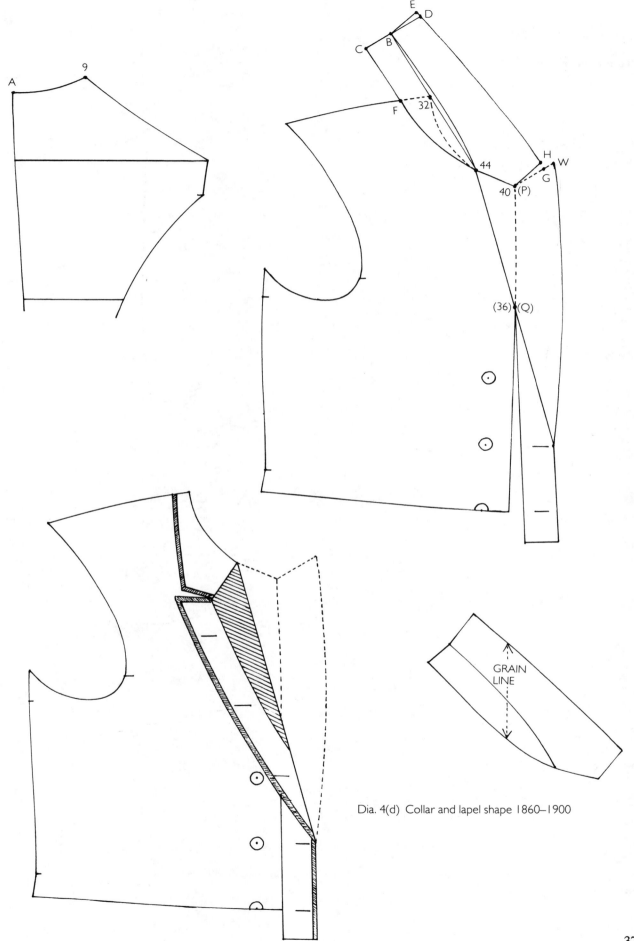

Dia. 4(d) Collar and lapel shape 1860–1900

GRAIN
LINE

Sleeve pattern, 1880–1900

Topsleeve (dia. 4(a))

1 = starting point.

Square across and down from 1.

2 from 1 is ⅛ scale minus 2cm (¾in) = 4cm (1⅝in).

3 from 2 = 12cm (4¾in) = same as 11 from 3 on the back pattern (see dia. 3(a)).

4 from 3 = 19cm (7½in).

5 from 2 is the sleeve length 82.5cm (32½in) minus the half back = 62cm (24⅜in).

At the top:

6 from 1 is ½ scale minus 3cm (1¼in) = 21cm (8¼in).

Square down from 6.

Square across from 2, 3, 4 and 5, and mark 7, 8, 9 and 10.

11 above 8 = 2.5cm (1in), same as 35 from 30 on the front pattern (see dia. 3(a)).

12 is the centre of 3 and 8.

Square up from 12 and mark 13 on the top line.

14 at an angle from 1 = 3cm (1¼in).

15 from 7 = 4cm (1½in).

Curve the sleevehead 2–14–13–15–11.

16 inside 4 = 1cm (⅜in).

17 from 5 = 7.5cm (3in).

Curve 3 – 16 – 17.

The back seam is 2 – 3 – 16 – 17.

18 above 10 = 2.5cm (1in).

Join 17 to 18 and continue the line.

19 from 18 = 2cm (¾in).

20 inside 9 = 1.3cm (½in).

Curve 11 – 20 – 19 for the front seam.

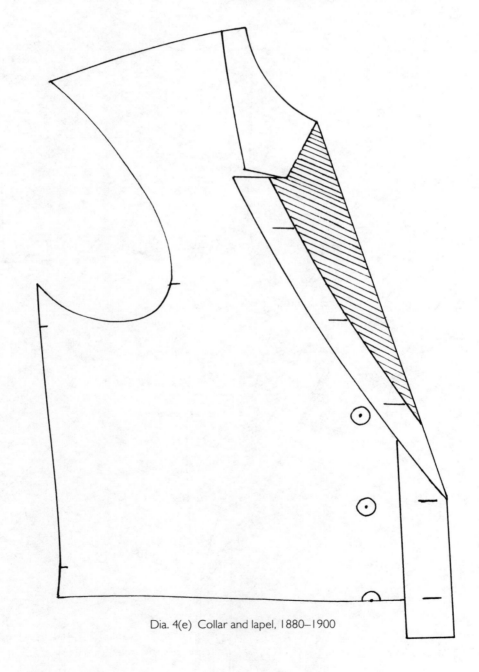

Dia. 4(e) Collar and lapel, 1880–1900

Undersleeve (dia. 4(b))

Using the topsleeve pattern as a basis, continue as follows:
21 above 12 = 2cm (¾in).
22 inside 2 = 1.3cm (½in).
Starting at 11, curve down to within 1cm (⅜in) of the line from 3, then curve up through 21 to 22.
23 from 3 = 1cm (⅜in).
Curve 22 – 23 into 16.
16 – 17 – 19 and the front seam are exactly the same as the topsleeve.

Note: The line A to B on the top and undersleeves is a seam placed round the sleeve, approx. 10cm (4in) above the cuff 17 to 19. It is referred to as a false or 'formed' cuff (see dia. 4(c)).

False or 'formed' cuff (dia. 4(a)-4(c))

This style of cuff (dia. 4(c)) can be seen on men's coats throughout the whole of the period dealt with in this book. It consists of a decorative seam round the sleeve, approximately 10cm (4in) above the cuff. The top and undersleeves are cut across as shown in dia. 4(c), and when sewn back together the seams are pressed downward (not opened) giving the impression of a turned back cuff.

For coats of the 1830s and 1840s the false cuff can be used together with the cuff 'vent' or opening. For the later periods, the sleeves can be made without the 'vent' and the buttons sewn on top of the sleeve.

Diagram 4(c) Following the top and undersleeve patterns of dia. 4(a)-(b) proceed as follows:
Cut across the pattern at A and B on the top and undersleeve.
Join the two parts of the cuff together at B and 19. The cuff is now in one piece with the front seam eliminated.
Add a turn-in of 5cm (2in) to the bottom edge of the cuff.

At A to B of the topsleeve and B to A of the undersleeve leave on an extra allowance of 5cm (2in) shown by points C and D. This extra allowance or 'inlay' remains inside the cuff and is available should the

sleeve require to be lengthened when the garment is fitted on the wearer.

The front seams of the main sleeve are sewn together and while the sleeve is open and flat the cuff is sewn across from A on the topsleeve to A on the undersleeve.

The usual seams must be added before cutting out the pattern.

Collar, 1860-1900 (dia. 4(d))

Place the front panel of dia. 3(a) to the front pattern as P to 40 and Q to 36.
Mark the points 32, 40, 44 and W.
Join 44 to 32 and continue the line.
B from 32 is the same as A to 9 on the back pattern (dia. 3(a)) = 8.5cm (3⅜in).
Square a line across from B.
C from B = 3cm (1¼in).
D from B = 4cm (1½in).
E from D = 1cm (⅜in).
Join E to B.
F from 32 = 3cm (1¼in).
Join C to F and gradually curve to 44, then a straight line to 40.
G inside W = 1.3cm (½in).
H above G = 1cm (⅜in).
Join E to H with a slight curve.

The undercollar is cut on the 'cross' of the fabric and stitched to a moderately firm interlining. The collar fits close to the neck and the 'crease' or folding line is well pressed. With only minor modification this type of collar has continued to the present day. The lower (left) diagram shows the collar shape and the lapel turned back. The edge of the silk facings runs parallel to the edge of the lapel, and the holes on the fronts and lapels are just decorative and not practical. The edges were often braided, especially during the 1860s and 1870s. From about 1890 the silk facings were extended further across the lapel and finished at the back of the buttonholes (dia. 4(e)).

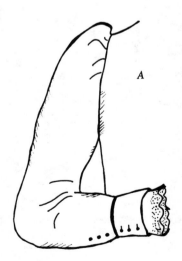 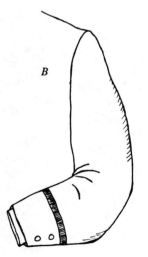 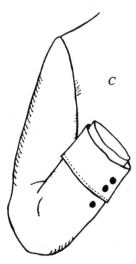

A   *B*   *C*

Ill. 73. (A) 1830. Puffed sleevehead and "formed" cuff. (B) 1860. Wide sleeve and narrow cuff and a row of braid above the cuff. (C) 1880. Moderate width of sleeve with stitching next to the seam of the "formed" cuff.

PLATE 11. 1835.   (L) The back view of a Frock coat with a full skirt pleated at the back. The deep collar has a seam
at the centre back. The Trousers are moderately wide from the knee to the shoe where they are secured by a strap under
the shoe. Note the spur attached to the heel. (R) Tail-Coat with the front curving away to a narrow skirt. The collar
and revers (lapels) are wide, the pocket flaps are on the waist seam, and (an unusual feature for this period) a narrow
welted pocket on the chest. The Vest is Double-breasted with a wide shawl collar and flaps on the pockets. The Trousers
are quite full from the knee to the bottom.

PLATE 12. 1830's. (L) *Single-breasted Frock Coat with a full skirt and cut to knee length. The large Collar rolls to the back of the neck with small revers at the front. The sleeves are narrow at the cuffs and shaped to fit over the hands. Trousers are strapped at the bottoms and display a wide stripe at the sideseams. (R) The front view of the Frock Coat showing the Vest which has a narrow Shawl Collar. Trousers are strapped at the bottom. Petit Courrier des Dames, January 1833.*

2 FROCK COATS AND MORNING COATS

Frock coat

If the dress coat could be described as the most elegant of nineteenth century male attire, then the frock coat must be the most dignified. Combined with the top hat, the general effect was very impressive.

From a technical point of view, the frock coat follows a similar development to the dress coat. The standard pattern has a panel at the front (double-breasted), a waist seam (1820s) and – by 1840 – it included the sidebody panel. Waist lines were raised or lowered and sleeve styles changed according to prevailing fashion. There were also variations in the coat length.

Apart from changes in the style of collar and lapel, the most notable difference in the frock coat from one period to another was in the style of the skirt. This ranged from being very full and flared in the earlier period to hanging straight with very little fullness from 1880 to 1900.

Towards the end of the century the frock coat was mainly replaced by the morning coat.

Frock coat, 1830 (fig. 5; dia. 5(a)-(c))

Measurements

	Height	Nape to waist	Full length	Half back	Sleeve length	Chest	Waist	Seat
cm	176	44.5	100	20.5	82.5	96	86	102
in	69	17½	39½	8⅛	32½	38	34	40

Scale is half the chest = 48cm (19in) : ⅛ scale = 6cm (2⅜in)
¼ scale = 12cm (4¾in)

Back pattern (dia. 5(a))

A = starting point.
Square across and down from A.
B from A = 10cm (4in).
C from A = 24cm (9½in).
D from A = nape to waist (44.5cm) plus 1cm = 45.5cm or 17½in plus ½in = 18in.
Square across from B, C and D.

At the top:
1 from A = 20.5cm (8⅛in) (half back measure).
Square down from 1 and mark 2 on the line from B and 3 on the line from C.

4 inside C = 1.5cm (⅝in).
5 inside D = 3cm (1⅛in).
Join A – 4 – 5.
Square a line down from 5.
6 from A = 100cm (39½in) (full length).
Square a line across at 6.
The centre back = A – 4 – 5 – 6.

At the top line:
7 from A is ⅛ scale plus 1.5cm (⅝in) = 7.5cm (3in).
8 squared up from 7 = 1.5cm (⅝in).
Curve 8 to A for the back neck.
Join 8 to 2 with a straight line.
Slightly hollow between 8 and 2 to complete the back shoulder.
9 above 3 is ¼ scale minus 2cm (¾in) = 10cm (4in).
Curve the back armhole from 2 to 9.
10 from 3 is ¼ scale = 12cm (4¾in).
10 is the back balance point for the sleeve.
11 from 4 is ¼ scale = 12cm (4¾in).
12 from 5 is ⅛ scale minus 1 cm (⅜in) = 5cm (2in).
Join 11 to 12 with a straight line.
E is half-way between 11 and 12.
F squared from E = 1cm (⅜in)
Curve 9 – 11 – F – 12.
13 from 6 = 7.5cm (3in).
Join 12 to 13.
G from 5 and H from 6 = 4.5cm (1¾in).
Join G to H.
I from 12 = 2.5cm (1in).
J from 13 = 4cm (1½in).
Join I to J.
Continue 1cm (⅜in) above I and join to 12.

Side edge

This was an ornamental flap shaped along the outside edge and inserted into the skirt pleat below point 12 with two or three buttons as decoration.

The side edge was a feature on many frock coats and dress coats before 1850. After that date, they were usually seen only on frock top coats, but became obsolete by 1880. However, side edges remained a part of livery coats and military tunics.

To keep the pattern parts separate and to avoid overlapping, add 5cm (2in) for turning in the bottom edge from H to J. Add 1cm (⅜in) seam to the rest of the pattern. Cut out the back pattern and place it back on the pattern paper, then proceed as in diagram 5(b).

For added visual reference see Illustrations G4 and G15.

(ii) back

*Ill. 53. 1836. Single-breasted
Frock Coat with very wide
revers. The body shape is very
waisted with a flared skirt.
The collar would have been in
velvet.*

Fig. 5   Frock coat, 1830

(i) front

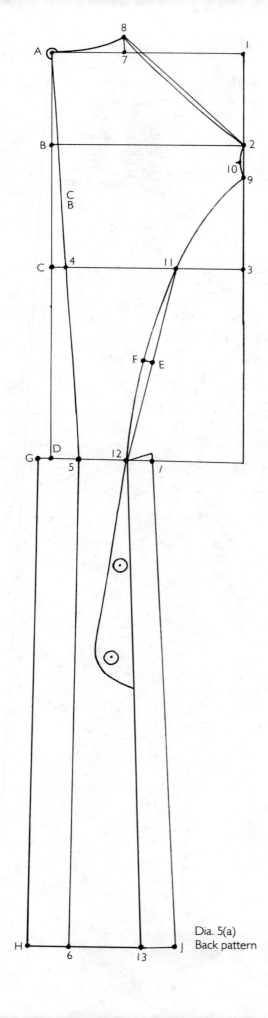

Front pattern (dia. 5(b))

Continue the lines across from A, C and D.

On the chest line from C, point 14 from 3 = 13cm (5in).

15 squared above 14 is the same as 9 from 3 plus 0.5cm (¼in) = 10.5cm (4¼in).

Square down from 14 and mark 16 on the waist line.

17 from 14 = 5.5cm (2¼in).

18 from 16 = 7cm (2¾in).

Join 15 – 17 – 18 with straight lines.

K is centre of 15 and 17.

L squared from K = 1cm (⅜in).

Curve 15 – L – 17 and continue with a moderate curve from 17 to 18.

18x continued from 18 = 0.5cm (¼in).

19 from 14 is ¼ scale plus 2cm (¾in), = 14cm (5½in).

Square up from 19 and mark 20 on the top line.

21 from 20 is ⅛ scale plus 1cm (⅜in), = 7cm (2¾in).

22 squared up from 21 = 1cm (⅜in).

Join 22 to 20 and continue the line.

23 from 22 is the back shoulder width 8 to 2 minus 1cm (⅜in) = 17cm (6⅝in).

Curve from 22 to 23 to complete the front shoulder.

24 above 19 = 2.5cm (1in). 24 is the front balance point for the sleeve.

Join 23 to 24 with a straight line.

M is centre of 23 to 24.

N squared from M = 2.5cm (1in).

O at an angle to 19 = 2cm (¾in).

P at an angle to 14 = 4.5cm (1¾in).

Curve the armhole 23–N–24–O, then down to the chest line and continue the curve up through P to 15.

25 from 19 is ½ scale minus 3.5cm (1½in) = 20.5cm (8in).

Square down from 25 and mark 26 on the waist line.

27 continued from 26 = 1.5cm (⅝in).

25 to 27 is the centre front.

28 from 27 = 2cm (¾in).

29 squared up from 28 = 19cm (7½in).

30 continued up from 29 = 18cm (7in).

31 squared down from 21 = 7cm (2¾in).

Join 31 to 30 and continue the line.

32 from 30 = 2cm (¾in).

Join 32 to 29 for the outside edge of the lapel.

33 opposite 22 = 3.5cm (1⅜in).

Join 33 to 29 and mark 34 at the neck line.

35 at an angle to 31 = 2.5cm (1in).

Curve front neck 22–35–34.

The neck dart is placed half-way between 34 and 32.

Mark 1.3cm (½in) to be sewn out at the top and make the dart 10cm (4in) long.

To complete the waist seam of the front:

36 from 16 = 7.5cm (3in).

37 squared up from 36 = 2cm (¾in).

38 from 26 = 9cm (3½in).

Curve 18x – 37 – 38 – 27 as in the diagram.

The buttons and buttonholes are marked on the centre front. The top hole and button position is opposite 29 and the bottom position at point 26. Divide the space between equally for the other two holes and buttons.

Dia. 5(a)
Back pattern

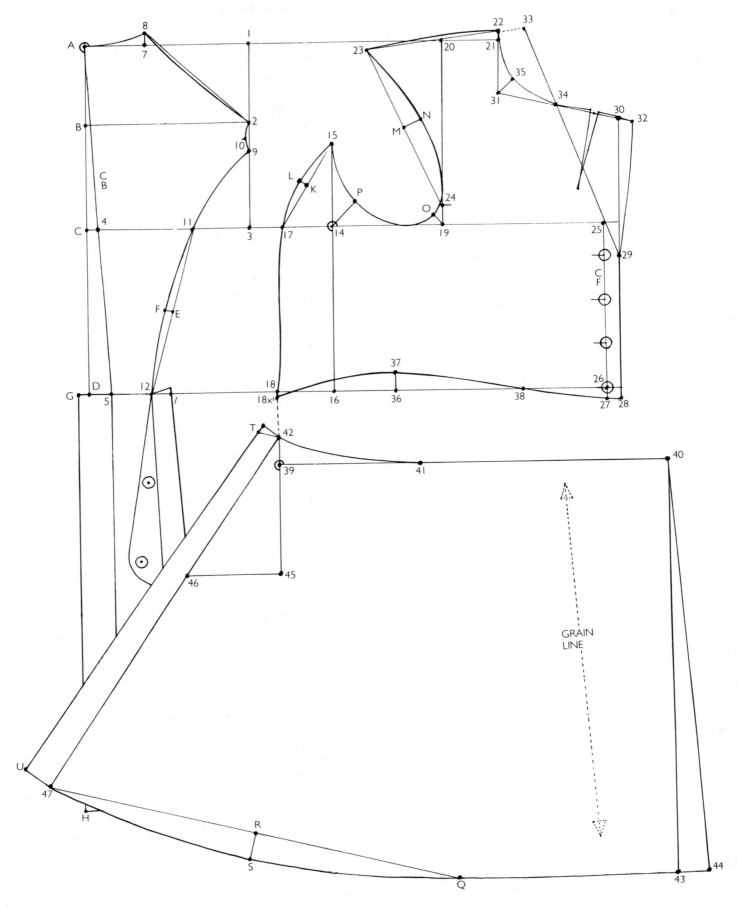

Dia. 5(b) Front and skirt

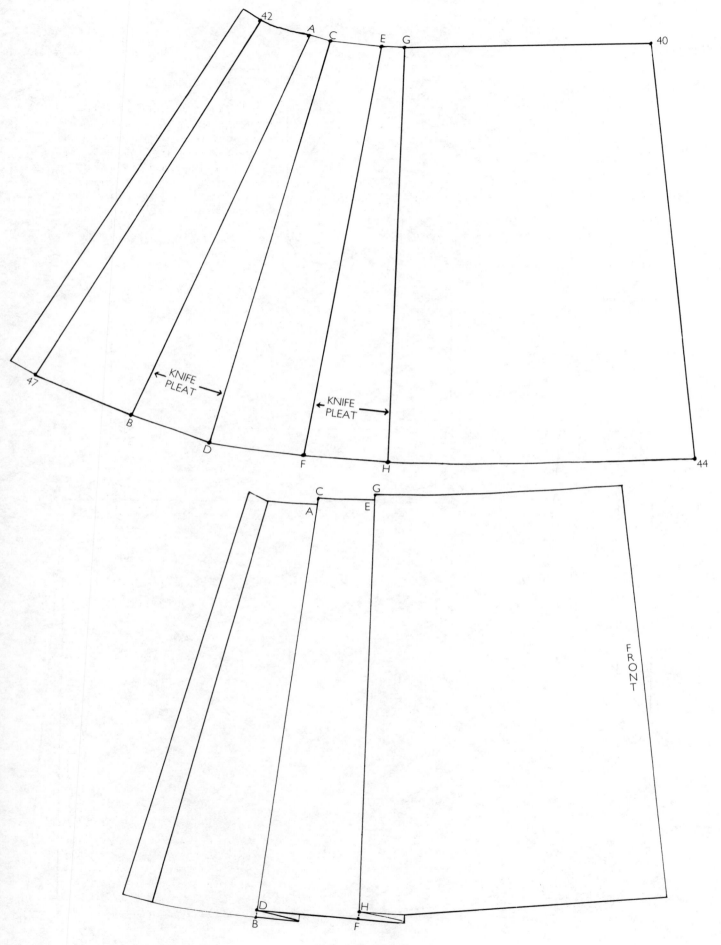

42
47
A
C
E
G
40
KNIFE
PLEAT
KNIFE
PLEAT
B
D
F
H
44

C
G
A
E
D
H
B
F
F
R
O
N
T

46

Dia. 5(c) Skirt pleats

Skirt pattern

Dia. 5(b)) Square a line down from 18x.

39 from 18x = 9cm (3½in).

Square across from 39.

For 40 from 39, measure the waist seam of the front (18x – 37 – 38 – 28) plus 5cm (2in) = 49.5cm (19½in).

41 from 39 = 18cm (7in).

42 above 39 = 3.5cm (1⅜in).

Join 42 to 41 with a moderate curve.

43 squared down from 40 is the same as 12 to 13 on the back (see dia. 5(a)) = 55cm (21½in).

44 squared from 43 = 4cm (1½in).

Join 40 to 44 for the front edge.

45 from 42 = 18cm (7in).

46 squared from 45 = 11.5cm (4½in).

Join 42 to 46 and continue the line.

47 from 42 is the same as 12 to 13 on the back (see dia. 5(a)) = 55cm (21½in).

To complete the bottom edge:

Square back from 43.

Q from 43 = 28cm (11in).

Join Q to 47 and mark R at the centre.

S squared from R = 4cm (1½in).

Curve Q – S – 47.

T from 42 – 2.5cm (1in).

U from 47 = 4cm (1½in).

Join T to U for the half pleat.

Continue 1cm (⅜in) above T and join to 42. (Continue to dia. 5(c)).

The grain line is parallel with the front edge 40 – 44.

For sleeve pattern see diagrams 1(d)–(f), pp. 19-20.

Dia. 5(c)) The skirt pattern has been constructed to include two deep knife pleats in addition to the standard pleat in the skirt seam. On the skirt pattern of dia. 5(b), mark as follows, as in dia. 5(c):

A from 42 = 6.5cm (2½in).

B from 47 = 13cm (5in).

C from A = 2.5cm (1in).

D from B = 10cm (4in).

Join A – B and C – D.

E from C = 6.5cm (2½in).

F from D = 13cm (5in).

G from E = 2.5cm (1in).

H from F = 10cm (4in).

Join E–F and G–H.

Before the skirt is sewn to the front waist seam the pleats are folded towards the back – as shown in the lower diagram.

C – D folds to A – B.

G – H folds to E – F.

Pin the pleats into position and sew a narrow row of stitching along the inside fold. The outside edges of the pleats (C – D and G – H) can be either pressed flat or allowed to 'roll'.

Note: Before cutting the pattern allow for seams and turn-ins.

Ill. 54. Frock Coats A/B.

A. 1855-1860. *Single-breasted Frock Coat with a three button front fastening. The coat length is well above the knees and the skirt is pleated for a "full" effect. The sleeves are gathered at the top to give a "puffed" sleeve head. The turned back cuffs are fastened with two buttons. A deep collar is required to balance the wide revers. Trousers are of a parallel style (i.e. the knee and bottom are of a similar width). At the bottom, the trousers are secured with a strap and buckle under the shoe. The figure wears a high crowned Top hat with a narrow brim.*

B. 1835-1840. *Short Double-breasted Frock Coat with a flared skirt. The sleeves have plain cuffs and at the sleeve head there is a "puffed" effect. There is a Vest beneath the coat which could be either Single- or Double-breasted. Trousers are narrow at the thigh and the knee and become a little wider at the bottom. The figure wears a Top hat with a curled brim.*

Double-breasted frock coat, 1840
(fig. 6; dia. 6 (a)-(b))

Measurements

	Height	Nape to waist	Full length	Half back	Sleeve length	Chest	Waist	Seat
cm	176	44.5	96	20.5	82.5	96	86	102
in	69	17½	38	8⅛	32½	38	34	40

Scale is half the chest = 48cm (19in) : ⅛ scale = 6cm (2⅜in)
¼ scale = 12cm (4¾in)

Back pattern (dia. 6(a))

A = starting point.
Square across and down from A.
B from A = 10cm (4in).
C from A = 24cm (9½in).
D from A = 44.5cm (17½in) (nape to waist).
E from D = 4cm (1½in) for dropped waist line.
Square across from B, C, D and E.

At the top:
1 from A = 20.5cm (8⅛in) (half back measure).
Square down from 1 and mark 2 on the line from B and point 3 on the line from C.
4 inside C = 1.5cm (⅝in).
5 inside D = 3cm (1⅛in).
6 inside E = 3cm (1⅛in).
Join A – 4 – 5 – 6.
Square down from 6.
7 from A = 96cm (38in) (full length).
The centre back = A – 4 – 5 – 6 – 7.
Square a line across at 7.

At the top line:
8 from A is ⅛ scale plus 1.5cm (⅝in) = 7.5cm (3in).
9 squared up from 8 = 1.5cm (⅝in).
Curve 9 to A for the back neck.
Join 9 to 2 with a straight line, then hollow the back shoulder.
10 above 3 is ¼ scale minus 2cm (¾in) = 10cm (4in).
Curve the back armhole from 2 to 10.
11 from 3 is ¼ scale = 12cm (4¾in) and 11 is the back balance point for the sleeve.
12 from 4 is ¼ scale minus 1cm (⅜in) = 11cm (4⅜in).
13 from 5 is ⅛ scale minus 1cm (⅜in) = 5cm (2in).
14 from 6 = ⅛ scale minus 1cm (⅜in) = 5cm (2in).
Join 13 to 14.
Join 12 to 13 with a straight line.
F is centre of 12 and 13.
G squared from F = 1cm (⅜in).
Curve 10 – 12 – G – 13.
15 from 7 = 6.5cm (2½in).
Join 14 to 15.
H from 6 and I from 7 = 4.5cm (1¾in).
Join H to I.
J from 14 = 2.5cm (1in).

NOTE:
Fig. 6. shows the more moderate skirt of the 1840's.

Fig. 6   Frock coat, 1840

48

K from 15 = 4cm (1½in).
Join J to K for the half pleat.
Continue up 1cm (⅜in) above J and join to 14.

Add 5cm (2in) for turning in the bottom edge from I to K and add 1cm (⅜in) to the rest of the pattern. Cut out the back pattern and re-place it on the pattern paper, then proceed as in dia. 6(b).

Sidebody (dia. 6 (b))

Continue the lines across from A, C, D and E.
Mark point 16 on the chest line.
17 squared up from 16 is the same as 10 from 3 plus 0.5cm (¼in),
    = 10.5cm (4¼in).
Square down from 16 and mark 18 on the waist line from D.
19 from 16 = ⅛ scale plus 1cm (⅜in) = 7cm (2¾in).
Join 17 to 19 with a straight line.
L is centre of 17 and 19.
M squared from L = 1cm (⅜in).
Curve 17 – M – 19.
20 from 18 = 9cm (3½in).
Join 19 to 20 and 'spring' out on to the dropped waist line.
Mark 21 just below the line.
22 from 16 = 3cm (1⅛in).
23 from 18 = 2cm (¾in).
Join 22 to 23 and 'spring' out below 23.
24 from 23 = 2.5cm (1in).
Curve 24 to 21.
25 continued above 22 = 2.5cm (1in).
Curve 25 to 17 for completion of sidebody.
26 from 22 = 2.5cm (1in).
27 from 23 = 4.5cm (1¾in).
Join 26 and 27 and 'spring' out below 27.
28 from 27 = 2.5cm (1in).
29 continued above 26 = 2.5cm (1in).
30 from 26 is ⅛ scale plus 5cm (2in) = 11cm (4⅜in).
Square up from 30 and mark 31 on the top line.
32 from 31 is ⅛ scale plus 1cm (⅜in) = 7cm (2¾in).
33 squared up from 32 = 1cm (⅜in).
Join 33 to 31 and continue the line.
For 34 from 33, measure 9 to 2 minus 1cm (⅜in) = 17cm (6⅝in).
Curve the front shoulder out gently from 33 to 34.
35 above 30 = 2.5cm (1in). 35 is the front balance point for the
    sleeve.
Join 34 to 35 with a straight line.
N is centre of 34 and 35.
O squared from N = 2.5cm (1in).
Curve the armhole: 34 – 0 – 35 then down to the chest line and up
    to 29.
36 from 30 is ½ scale minus 3.5cm = 20.5cm or 9½in minus 1½in
    = 8in.
Square down from 36.
Mark 37 on the waist line and continue the line.
38 below 37 = 5cm (2in).
39 from 32 = 11.5cm (4½in).
Join 39 to 36.
40 from 39 = 9cm (3½in).
Join 40 to 36 with a moderate curve.
Centre front (CF)= 40 – 36 – 37– 38.

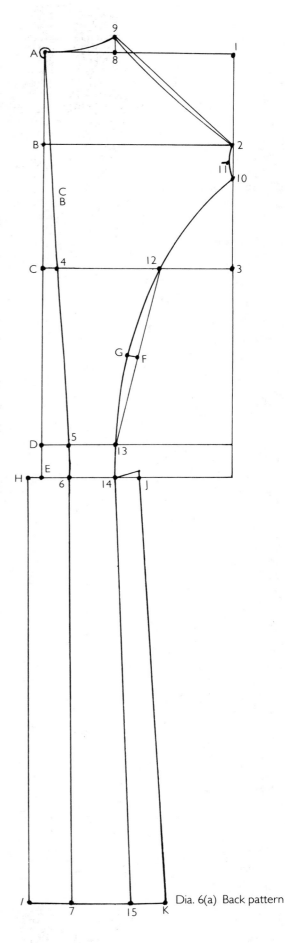

Dia. 6(a) Back pattern

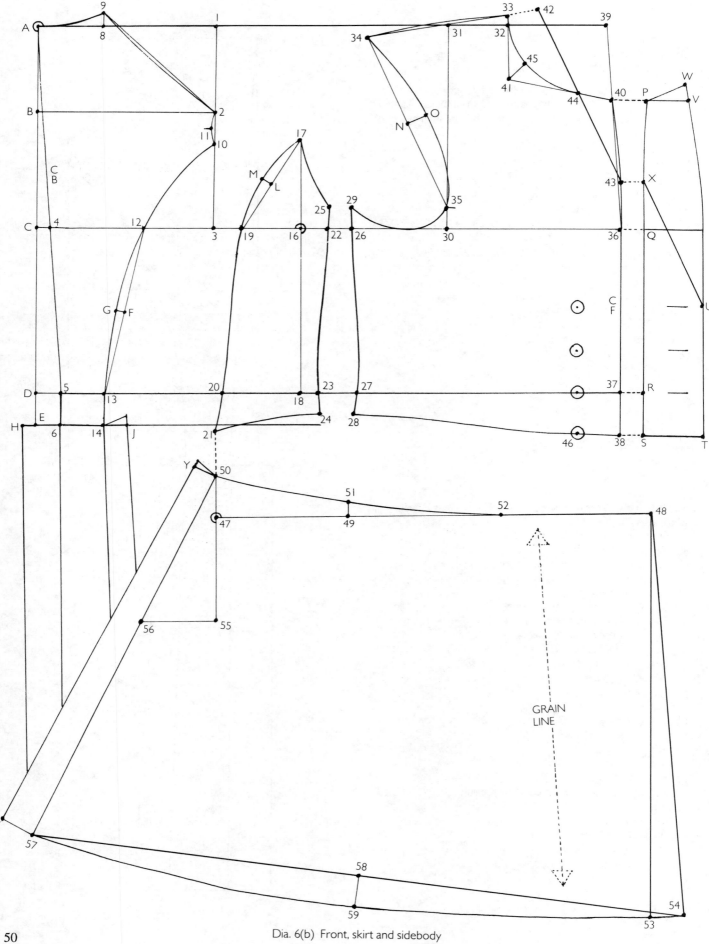

50   Dia. 6(b) Front, skirt and sidebody

41 squared down from 32 = 6.5cm (2½in).
Join 40 to 41.
42 opposite 33 = 3.5cm (1⅜in).
43 above 36 = 5cm (2in).
Join 42 to 43 and mark 44 on the neck line.
45 at an angle to 41 = 2.5cm (1in).
Curve the front neck 33 – 45 – 44.

To complete the waist seam of the front:
46 squared back from 38 = 5cm (2in).
Curve 28 to 46 as in diagram.

Front panel (dia. 6(b))

P on a level with 40 = 4cm (1½in).
Q from 36 = 2.5cm (1in).
Curve P to Q.
Square down from Q and mark R and S.
T squared from S = 7cm (2¾in).
U squared up from T = 15cm (6in).
V on a level with P = 5cm (2in)
Join U to V and continue the line.
W from V = 2cm (¾in).
Join W to P.
Curve the outer edge of the lapel from W to U
X above Q = 4.5cm (1¾in).
Join U to X with a straight line.

The buttonholes are 5cm (2in) apart and 2cm (¾in) from the front edge. The buttons are placed 5cm (2in) back from the centre front.

Skirt pattern

47 squared down from 21 = 10cm (4in).
Square across and down from 47.
Measure 21 – 24 plus 28 – 38 plus S – T = 51cm (20in).
48 from 47 = 51cm (20in).
49 from 47 = 15 (6in).
50 above 47 = 5cm (2in).
51 above 49 = 2cm (¾in).
52 is centre of 48 and 49.
Join 50 – 51 – 52 and continue to 48.
Square down from 48.
53 from 48 is the same as 14 to 15 on the back (see dia. 6(a))
    = 48cm (19in).
54 squared from 53 = 4cm (1½in).
Join 48 to 54 for the front edge of the skirt.
55 from 50 = 18cm (7in).
56 squared from 55 = 9cm (3½in).
Join 50 to 56 and continue the line.
57 from 50 is the same as 14 to 15 on the back (see dia. 6(a)) =
    48cm (19in).
Join 54 to 57 with a straight line.
58 is centre of 54 to 57.
59 squared from 58 = 4cm (1½in).
Curve the bottom edge of the skirt from 54 to 57.
Y from 50 = 2.5cm (1in).

Z continued from 57 = 4cm (1½in).
Join Y to Z for the half pleat.
Continue 1cm (⅜in) above Y and join to 50.
The grain line is level with 48 and 54.
Sleeve pattern as in diagrams 2(b) and 2(c), p. 26.

Single-breasted frock coat, 1860–1870s
(fig. 7; dia. 7)

Measurements

	Height	Nape to waist	Full length	Half across back	Sleeve length	Chest	Waist	Seat
cm	176	44.5	100	20.5	82.5	96	86	102
in	69	17½	39½	8⅛	32½	38	34	40

Scale is half the chest = 48cm (19in) : ⅛ scale = 6cm (2⅜in)
                                          ¼ scale = 12cm (4¾in)

Back pattern (dia. 7)

A = starting point.
Square across and down from A.
B from A = 7.5cm (3in).
C from A = 24cm (9½in).
D from A = 44.5cm (17½in) (nape to waist).
E from D = 4cm (1½in).
Square across from B, C, D and E.

At the top:
1 from A is the half back plus 1cm (⅜in) = 21.5cm (8½in).
Square down from 1, marking 2 opposite B and 3 opposite C.
4 inside C = 1.5cm (⅝in).
5 from D = 3cm (1⅛in).
6 from E = 3cm (1⅛in).
Join A – 4 – 5 – 6.
Square down from 6.
7 from A = 100cm (39½in) (full length).
Square across from 7.

At the top:
8 from A is ⅛ scale plus 2cm (¾in) = 8cm (3⅛in).
9 squared up from 8 = 2cm (¾in).
Curve 9 to A for the back neck.
10 squared from 2 = 1cm (⅜in).
Join 9 to 10 and slightly hollow the back shoulder.
11 from 3 is ¼ scale = 12cm (4¾in).
Curve the back armhole from 10 to 11. 11 is the sleeve balance
    point.
12 from 4 is ¼ scale minus 1cm (⅜in) = 11cm (4⅜in).
13 from 5 is ⅛ scale minus 1cm (⅜in) = 5cm (2in).
14 from 6 = ⅛ scale minus 1cm (⅜in) = 5cm (2in).
Join 12 – 13 – 14.

Ill. 55 and Ill. 56 are both single-breasted Frock-coats with a three button fastening. The length of the coat, Ill. 55, is just below the knee while Ill. 56 is thigh length. Re-drawn from Demorest Magazine, 1879, by William-Alan Landes.

Ill. 55

Ill. 56

Fig. 7   Single-breasted frock coat, 1860–70s

F is centre of 12 – 13.
G squared from F = 1cm (³⁄₈in).
Curve 11 – 12 – G – 13.
Square down from 14 and mark 15 on the bottom line.
H from 6 and I from 7 = 4.5cm (1³⁄₄in).
Join H to I.
J from 14 = 2cm.
K from 15 = 2cm.
Join J to K for the half pleat.
Continue 1cm (³⁄₈in) above J and join to 14.

Sidebody

16 from 3 = 10cm (4in).
17 squared up from 16 is the same as 11 from 3 plus 0.5cm (¹⁄₄in)
   = 12.5cm (5in).
Square down from 16 and mark 18 on the waist line from D.
19 from 16 = ¹⁄₈ scale plus 1.5cm (⁵⁄₈in) = 7.5cm (3in).
Join 17 to 19 with a straight line.
L is centre of 17 and 19.
M squared from L = 1.3cm (¹⁄₂in).
Curve 17 – M – 19.
20 from 18 = 9.5cm (3³⁄₄in).
Join 19 to 20, 'spring' out below 20 and mark 21 just below the
   dropped waist line.
22 from 16 = 3cm (1¹⁄₈in).
23 from 18 = 2cm (³⁄₄in).
Join 22 to 23 and 'spring' out below 23.
24 from 23 = 2.5cm (1in).
Curve 24 to 21.
25 continued above 22 = 2.5cm (1in).
Curve 25 to 17 to complete the sidebody.

Front (dia. 7)

26 from 22 = 2.5cm (1in).
27 from 23 = 4.5cm (1³⁄₄in).
Join 26 to 27 and 'spring' out below 27.
28 from 27 = 2.5cm (1in).
29 continued above 26 = 2.5cm (1in).
30 from 26 is ¹⁄₈ scale plus 4.5cm (1³⁄₄in) = 10.5cm (4¹⁄₈in).
Square up from 30 and mark 31 on the top line.
32 from 31 is ¹⁄₈ scale plus 1cm (³⁄₈in) = 7cm (2³⁄₄in).
33 below 31 = 1.5cm (⁵⁄₈in).
Join 32 to 33 and continue the line.
For 34 from 32, measure 9 to 11 minus 1cm (³⁄₈in) = 16.5cm
   (6¹⁄₂in).
Curve the front shoulder from 32 to 34.
35 above 30 = 2.5cm (1in). 35 is front balance point for the sleeve.
Join 34 to 35.
N is centre of 34 and 35.
O squared from N = 2cm (³⁄₄in).
Curve the armhole 34 – O – 35, continue the curve down to the
   chest line and up to 29.
36 from 30 is ¹⁄₂ scale minus 3.5cm = 20.5cm or 9¹⁄₂in minus
   1¹⁄₂in = 8in.

Square down from 36. Mark 37 on the waist line and continue
   the line.
38 from 37 = 4.5cm (1³⁄₄in).
Curve 28 to 38.
39 from 38 = 2cm (³⁄₄in).
40 from 36 = 2cm (³⁄₄in).
Join 40 to 39 for the front edge.
(Note: 36 – 37 – 38 is the centre front (CF).)
41 squared up from 40 = 15cm (6in).
42 squared down from 32 = 6.5cm (2¹⁄₂in).
Join 42 to 41 and continue the line.
43 from 41 = 1cm (³⁄₈in).
Join 43 to 40 for the edge of the lapel.
44 from 32 = 3cm (1¹⁄₄in).
Join 44 to 40 and mark 45 at the neck line.
46 from 42 = 2.5cm (1in).
Curve the front neck 32 – 46 – 45.
The neck dart is placed half-way between 43 and 45.
Mark to sew out 1.3cm (¹⁄₂in) at the top and make the dart
   10cm (4in) long.

The buttons and holes are marked on the centre front. The top
position is at 36 and the lowest hole and button is at 38. Divide the
other two holes and buttons equally between 36 and 38.

Skirt pattern (dia. 7)

47 squared down from 21 = 7.5cm (3in).
For 48 squared across from 47, measure 21 – 24 plus 28 to 39 plus
   2cm (³⁄₄in) = 47.5cm (18³⁄₄in).
49 from 47 = 15cm (6in).
50 above 47 = 2.5cm (1in).
51 above 49 = 1cm (³⁄₈in).
Curve 50 to 51 and join 51 to 48.
Square down from 48.
52 from 48 is the same as 14 to 15 on the back = 51.5cm (20¹⁄₂in).
53 squared from 52 = 2cm (³⁄₄in).
Join 48 to 53 for front edge of the skirt.
54 squared down from 50 = 18cm (7in).
55 squared from 54 = 6.5cm (2¹⁄₂in).
Join 50 to 55 and continue the line.
56 from 50 is the same as 14 to 15 = 51.5cm (20¹⁄₂in).
Join 53 to 56 with a straight line.
P is centre of 53 and 56.
Q from P = 2.5cm (1in)
Curve the bottom edge of the skirt from 53 to 56.
R from 50 and S from 56 = 2cm (³⁄₄in).
Join R to S for the half skirt pleat.
Continue 1cm (³⁄₈in) above R and join to 50.
The grain line is parallel with 48–53.

Sleeve pattern as in diagrams 3(b) and 3(c), p. 32.

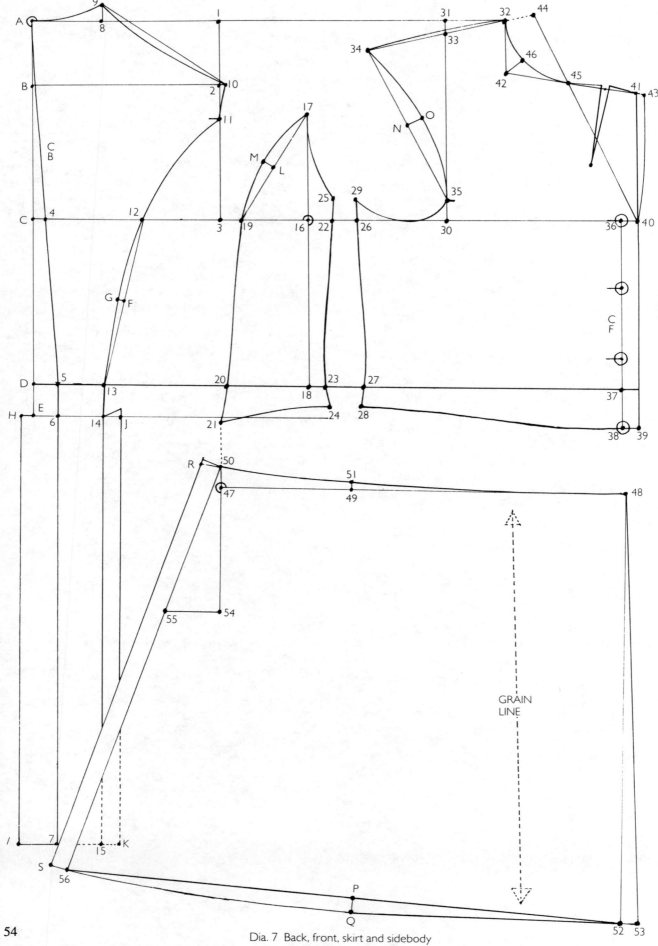

54 Dia. 7 Back, front, skirt and sidebody

Double-breasted frock coat, 1880–1900
(fig. 8; dia. 8)

The measurements are the same as the single-breasted frock coat (1860s–70s) p. 51.

Back pattern: as in dia. 7.

Sidebody pattern: as in dia. 7.

Scale is half chest = 48cm (19in) :   ⅛ scale = 6cm (2⅜in)
                                       ¼ scale = 12cm (4¾in)

Front pattern (dia. 8)

26 from 22 = 2.5cm (1in).
27 from 23 = 4.5cm (1¾in).
Join 26 to 27 and 'spring' out below 27.
28 from 27 = 2.5cm (1in).
29 continued above 26 = 2.5cm (1in).
30 from 26 is ⅛ scale plus 4.5cm (1¾in), = 10.5cm (4⅛in).
Square up from 30 and mark 31 on the top line.
32 from 31 is ⅛ scale plus 1cm (⅜in) = 7cm (2¾in).
33 below 31 = 1.5cm (⅝in).
Join 32 to 33 and continue the line.
For 34 from 32, measure the back shoulder 9 to 11 minus 1cm (⅜in) = 16.5cm (6½in).
Curve the front shoulder out slightly from 32 to 34.
35 above 30 = 2.5cm (1in). 35 is front balance point for the sleeve.
Join 34 to 35 with a straight line.
N is the centre of 34 and 35.
O squared from N = 2cm (¾in).
Curve the armhole 34 – 0 – 35, continue the curve down to the chest line and up to 29.
36 from 30 is ½ scale minus 3.5cm = 20.5cm or 9½in minus 1½in = 8in.
Square down from 36 and mark 37 on the waist line.
38 continued below 37 = 5cm (2in).
Curve the waist seam from 28, keeping the line straight just before it reaches 38.

At the top line:
39 from 32 = 11.5cm (4½in).
Join 39 to 36.
40 from 39 = 10cm (4in).
Curve from 40 to 36. Centre front (CF) = 40–36–37–38.
41 squared down from 32 = 7cm (2¾in).
Join 40 to 41.
42 opposite 32 = 3cm (1¼in).
Join 42 to 36 and mark 43 on the neck line.
44 at an angle to 41 = 2.5cm (1in).
Curve the front neck 32 – 44 – 43.

Front panel

P on a level with 40 = 4cm (1½in).
Q from 36 = 2.5cm (1in).
Curve P to Q.
Square down from Q and mark R level with 38.
S squared from R = 5cm (2in).
Square up from S for the front edge.
T from S = 10cm (4in).
U is on a level with Q = 5.5cm (2¼in).
V on a level with P = 4.5cm (1¾in).
W above V = 4cm (1½in).
Join W to P.
Complete the outer edge of the lapel with a moderate curve from W to T.
Join Q to T with a straight line.

The buttonholes are 2cm (¾in) inside the front edge and placed level with S and T. The buttons are 3cm (1¼in) back from the centre front and level with the holes. The 'show' button is directly above the top button.

Skirt pattern

Square down from 21.
45 from 21 = 7.5cm (3in).
Square across from 45.
For 46 from 45, measure 21 – 24 plus 28 – 38 plus R – S plus 2cm (¾in) = 51cm (20in).
Note: The 2cm (¾in) added to the waist seam measurement is for fullness when the skirt seam is sewn to the sidebody and front.
47 from 46 = 9cm (3½in).
48 above 45 = 12.5cm (5in).
49 above 45 = 1.3cm (½in).
50 above 48 = 2cm (¾in).
Curve 49 – 50 – 47 (47 to 46 remains a straight line).
51 squared down from 46 is the same as 14 to 15 on the back = 51.5cm (20½in).
52 squared from 51 = 2cm (¾in).
Join 46 to 52 for the front edge of the skirt.
53 from 49 = 18cm (7in).
54 squared from 53 = 4.5cm (1¾in).
Join 49 to 54 and continue the line.
55 from 49 is the same as 14 to 15 = 51.5cm (20½in).
X from 54 = 1cm (⅜in).
Curve 49–X–55.
Join 52 to 55 with a straight line.
Complete the bottom edge with a moderate curve from 52 to 55.
Y from 49 and Z from 55 are both 2cm (¾in).
Join Y to Z with a parallel curve to 49–X–55.
Continue 1cm (⅜in) above Y and join to 49.
The grain line is parallel to 46 and 52.

Sleeve pattern as in diagrams 4(a) and 4(b), p. 35.

(ii) back

Fig. 8   Double-breasted frock coat, 1880–1900 (i) front

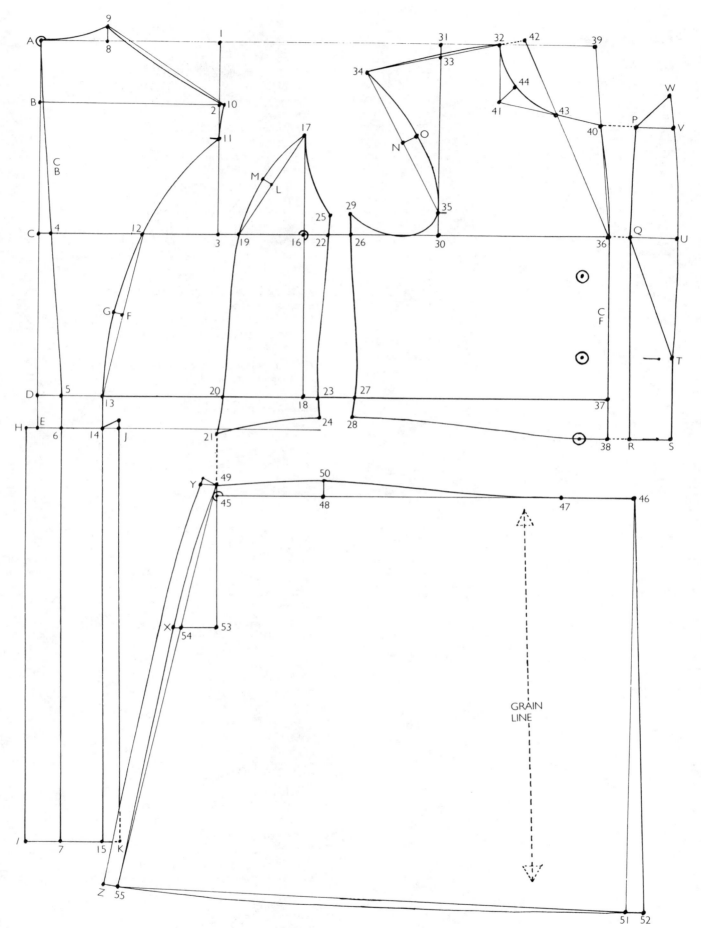

Dia. 8 Back, front, skirt and sidebody

57

Morning coat

This garment was originally known as a riding coat, as it was worn by the gentry when out for their morning ride. Thus it came to be called the morning coat. Although the skirt was continuous with the front edge (as in the frock coat) it was cut away from above the waist line. For practical purposes it had flaps and pockets on the waist seam – also an outbreast pocket on the left side. In all other respects it was cut on similar lines to tail coats of the period.

From c. 1850, the morning coat became popular for day wear, but towards the end of the century it was only worn on formal occasions. By this time the flap pockets at the waist seam had been discarded in order to present a more graceful line. However, unlike the dress and frock coats, it still retained the outbreast pocket.

For the period 1830–1900 the morning coat style remained basically unaltered. The fronts would be either single- or double-breasted with the buttoning high or low, according to prevailing fashion. The skirt was often quite short, almost to a jacket length or, at times, similar in length to the frock coat. At different periods it was known by various names: originally 'riding coat', then 'morning walking coat', 'cut-away', 'Newmarket' and finally 'morning coat'. In the 1870s there was also a form of morning coat known as a 'university' coat.

Double-breasted morning coat, 1860

(fig. 9; dia. 9) (same style for riding coat)

Except for the full length, the measurements are the same as the single-breasted frock coat (1860–70s), p. 51.

Back pattern: as in dia. 7 (make 7 from A = 96cm (38in)).

Sidebody pattern: as in dia. 7.

Front pattern: as in dia. 7, from 26 to 37.

Then continue the front pattern using diagram 9.

38 continued below 37 = 6.5cm (2½in).
39 below 36 = 4cm (1½in).
40 from 39 = 7.5cm (3in).
36–39–40–41–37 is centre front (CF).
41 from 40 = 7.5cm (3in).
Square across from 39, 40 and 41.
42 from 39 = 7cm (2¾in).
43 from 40 = 6cm (2¼in).
44 from 41 = 4.5cm (1¾in).
45 inside 38 = 1cm (⅜in).
Join 42–43–44–45 for the front edge.

Front neck and lapel

46 squared up from 42 = 19cm (7½in).
47 squared down from 32 = 6.5cm (2½in).
Join 46 to 47.
48 opposite 32 = 2.5cm (1in).
Join 48 to 42.
Mark 49 on the neck line.
50 at an angle from 47 = 2.5cm (1in).
Curve the neck 49–50–32.
P from 46 = 2cm (¾in).
Curve from 42 to P and continue the line.
Q from P = 5cm (2in).
R from P = 4.5cm (1¾in).
Join R to Q.
The neck dart is half-way between 49 and R.
Take out 1.3cm (½in) at the top and make the length of the dart 9cm (3½in).

The buttonholes are 2cm (¾in) inside the front edge.
The top button is 5cm (2in) from the centre front.
The middle button is 4cm (1½in) from the centre front.
The bottom button is 2.5cm (1in) from the centre front.

NOTE: *Fig. 9 shows only a two button front fastening instead of three as in Dia. 9.*

Outbreast welt pocket

On the chest line:
S from 30 = 3cm (1¼in).
T from S = 10cm (4in).
U squared down from T = 2cm (¾in).
Join U to S.
V squared up from S = 2cm (¾in).
Join V to T.

Skirt pattern

Square a line down from 21.
51 from 21 = 6.5cm (2½in).
Square across from 51.
52 from 51 is 21 to 24 plus 28 to 38 plus 2cm (¾in) = 47.5cm (18¾in).
53 from 52 = 15.5cm (6in).
54 squared down from 52 = 2.5cm (1in).
Curve 51 to 53 and continue the curve to 54.
55 squared down from 51 = 18cm (7in).
56 squared from 55 = 2.5cm (1in).
Join 51 to 56 and continue the line.
Measure 14 to 15 on the back pattern of dia. 9 which is 48cm (19in).
    Apply this measurement from 51 and mark 57.
Draw a line across from 57.
W from 56 = 1cm (⅜in).
Curve 51–W–57.
X from 51 and Y from 57 = 2cm (¾in).
Join X to Y parallel with 51 – W – 57.
Continue 1cm (⅜in) above X and join to 51.
58 from 57 = 23cm (9in).
Join 54 to 58 and curve the corner of 58.
The grain line of the skirt is squared from the line 51 to 52.

Flap pocket in waist seam
Point 53 is the front of the flap.
Z from 53 = 18cm (7in).
The width of the flap is 6.5cm (2½in).
The front and back of the flap are sloping, as shown in the diagram

For sleeve pattern see diagrams 3(b) and 3(c), p. 32.

NOTE:
*Variations on the Double-breasted
Morning Coat for 1870-1880 can be
found on Page 61.*

Fig. 9   Double-breasted morning coat, 1860

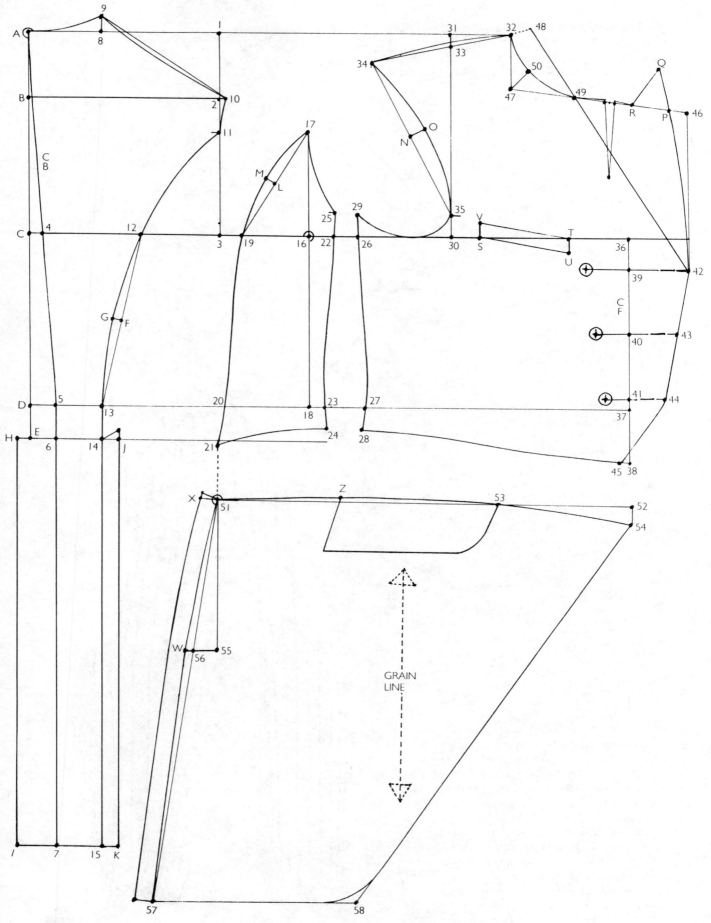

60   Dia. 9 Back, front, skirt and sidebody

Single-breasted morning coat, 1880–1900
(fig. 10; dia. 10)

Measurements are the same as for the single-breasted frock coat (1860s–70s), p. 51 (dia. 7).

Back pattern: as in dia. 7.

Sidebody pattern: as in dia. 7.

Front pattern: as in dia. 7, from 26 to 37.

Then continue the front pattern using diagram 10.

38 below 37 = 5cm (2in).
39 from 36 = 2cm (¾in).
Square down from 39.
40 from 39 = 4cm (1½in).
41 below 40 = 14cm (5½in).
42 from 38 = 1cm (⅜in).
Curve the front 40–41–42.
Curve the waist seam from 28 to 42
43 squared up from 39 = 16.5cm (6½in).
44 squared down from 32 = 6cm (2½in).
Join 43 to 44.
45 from 32 = 3cm (1¼in).
Join 45 to 40 and mark 46 on the neck line.
47 at an angle to 44 = 2.5cm (1in).
Curve the front neck 32–47–46.
Curve the outside edge of the lapel from 43 to 40.
The neck dart is half-way between 43 and 46.
Mark 1.3cm (½in) at the top and make the dart 10cm (4in) long.
The holes and buttons are placed on the centre front opposite 40 and 41.
Mark the centre button and hole.

Outbreast welt pocket

48 from 30 = 3cm (1¼in).
Proceed as instructions for dia. 9.

Note: although the pattern shows a single-breasted lapel, the double-breasted lapel was also fashionable.

Skirt pattern

Square down from 21.
49 from 21 = 6.5cm (2½in).
Square across from 49.
For 50 from 49, measure 21 to 24 plus 28 to 38 plus 2cm (¾in) = 44cm (17¼in).
51 squared from 50 = 2cm (¾in).
P is centre of 49 and 50.
Curve 49 out to P and continue the curve in to 51.
Q from 49 = 18cm (7in).
R from Q = 2.5cm (1in).
Join 49 to R and continue the line.
S from 49 is the same as 14 to 15 on the back pattern = 51.5cm (20½in).
T from R = 1cm (⅜in).
Curve 49 – T – S.
Draw a line across from S.
U from S = 30.5cm (12in).
Join 51 to U.
V at an angle to U = 10cm (4in).
Curve the front of the skirt, 51 – V – S.
W from 49 and X from S = 2cm (¾in).
Join W to X parallel to the curve of 49 to S.
Continue 1cm (⅜in) above W and join to 49.

The grain line is squared from the line 49 to 50.

Use sleeve pattern as in diagrams 4(a) and 4(b), p. 35.

*Ill. 57/58. 1870-1880. The two figures show a semi-double-breasted style of Morning coat, where the fronts cross-over at the top button only. **Note the different shapes of the collar and revers (lapel) between Ill. 57 and Ill. 58. Ill.57 has a** peaked or double-breasted collar and lapel while Ill. 58 shows a notch or single-breasted collar and rever. The outbreast pocket is placed at an acute angle, and the edges of the coat and the cuffs are decorated with a narrow braid. A Vest is worn with both outfits and can just be seen below the front of the coat. The Trousers have a fly front fastening, and the legs are of similar width at the knee and the bottom.*

Ill. 59. Single-breasted Morning coat 1880-1890. High buttoning fronts with flapped pockets on a low waist seam. Bloomingdale Brothers Catalogue 1886.

NOTE:

Ill. 59. Shows the morning coat style at the beginning of the period 1880-1900. By 1890 the high front fastening was placed at a lower level as shown in Fig. 10. The flaps and pockets on the waist-seam were mainly discontinued, but the top welt pockets remained and there would also be a pocket inside the right front at chest level (inbreast pocket). For another example of the 1880's Morning coat style refer to G.41.

Fig. 10 Single-breasted morning coat, 1880–1900

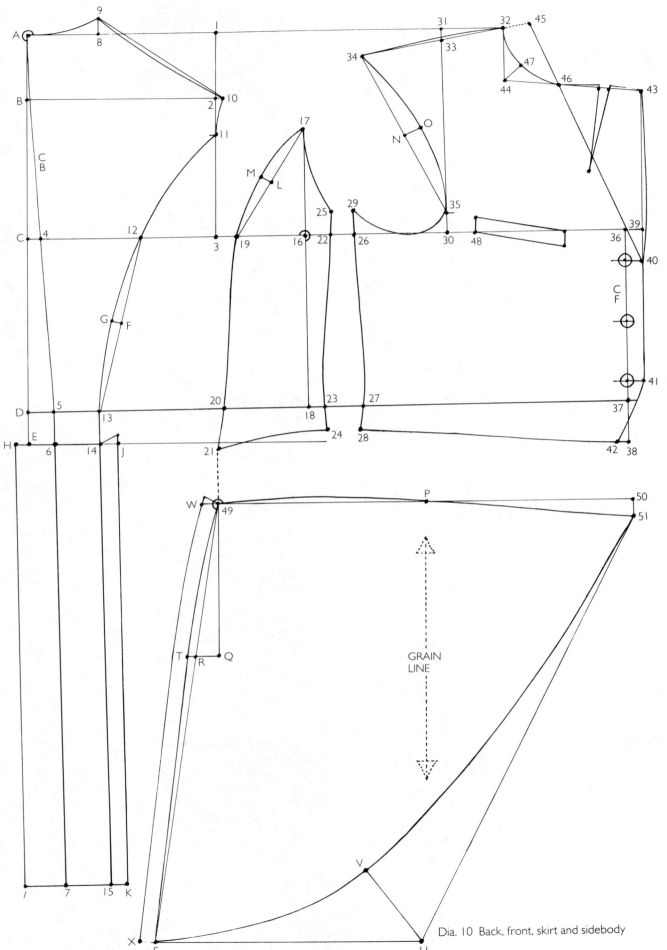

Dia. 10 Back, front, skirt and sidebody

63

3 JACKETS

Although the frock coat was in general use for daywear, there were variations of this garment which gave the wearer more freedom of movement for leisure or sport.

By 1860 a coat with a centre back seam and side seams, known as a 'three seamer' had become quite popular, and the 'Tweedside' (see fig. 11) is an example of this loose-fitting style. From about 1870 a seam from the base of the armhole to the pocket (known as the underarm seam) gave the garment a more fitted and, consequently, a more graceful appearance. Combined with matching waistcoat and trousers, the 'lounging' or 'lounge' jacket was worn not only as leisure wear but also for fashionable daily attire. It is interesting to note that the term 'lounge jacket' was being used as a trade term until very recently.

By the late 1880s the frock coat was fading into obscurity, having been replaced by the morning coat, but it was the jacket that finally won the day. By the latter part of the nineteenth century, tailoring skills had developed to a very high standard and this – coupled with the fact that the jacket was both smart in appearance and comfortable to wear – ensured its lasting popularity.

'Tweedside', 1860s (fig. 11; dia. 11(a)-(b))

Measurements

	Height	*Nape to waist*	*Full length*	*Half across back*	*Sleeve length*	*Chest*	*Waist*	*Seat*
cm	176	44.5	84	20.5	82.5	96	86	102
in	69	17½	33	8⅛	32½	38	34	40

Scale half chest = 48cm (19in) : ⅛ scale = 6cm (2⅜in)
¼ scale = 12cm (4¾in)

Back pattern (dia. 11(a))

A = starting point.
Square across and down from A.
B from A = 7.5cm (3in).
C from A = 24cm (9½in).
D from A = nape to waist (44.5cm) plus 1.5cm = 46cm (or 17½in plus ½in = 18in).
E from D = 20cm (8in) (for seat line).
F from A = 84cm (33in) (full length).
Square a short line across from B.
Square a long line across from C, D, E and F.
1 from A = 20.5cm (8⅛in) (half back)
Square down from 1 to the bottom line.
Mark 2 opposite B, 3 opposite C, 4 opposite D and 5 opposite F.

Centre back seam

6 inside D = 1.5cm (⅝in).
Join B – 6 – F.
Centre back (CB) = A – B – 6 – F.

Back neck

7 from A = ⅛ scale plus 2cm (¾in) = 8cm (3⅛in).
8 squared up from 7 = 2cm (¾in).
Curve 8 to A.

Back shoulder

9 squared from 2 = 1.3cm (½in).
Join 8 to 9, and slightly hollow the shoulder between 8 and 9.
10 above 3 = ⅛ scale minus 1cm (⅜in) = 5cm (2in).
11 squared from 10 = 1cm (⅜in).
Curve 9 to 11 for the back armhole.
12 from 3 is ¼ scale = 12cm (4¾in). 12 is the back sleeve balance point.

Sideseam

13 inside 4 = 1.3cm (½in).
Join 11 – 13 – 5.
Hollow slightly from 11 to 13.

Front pattern

14 from 3 = 7.5cm (3in).
15 from 11 = 7cm (2¾in).
16 from 4 = 7cm (2¾in).
17 from 5 = 2.5cm (1in).
Join 15–14–16–17 for the side seam.

Front shoulder and armhole

18 from 14 = ¼ scale, i.e. 12cm (4¾in).
19 on the top line is squared up from 18.
20 from 19 is ⅛ scale plus 2cm (¾in) = 8cm (3⅛in).
21 below 19 = 1.5cm (⅝in).
Join 20 to 21 and continue the line.
22 from 20 = 16.5cm (6½in).
Curve the front shoulder 20 to 22 as in the diagram.
23 above 18 = 2.5cm (1in).
Join 22 to 23 with a straight line.
G is centre of 22 and 23.

Ill. 61. 1863. Long Single-breasted jacket with braid on the coat edges and flaps. Fronts have four holes and buttons but only the top button is fastened. Sleeves are wide at the elbows and narrow at the cuffs. Single-breasted Vest. Trousers are wide at the thigh and knee, then taper down to a narrow bottom. Top hat.

NOTE:
The Tweedside style had a distinctive collar and straight welt pockets as shown in Fig. 11. The small figure resembles the Tweedside in the length of the coat but having a rever and notch (single-breasted) collar, it would seem, to have more in common with the lounge jacket. **The flapped pockets are also an indication of the jacket style that was becoming increasingly popular for everyday wear.** *Another example of the Tweedside is shown in Illustration G28.*

Fig. II 'Tweedside', 1860s

Ill. 60. 1863. Single-breasted jacket. Long loose style with high buttoning fronts. Flapped pockets at the sides and a flap on the top pocket. (Italian magazine, Corriere delle Dame.)

65

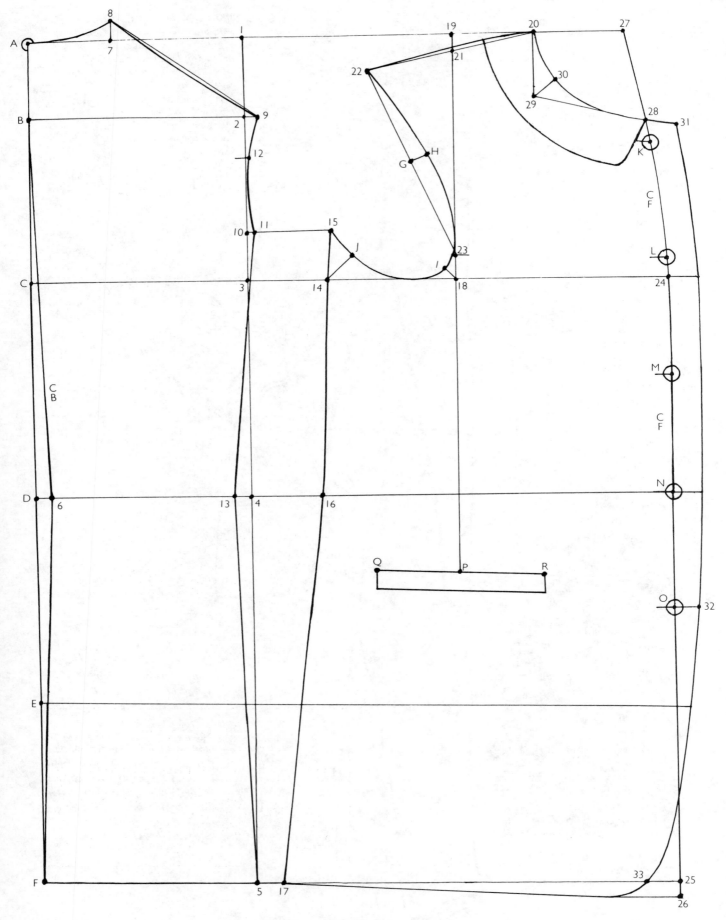

66   Dia. 11(a) Back and front

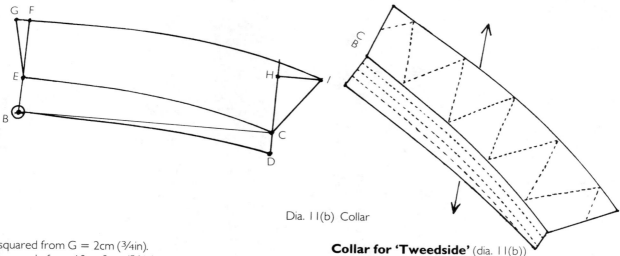

Dia. 11(b) Collar

Completion of fronts

H squared from G = 2cm (¾in).
I at an angle from 18 = 2cm (¾in).
J at an angle from 14 = 2.5cm (1cm).
Curve the armhole 22 – H – 23 – I – J.

Completion of fronts

24 from 18 = ½ scale (24cm) minus 3.5cm = 20.5cm, (or 9½in minus 1½in = 8in).
Square down from 24.
25 is located on the bottom line.
26 below 25 = 2cm (¾in).
Join 26 to 17.

At the top line:
27 from 20 = 8.5cm (3¼in).
Curve 27 to 24.

Front neck

28 from 27 = 9cm (3½in) (centre front is 28–24–26).
29 squared down from 20 = 6.5cm (2½in).
Join 28 to 29.
30 at an angle from 29 = 2.5cm (1in).
Curve the neck 20 – 30 – 28.
Mark the button and buttonhole positions K to O:
K from 28 = 2cm (¾in).
K, L, M, N and O are 11.5cm (4½in) apart.

Front edge

31 continued from 28 = 2.5cm (1in).
32 from O = 2.5cm (1in).
Curve the front edge from 31 through to 32 and finishing with a curve at the bottom line, 17 – 26.

Pocket position

Square down from 18 and mark P for the centre of the pocket = 28cm (11in).
Draw a line across from P, level with 17 and 26.
Q from P = 8cm (3⅛in).
R from P = 8cm (3⅛in).
The pocket shown on the diagram is a narrow welt approx. 2cm (¾in) wide below Q and R.

Use sleeve pattern as in diagrams 3(b) and 3(c), p. 32.

Collar for 'Tweedside' (dia. 11(b))

B = starting point.
Square up and across from B.
C from B is A to 8 at the back neck plus 20 round to 28 at the front neck = 23cm (9in) (see dia. 11(a)).
D squared below C = 2cm (¾in).
Curve B to D.
E squared from B = 3cm (1¼in).
Join E to C with a gradual curve.
F continued above E = 5cm (2in).
G squared from F = 1cm (⅜in).
Join G to E.
H continued above C = 5cm (2in).
I squared from H = 4cm (1½in).
Join I to C.
Curve G to I to complete the outside edge.
The centre back is G – E – B.

The undercollar is cut on the 'cross' of the material and is stitched to a moderately firm interlining which is also cut on the 'cross'. The 'stand' has three or four rows of stitching to give it firmness, whilst the 'fall' has a zigzag pattern stitching to give it flexibility. If more length is required along the outside edge, this can be stretched with the iron.

Single-breasted lounge jacket
1870–1900 (fig. 12; dia. 12)

Measurements

	Height	Nape to waist	Full length	Half across back	Sleeve length	Chest	Waist	Seat
cm	176	44.5	76	20.5	82.5	96	86	102
in	69	17½	30	8⅛	32½	38	34	40

Scale is half chest = 48cm (19in) : ⅛ scale = 6cm (2⅜in)
¼ scale = 12cm (4¾in)

Back pattern (dia. 12)

A = starting point.
Square across and down from A.
B from A = 7.5cm (3in).
C from A = 24cm (9½in).
D from A = nape to waist = 44.5cm (17½in).
E from D = 20cm (8in) for seat line.
F from A = full length = 76cm (30in).
Square a short line across from B.
Square a long line across from C, D, E and F.
1 from A = half back: 20.5cm (8⅛in).
Square down from 1 to the bottom line.
Mark 2, 3, 4, 5 and 6 as in the diagram.

Centre back seam

7 inside C = 1cm (⅜in).
8 inside D = 2.5cm (1in).
9 inside E = 2cm (¾in).
10 inside F = 1.5cm (⅝in).
Join B – 7 with a moderate curve, continue to 8 – 9 – 10 with straight lines.
The centre back (CB) = A – B – 7 – 8 – 9 – 10.

Back neck

11 from A = ⅛ scale plus 2cm (¾in) = 8cm (3⅛in).
12 squared up from 11 = 2cm (¾in).
Curve 12 – A for the back neck.

Back shoulder

13 squared from 2 = 1cm (⅜in).
Join 12 to 13 with a slight hollow.
14 above 3 = ⅛ scale = 6cm (2⅜in).
Curved the back armhole 13 to 14.
15 from 3 is ¼ scale = 12cm (4¾in). 15 is the back sleeve balance point.
16 inside 3 = 1cm (⅜in).
17 inside 4 = 3cm (1⅛in).
18 inside 5 = 2cm (¾in).
19 inside 6 = 1.5cm (⅝in).
Curve 14 – 16 – 17 – 18 – 19 as in the diagram to complete the back pattern.

Front pattern

20 from 3 = 7.5cm (3in).
21 squared across from 14 = 8.5cm (3⅜in).
22 from 4 = 7.5cm (3in).
23 from 5 = 4.5cm (1¾in).
24 from 6 = 3cm (1⅛in).
Curve 21–20–22–23–24 for the side seam of the front pattern.
When joining 20 – 22 the waist hollow occurs *above* point 22.

Front shoulder and armhole

25 from 20 is ¼ scale plus 2cm (¾in) = 14cm (5½in).
26 is squared up from 25 and located on the top line.
27 from 26 is ⅛ scale plus 1cm (⅜in) = 7cm (2¾in).
28 below 26 = 1.3cm (½in).
Join 27 to 28 and continue the line.
29 from 27 = 16cm (6¼in). (This is calculated by measuring 12 to 13 – then minus 1cm (⅜in).)
Curve front shoulder 27 – 29 as in the diagram.
30 above 25 = 2.5cm (1in).
Join 29 – 30 with a straight line.
G is half-way between 29 and 30.
H squared from G = 2cm (¾in).
I at an angle from 25 = 2cm (¾in).
J at an angle to 20 = 4cm (1½in).
Curve the armhole 29 – H – 30 – I – J – 21.

Completion of fronts

31 from 25 = ½ scale (24cm) minus 3.5cm = 20.5cm or 9½in minus 1½in = 8in.
Square down from 31.
32 is located on the waist line.
33 is located on the bottom line across from F.
34 below 33 = 2.5cm (1in).
The centre front (CF) = 31 – 34.
35 from 31 = 2cm (¾in).
36 from 32 = 2cm (¾in).
37 from 33 = 6.5cm (2½in).
Join 35 to 36. Curve from 36 to 37 and continue on to the bottom line 24 – 34 to complete the front edge.
38 squared up from 35 = 16.5cm (6½in).
Curve lapel 38 to 35.
39 squared down from 27 = 6.5cm (2½in).
Join 38 to 39.
40 from 27 = 2.5cm (1in).
Join 40 to 35 and mark 41 on the neck line.
42 at an angle to 39 = 2.5cm (1in).
Curve 27 – 42 – 41.
The neck dart is placed half-way between 38 and 41.
Mark 1.3cm (½in) at the top of the dart and make the dart 9cm (3½in) long. The dart is sewn together on the lines.
The top button and hole are placed at point 31.
The other holes and buttons are 10cm (4in) apart.

Side pockets

Square a line down from 25.
K from 25 = 28cm (11in).
Draw a line across through K, parallel with the bottom line 24 – 34.
L from K and M from K are 7.5cm (3in) each.
The flap is 5.5cm (2¼in) wide and 'sloped' at the front and back.

NOTE:
For other single-breasted Jacket styles of the period, see Gallery pages xxii, xxiii and xxiv.

Ill. 62.   1890's Single-breasted lounge jackets. Figure A has the cut-away front similar to Fig. 12. Figure B has the straight front that remained popular into the early 1900's. Both styles show side pocket flaps, top pocket flap and a 'ticket' flap above the right side pocket. A single-breasted Vest would normally be worn under the jacket. Moderate width of trousers with creases pressed into the centre of the leg at the front and back. Bowler hats are worn by both figures. (Montgomery Ward Catalogue 1895.)

Ill. 63. 1850. A single-breasted lounge Jacket with flapped pockets. The inside lining extends over the collar and the revers for a decorative effect. The jacket is well ahead of fashion and was to become more generally worn in the 1860's. The Vest is single-breasted with a wide space between the buttons. Trousers are narrow all through the legs and are shaped over the shoe at the bottom.

Fig. 12 Single-breasted lounge jacket, 1870–1900

69

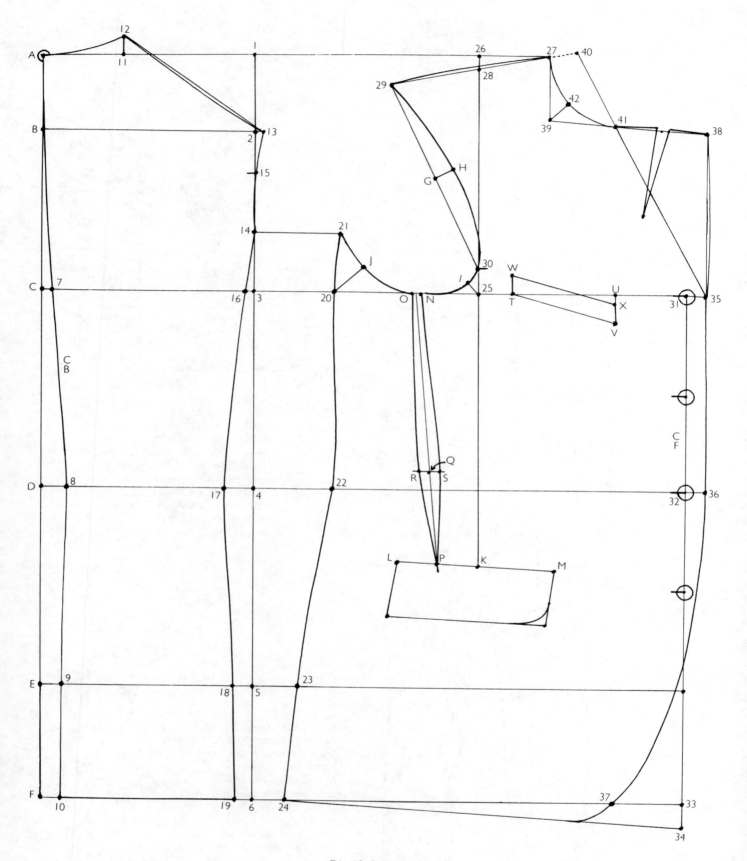

Dia. 12 Back and front

Underarm dart

N from 25 = 5.5cm (2¼in).
O from N = 1cm (⅜in).
P from K = 4cm (1½in).
From the centre of O – N draw a straight line to P.
Q is 2cm (¾in) above the waist line (22–32).
R from Q = 1cm (⅜in).
S from Q = 1cm (⅜in).
Join N – S – P and O – R – P to complete the dart which is sewn
   together on these lines.

Outbreast welt pocket

T from 25 = 3cm (1¼in).
U from T on the chest line = 10cm (4in).
V squared down from U = 3cm (1¼in).
Join T to V.
W squared up from T = 2cm (¾in).
X squared up from V = 2cm (¾in).
Join W to X to complete the welt pocket.

Use Sleeve pattern as in diagrams 4(a) and 4(b), p. 35.

Double-breasted reefer, 1870–1900

(fig. 13; dia. 13(a)-(c))

Use measurements as in diagram 12.

Scale is 48cm (19in) : ⅛ scale = 6cm (2⅜in)
                          ¼ scale = 12cm (4¾in)

Back pattern:

The instructions for this are exactly the same as for diagram 12,
A to F and 1 to 19.

Front pattern

The instructions for this are exactly the same as for diagram 12,
points 20 to 30 up to the centre front 31 – 32 – 33.

Now continue with diagram 13(a) for the double-breasted front:
34 continued below 33 = 2cm (¾in).
35 squared from 34 = 7.5cm (3in).
Join 24 to 34 with a slight curve as in diagram.
24 – 34 – 35 is the bottom edge of the front pattern.

At the chest line:
36 from 31 = 7.5cm (3in).
Join 36 to 35 for the front edge.
K below 36 = 4cm (1½in) for the top buttonhole position.
37 squared up from 36 = 16cm (6¼in).
38 squared down from 27 = 6.5cm (2½in).
Join 37 to 38.

39 at an angle to 38 = 3cm (1⅛in).
40 from 27 = 2.5cm (1in).
Join 40 to K and mark 41 at the neck.
Curve 27 – 39 – 41 for the front neck.
42 from 37 = 2cm (¾in).
Join K – 42 and continue the line.
43 from 42 = 5cm (2in).
Curve lapel K to 43.
44 from 42 = 4.5cm (1¾in).
Join 43 to 44 to complete the lapel 'point'.
The neck dart (of which the centre is at 45) is 2.5cm (1in) from 44.
Take out 1.5cm (½in) at 45.
The dart is approx. 9cm (3½in) long.

Buttons and buttonholes

K, L, M and N are 9cm (3½in) apart.
The buttonholes are 2cm (¾in) inside K, L, M and N.
The buttons are opposite the buttonholes and are 5.5cm (2¼in)
   from the CF.

Side pockets

Square down from 25.
O from 25 = 28cm (11in).
Draw a line across through O, parallel with the bottom edge 24 – 34.
P from O and Q from O = 8cm (3⅛in) each.
The flap is 5cm (2in) wide.

Underarm dart

R from 25 = 5.5cm (2¼in).
S from R = 1cm (⅜in).
T from O = 4cm (1½in).
From the centre of S – R draw a straight line to T.
U is 2cm (¾in) above the waist line.
V from U = 1cm (⅜in).
W from U = 1cm (⅜in).
Join R – W – T and S – V – T to complete the dart which is sewn
   together on these lines.

Outbreast welt pocket

46 from 25 = 3cm (1¼in).
X from 46 on the chest line = 10cm (4in).
Y squared from X = 2cm (¾in).
Join Y to 46.
Z squared up above 46 = 2cm (¾in).
Join Z to X to complete the welt pocket.

Use sleeve pattern as in diagrams 4(a) and 4(b), p. 35.

Collars for jackets

Single-breasted collar (dia. 13(b))
Close up the neck dart.
Mark points 27, 41 and 38 on the front neck.
Join 41 to 27 and continue the line.
B from 27 is the same as the back neck A to 12 = 8.5cm (3⅜in)
   (see inset, dia. 13(b)).
Square across from B.
C from B = 3cm (1¼in).
D from B = 4cm (1½in).

PLATE 13. 1895. "Single-breasted Cut-away Jacket with a three button fastening. The four outside pockets have flaps with rounded corners. There is a single row of stitching on the edges, flaps and cuffs. At the centre back there is a short slit.

PLATE 14. 1896 Double-breasted jacket based on the Naval Reefer (see Plate 15). There are four outside pockets with square cornered flaps. The back view shows the short slit at the sideseams. A single row of stitching on the edges and the flaps with a double row on the cuffs.

PLATE 15. *A Double-breasted naval Reefer Jacket of the 19th century. It has three buttons to fasten and three to "show," with deep cuffs on the sleeves. Usually with short slits at the bottom of each sideseam. This garment was the forerunner of the Double-breasted lounge jacket.*

Fig. 13 Double-breasted
reefer, 1870–1900

Ill. 64   Double-breasted jacket
with 3 front buttons and 3 to show.
There is a row of stitching inside
the coat edges and round the 4
pocket flaps. (Montgomery Wards
Catalogue, 1895.)

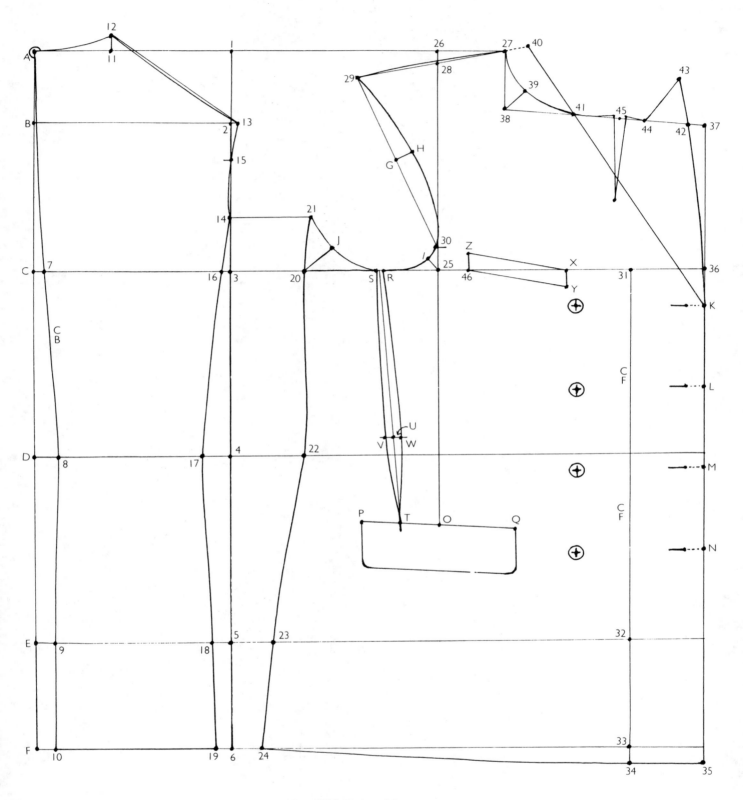

Dia. 13(a) Back and front

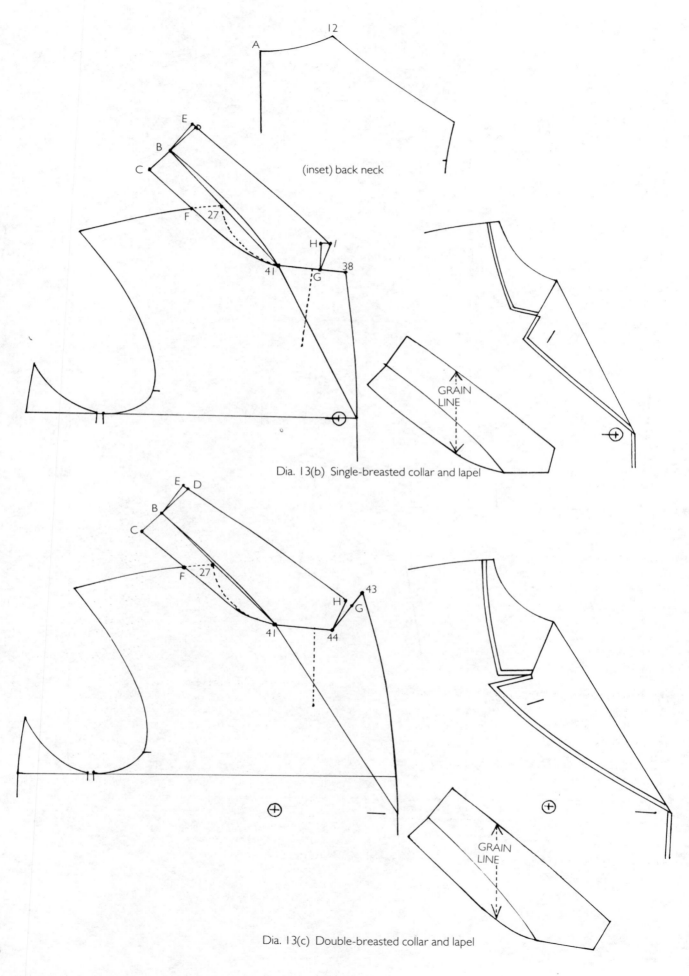

(inset) back neck

Dia. 13(b) Single-breasted collar and lapel

GRAIN LINE

Dia. 13(c) Double-breasted collar and lapel

GRAIN LINE

E squared from D = 0.6cm (¼in).
Join E – B.
Curve B – 41.
F from 27 = 3cm (1¼in).
Join C – F and curve F – 41.
G from 38 = 3cm (1¼in).
Complete the collar line by continuing along the lapel from 41 to G, as shown in the diagram.
H squared up from G = 2.5cm (1in).
I squared from H = 1cm (⅜in).
Join *I* to G.
Join E to *I* with a slight curve.
Centre back = C–B–E.

The coat and collar edges can be finished with a narrow stitching.

Double-breasted collar (dia. 13(c))
Close up the neck dart.
Mark the points 27, 41, 44 and 43.
Join 41 – 27 and continue the line.
B from 27 is the same as the back neck A to 12 = 8.5cm (3⅜in) (see inset, dia. 13(b)).
Square across from B.
C from B = 3cm (1¼in).
D from B = 4cm (1½in).
E squared from D = 0.6cm (¼in).
Join E – B.
Curve B – 41.
F from 27 = 3cm (1¼in).
Join C – F and curve F – 41.
G from 43 = 2cm (¾in).
H from G = 1cm (⅜in).
Join E to H with a slight curve.
Centre back = C–B–E.

The jacket undercollars are always cut on the 'cross' or bias of the fabric which is usually of a plain thin Melton fabric that matches the jacket material.

The interlining is of a moderate stiffness (collar canvas) and is also cut on the 'cross'.

Single-breasted dinner jacket (tuxedo) 1880–1900 (fig. 14; dia. 14(a)-(b))

Measurements

	Height	*Nape to waist*	*Full length*	*Half across back*	*Sleeve length*	*Chest*	*Waist*	*Seat*
cm	176	44.5	74	20.5	82.5	96	86	102
in	69	17½	29	8⅛	32½	38	34	40

Scale is half chest 48cm (19in) : ⅛ scale = 6cm (2⅜in)
¼ scale = 12cm (4¾in)

Back pattern (dia. 14(a))

A = starting point.
Square across and down from A.
B from A = 7.5cm (3in).
C from A = 24cm (9½in).
D from A = 44.5cm (17½in) (nape to waist).
E from D = 20cm (8in) (for seat line).
F from A = 74cm (29in) (full length).
Square a short line across from B.
Square a long line across from C, D, E and F.
1 from A = 20.5cm (8⅛in) (half back).
Square down from 1 to the bottom line.
Mark 2, 3, 4, 5 and 6.
7 inside C = 1cm (⅜in).
8 inside D = 2.5cm (1in).
9 inside E = 2cm (¾in).
10 inside F = 1.5cm (⅝in).
Join B–7–8–9–10 as in the diagram.
The centre back = A–B–7–8–9–10.
11 from A = ⅛ scale plus 2cm (¾in) = 8cm (3⅛in).
12 squared up from 11 = 2cm (¾in).
Curve 12 – A for the back neck.
13 squared from 2 = 1cm (⅜in).
Join 12 – 13 with a slight hollow.
14 above 3 = ⅛ scale = 6cm (2⅜in).
Curve the back armhole 13 – 14.
15 from 3 is ¼ scale = 12cm (4¾in). 15 is the back sleeve balance point.
16 inside 3 = 1cm (⅜in).
17 inside 4 = 3cm (1⅛in).
18 inside 5 = 2cm (¾in).
19 inside 6 = 1.5cm (⅝in).
Curve 14–16–17–18–19 as in diagram to complete the back pattern.

Front pattern

20 from 3 = 7.5cm (3in).
21 squared across from 14 = 8.5cm (3⅜in).
22 from 4 = 7.5cm (3in).
23 from 5 = 4.5cm (1¾in).
24 from 6 = 2.5cm (1in).
Join 21 – 20 – 22 – 23 – 24 for the side seam of the front pattern.

Front shoulder and armhole
25 from 20 is ¼ scale plus 2cm (¾in) = 14cm (5½in).
26 is squared up from 25 and located on the top line.
27 from 26 is ⅛ scale plus 1.5cm (⅝in) = 7.5cm (3in).
28 below 26 = 1.3cm (½in).
Join 27 – 28 and continue the line.
29 from 27 = 16cm (6¼in).
(This is calculated by measuring 12 to 13 – then minus 1cm (⅜in).)
Curve front shoulder 27 – 29, as in the diagram.
30 above 25 = 2.5cm (1in).
Join 29 – 30 with a straight line.
G is half-way between 29 – 30.
H squared from G = 2cm (¾in).
I at an angle from 25 = 2cm (¾in).
J at an angle from 20 = 4cm (1½in).
Curve the armhole 29 – H – 30 – *I* – J – 21.

The Dinner Jacket achieved
popularity during the late
1880's. The two button front
and shawl collar, as shown in
Fig. 14, remained until the end
of the century when the button
one style became fashionable.
The braid down the side of the
trousers has remained a
necessary part of 'Dinner' wear.

Fig. 14 Single-breasted dinner jacket
(tuxedo), 1880–1900

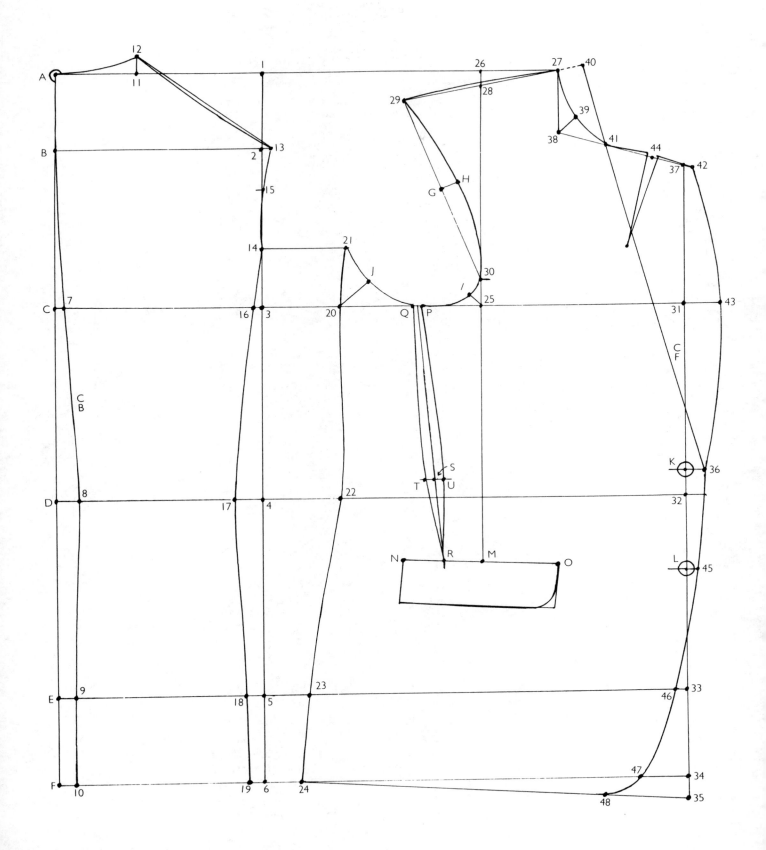

Dia. 14(a) Back and front

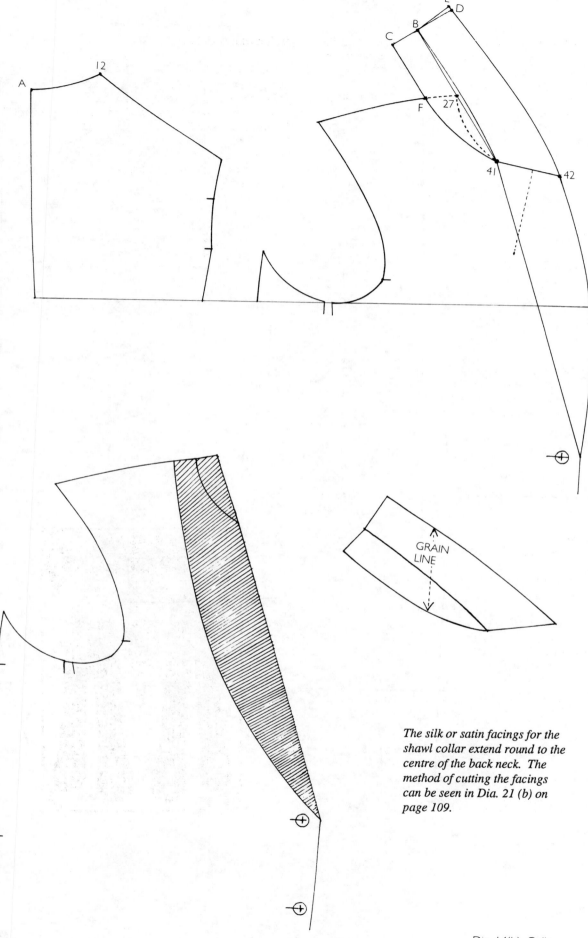

The silk or satin facings for the
shawl collar extend round to the
centre of the back neck. The
method of cutting the facings
can be seen in Dia. 21 (b) on
page 109.

Dia. 14(b) Collar

Completion of fronts

31 from 25 = ½ scale minus 3.5cm = 20.5cm, or 9½in minus
1½in = 8in.

Square down from 31.

Mark 32 on the waist line.

Mark 33 on the seat line.

Mark 34 on the bottom line from F.

35 below 34 = 2.5cm (1in).

The centre front (CF) = 31 – 35.

Join 35 to 24.

K above 32 = 2.5cm (1in) for top button and hole position.

L below K = 10cm (4in) for second button and hole position.

36 squared from K = 2cm (¾in).

37 continued above 31 = 14cm (5½in).

38 squared down from 27 = 6.5cm (2½in).

Join 37 to 38.

39 at an angle to 38 = 2.5cm (1in).

40 from 27 = 2.5cm (1in).

Join 40 to 36.

Mark 41 on the neck line.

Curve 27–39–41.

42 continued from 37 = 1cm (⅜in).

43 from 31 = 3cm (1¼in)

Curve 36 – 43 – 42 for the outside edge of the roll collar.

44 is the neck dart located half-way between 41 and 42.

Take out 1.5cm (½in) at the top of the dart.

Mark the dart 9cm (3½in) long.

Front edge

45 from L = 1.5cm (⅝in).

46 inside 33 = 1cm (⅜in).

47 from 34 = 5cm (2in).

Curve 36 – 45 – 46 – 47 and continue the curve to 48 at the bottom
edge of the pattern.

Side pockets

Square a line down from 25.

M from 25 = 27cm (10½in).

Draw a line across through M, parallel with the bottom edge,
i.e. 24 – 48.

N from M and O from M = 7.5cm (3in) each side.

The flap is 4.5cm (1¾in) wide.

Underarm dart

P from 25 = 5.5cm (2¼in).

Q from P = 1cm (⅜in).

R from M = 4cm (1½in).

Draw a line from the centre of Q – P to R.

S above the waist line = 2cm (¾in).

T from S and U from S = 1cm (⅜in) each side.

Join Q – T – R and P – U – R to complete the dart.

Note: The dinner jacket has no outbreast pocket.

Use sleeve pattern as in diagrams 4(a) and 4(b), p. 35.

Roll collar (dia. 14(b))

Close up the neck dart.

Mark points 27 – 41 – 42 on the front neck.

Join 41 to 27 and continue the line.

B from 27 is the same as the back neck A – 12, i.e. 8.5cm (3⅜in).

Square across from B.

C from B = 3cm (1¼in).

D from B = 4.5cm (1¾in).

E squared from D = 6mm (¼in).

Join E to B.

Curve B to 41.

F from 27 = 3cm (1¼in).

Join C to F and curve F to 41.

Continue the collar line 41 to 42, which is the same as the neck
line of the dinner jacket in dia. 14.

Complete the outer edge by curving from E to 42.

The centre back = C – B – E.

Styles for Men and Boys.

PLATE 16. 1892. An illustration from the Delineator, June 1892. Called an "Outing" suit which might be termed "casual" for that period. The Blazer has three patch pockets and a soft-rolling lapel. There are two rows of stitching on the edges and patches but only one row round the cuffs. The garment around the waist is called a "sash-Vest" and is made of black silk. It is stiffened at the front with whalebone and there are two pockets similar to a vest. Trousers have plain fronts and there are no creases. The Cap is described as a "Commodore" and is based on a peaked yachting style cap.

Single-breasted blazer, 1890–1900

(fig. 15; dia. 15)

Measurements as for diagram 14(a).

Scale is half chest 48cm (19in) : 1/8 scale = 6cm (2⅜in)
1/4 scale = 12cm (4¾in)

Back pattern (dia. 15)

A = starting point.
Square across and down from A.
B from A = 7.5cm (3in).
C from A = 24cm (9½in).
D from A = 44.5cm (17½in) (nape to waist).
E from D = 20cm (8in) (seat line).
F from A = 74cm (29in) (full length).
Square a short line across from B.
Square a long line across from C, D, E and F.
1 from A = 20.5cm (8⅛in) (half back).
Square down from 1 to the bottom line.
Mark 2, 3, 4, 5 and 6.
There is no seam at the centre back (CB) which is cut on the fold of
   the material.
7 inside D = 1cm (⅜in).
Draw a straight line from A to 7 and continue to point 8 on the
   bottom line.
The centre back (CB) is A–7–8.
9 from A is 1/8 scale plus 2cm (¾in) = 8cm (3⅛in).
10 squared up from 9 = 2cm (¾in).
Curve the back neck 10–A.
11 squared from 2 = 1cm (⅜in).
Join 10 – 11 with a slight hollow.
12 above 3 = 1/8 scale = 6cm (2⅜in).
Curve the back armhole 11 to 12.
13 from 3 is 1/4 scale 12cm (4¾in). 13 is the back sleeve balance
   point.
14 from 4 = 2cm (¾in).
15 from 6 = 1cm (⅜in).
Join 12–14–15.

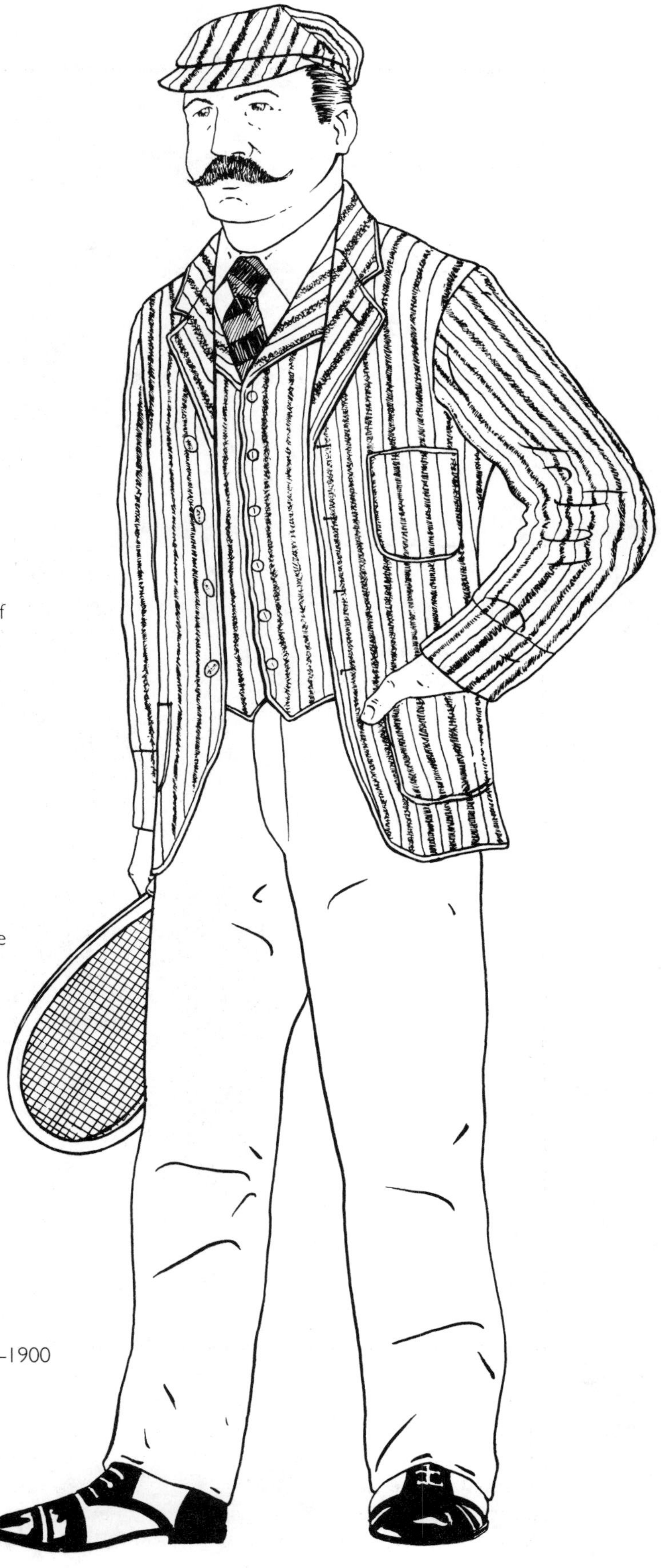

Fig. 15 Single-breasted blazer, 1890–1900

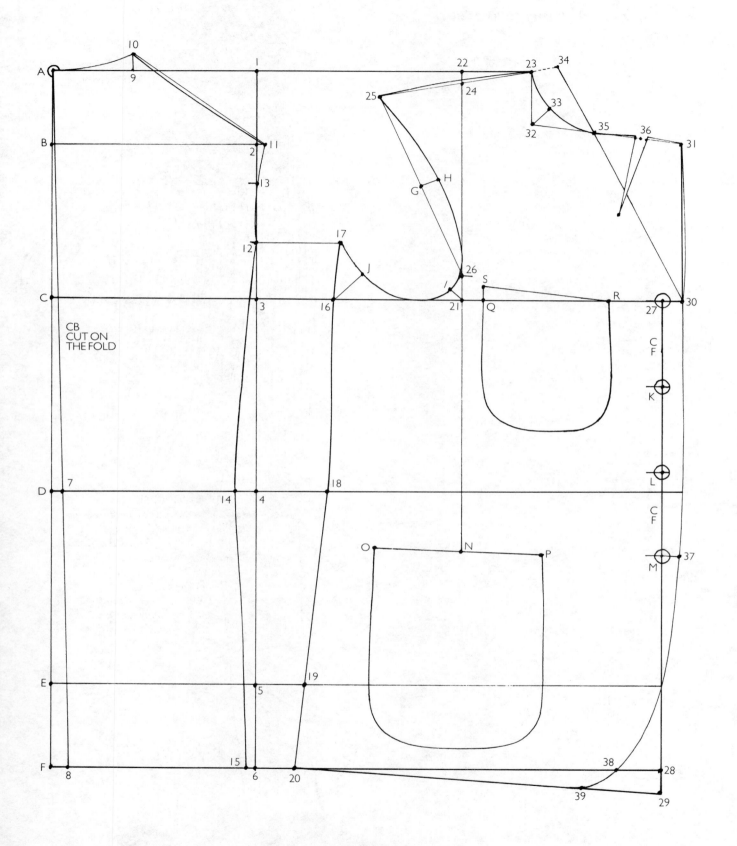

Dia. 15 Back and front

Front pattern

16 from 3 = 7.5cm (3in).
17 squared across from 12 = 8.5cm (3⅜in).
18 from 4 = 7cm (2¾in).
19 from 5 = 4.5cm (1¾in).
20 from 6 = 4cm (1½in).
Join 17–16–18–19–20.
21 from 16 is ¼ scale plus 2cm (¾in) = 14cm (5½in).
22 is squared up from 21 and located on the top line.
23 from 22 is ⅛ scale plus 1cm (⅜in) = 7cm (2¾in).
24 below 22 = 1.5cm (½in).
Join 23 to 24 and continue the line.
25 from 23 = 16cm (6¼in). This is calculated by measuring
    10 to 11, then minus 1cm (⅜in).
Curve the front shoulder 23–25, as in diagram.
26 above 21 = 2.5cm (1in) 26 is the front sleeve balance point.
Join 25 to 26 with a straight line.
G is centre of 25 and 26.
H squared from G = 2cm (¾in).
I at an angle from 21 = 1.3cm (½in).
J at an angle from 16 = 4cm (1½in).
Curve the armhole 25–H–26–I–J–17.

Completion of fronts

27 from 21 = ½ scale minus 3.5cm = 20.5cm, or 9½in minus
    1½in = 8in.
Square down from 27.
28 is located on the line from F.
29 below 28 = 2.5cm (1in).
The centre front (CF) = 27–28–29.
Join 29 to 20.
30 from 27 = 2cm (¾in).
Square up from 30.
31 from 30 = 16.5cm (6½in).
32 squared down from 23 = 5.5cm (2¼in).
Join 31 to 32.
Curve 31 to 30.
33 at an angle to 32 = 2.5cm (1in).
34 from 23 = 2.5cm (1in).
Join 34 to 30.
Mark 35 on the neck line.
Curve 23 – 33 – 35.
The neck dart is half-way between 31 and 35.
Mark 36 as in diagram.
At 36 take out 1.3cm (½in).
The dart is 7.5cm (3in) long.

The top button and buttonhole are at 27.
27, K, L and M are 9cm (3½in) apart.
37 from M = 2cm (¾in).
38 inside 28 = 4.5cm (1¾in).
Draw the front edge from 30 to 37 parallel with the centre front (CF).
Then from 37 curve through 38 to 39 at the bottom edge.

Side patch pockets

Square down from 21.
N from 21 = 26.5cm (10½in).
Draw a line across N parallel with 20 and 39.
O from N and P from N = 8.5cm (3⅜in).
The patch pocket is 20.5cm (8in) deep.

Outbreast patch pocket

Q from 21 = 2cm (¾in).
R from Q = 12.5cm (5in).
S squared up from Q = 1.5cm (⅝in).
Join S to R for mouth of pocket.
The patch pocket is 14cm (5½in) deep at the centre.

Note: For a closer fitting the underarm dart can be included.

Use sleeve pattern as in diagrams 4(a) and 4(b), p. 35.

TAILOR'S NOTE

*To match the stripe on the back
and front shoulders of the
Blazer, it is necessary to adjust
the shoulder angles.*
1. *Add 2.5 cm (1 in.) to the
    back shoulder.*
2. *Reduce 2.5 cm (1 in.) from
    the front shoulder (see Dia.
    15(a), below).*

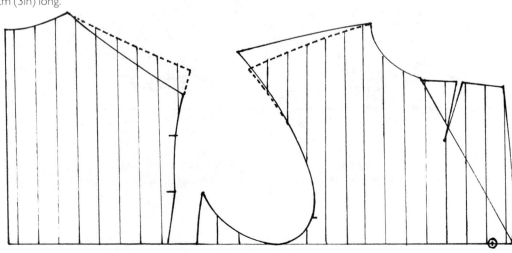

PLATE 17. 1896. (L) *The man wears the complete Norfolk outfit which includes a Jacket, Knicker Breeches, Long Socks and a segmented Cap. His lady friend is appropriately dressed for the period. The Delineator, April 1896.*

(ii) back

Ill. 65. 1880-1900. Norfolk Jacket and trousers. This type of outfit was usually made from a strong tweed material. Bloomingdale Brothers Catalogue, 1886.

NOTE

Illustration G50, shows the Norfolk jacket with alternative pockets to Fig. 16. Another difference is that the woollen stockings cover the bottom of the knicker-breeches whereas in Fig. 16 the breeches are fastened outside the stockings.

Fig. 16 Norfolk jacket,
1880–1900
(i) front

87

Norfolk jacket, 1880–1900

(fig. 16; dia. 16)

Measurements as for diagram 12.

Scale is half the chest 48cm (19in) : 1/8 scale = 6cm (2⅜in)
                                                    1/4 scale = 12cm (4¾in)

Back pattern

Follow dia. 12 for A – B – C – D – E – F and 1 – 2 – 3 – 4 – 5 – 6 (as
    for previous jackets).

Then, using dia. 16, proceed as follows:
7 from C = 0.5cm (¼in).
8 from D = 2cm (¾in).
9 from F = 1.3cm (½in).
Join B – 7 – 8 – 9.
A – B – 7 – 8 – 9 = centre back (CB).
10 from A = 8cm (3⅛in) (as in previous diagrams).
11 squared up from 10 = 2cm (¾in).
Curve 11 to A.
12 squared from 2 = 1cm (⅜in).
Join 11 – 12 and hollow slightly.
13 above 3 = 1/8 scale = 6cm (2⅜in).
Curve 12 to 13.
14 from 3 is 1/4 scale = 12cm (4¾in). 14 is back sleeve balance
    point.
15 inside 4 = 2cm (¾in).
16 inside 6 = 1.3cm (½in).
Join 13–15–16.

Front pattern

17 from 3 = 7.5cm (3in).
18 squared from 13 = 8cm (3¼in).
19 from 4 = 7.5cm (3in).
20 from 5 = 4.5cm (1¾in).
21 from 6 = 3cm (1¼in).
Join 18 – 17 – 19 – 20 – 21 for the side seam.
22 from 17 is 1/4 scale plus 1cm (⅜in) = 13cm (5⅛in).
23 is squared up from 22 and located on the top line.
24 from 23 is 1/8 scale plus 2cm (¾in) = 8cm (3⅛in).
25 below 23 = 1.5cm (½in).
Join 24 to 25 and continue the line.
26 from 24 = 16cm (6¼in). (Front shoulder is 1cm (⅜in) less
    than back shoulder 11 to 12.)
Curve front shoulder 24 – 26.
27 above 22 = 2.5cm (1in).
Join 26 to 27 with a straight line.
G is halfway between 26 and 27.
H squared from G = 2cm (¾in).
I at an angle to 22 = 2cm (¾in).
J at an angle to 17 = 4cm (1½in).
Curve the armhole 26 – H – 27 – I – J – 18.
28 from 22 is ½ scale minus 3cm = 21cm or 9½in minus 1¼in =
    8¼in.

Square down from 28 and mark 29 on the line squared from F.
30 from 29 = 2cm (¾in).
Join 30 to 21.
31 from 28 = 2cm (¾in).
32 squared up from 31 = 16.5cm (6½in).
Curve 32 to 31.
33 squared down from 24 = 6.5cm (2½in).
Join 32 to 33.
34 at an angle to 33 = 2.5cm (1in).
35 from 24 = 2.5cm (1in).
Join 35 to 31.
Mark 36 on the neck line.
Curve 24 – 34 – 36.
37 from 30 = 2cm (¾in).
Join 31 to 37 and curve the corner at 37.
The top button and buttonhole are located at 28.
28, K, L and M are 10cm (4in) apart.

Side patches with flaps

To allow space for the front 'pleat' the pocket is moved back
    towards the side seam.
N from 22 = 2cm (¾in).
Square down from N.
O from N = 29cm (11½in).
Draw a line across O, parallel to 21–30.
P from O and Q from O = 8.5cm (3⅜in) each.
The flap is 7cm (2¾in) deep and placed 2cm (¾in) above the
    patch pocket.
The depth of the patch pocket is 20.5cm (8in).

Back and front 'pleats'

Originally, the pleats were included as part of the pattern in the form
of box pleats. A similar effect can be achieved by cutting separate
bands of fabric to finish approx. 4.5cm (1¾in) wide. A straight band
is sewn on top of the centre back seam and a curved band is sewn
down each front. These bands are left open at the waist position so
that the belt can be threaded through.

The belt fastens at the front with a hole and button.

Note: The shaded section of the back in diagram 16 shows only half
of the back 'pleat' or 'band'.

Use sleeve pattern as in dia. 4(a) and 4(b), p. 33.

PLATE 18. 1896. *Norfolk Jacket with a yoke back and
front. There is a Box Pleat at the centre back and a pleat
each side at the front. Always in a Single-breasted style and
a four button fastening. The wide cloth belt fastens with a
hole and button. The Delineator, January 1896.*

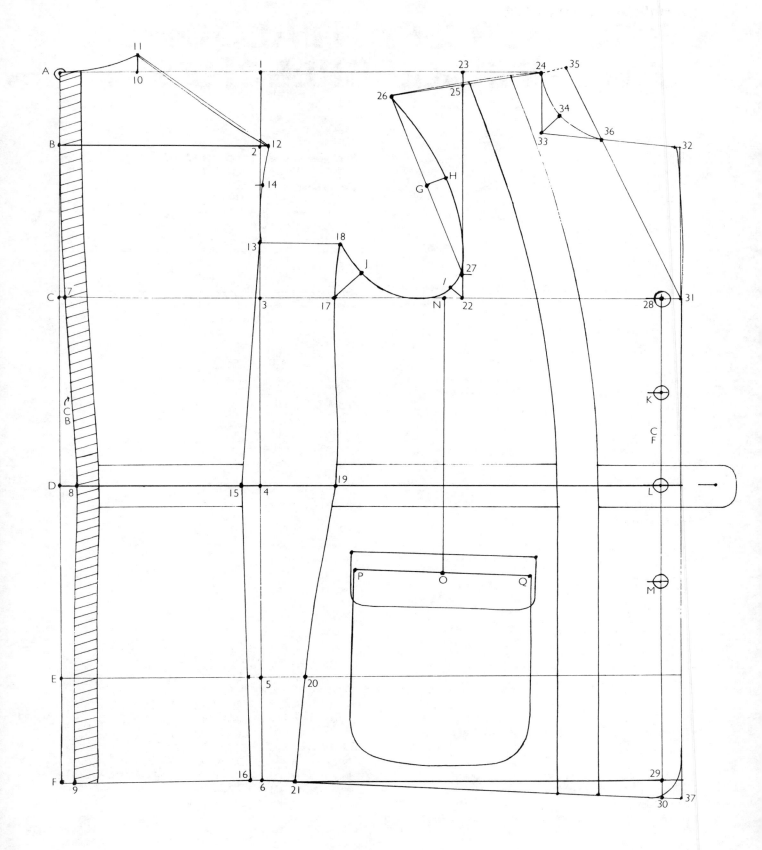

Dia. 16 Back and front

4 TROUSERS, PANTALOONS AND KNICKERBREECHES

By 1830 these were in general use for daywear and had already replaced the knee breeches. Another innovation at this period was the introduction of the fly front fastening, which by the end of the 1830s had taken the place of the flap or 'fall' front.

The bottoms of the trousers were secured under the shoe by means of a strap, but this feature was discontinued after 1850.

The patterns shown in diagrams 17(a) and 17(b) are the basic trouser construction, which applies to the period 1830 to 1900. Although there were variations of style throughout this period, these were mainly concerned with the width of the leg at the knee and the bottom, and the pattern can easily be adapted to meet these requirements.

It is important to note that back and front creases and turn-ups did not appear until the end of the nineteenth century.

'Gathered' or 'pleated' trousers ('Cossacks')
(fig. 18)

This style is included as a useful alternative to the plain-fronted trousers. It was based on an earlier style, which was gathered at the waist and the bottom of the trouser leg and known as 'Cossack' trousers. From 1830 there was a strap at the bottom, secured under the shoe as on the standard trousers. 'Cossacks' ceased to be fashionable after 1850.

Pantaloons (fig. 19)

Pantaloons were worn with evening wear – the earlier style (1830s) was secured at the bottom of the legs with holes and buttons at the side seam and finished just below the calf. From about 1840 they were cut to ankle length and secured with a strap under the foot. They should be made from a fabric that has a certain amount of 'stretch' to the weave as they fitted closely at the thigh and the leg. By 1850, pantaloons were replaced by trousers for evening wear and were no longer in vogue after that date.

Knickerbreeches (also known as Knickerbockers)
(fig. 20)

Introduced in about 1860, they were fastened below the knee and were a looser and longer version of the knee breeches. They were used for country wear and, combined with the Norfolk jacket and a waistcoat, this ensemble became known as the 'Norfolk suit'. With slight modifications, knickerbreeches continued to be worn (for sporting pursuits) after 1900.

Trousers: standard method (fig. 17; dia. 17(a)-(b))

Measurements

	Outside leg	Inside leg	Waist	Seat	Knee	Bottom width
cm	112	80	86	102	50	43
in	44	31½	34	40	19½	17

Rise = 32cm (12½in) (difference between outside leg and inside leg)
Scale is half the seat measure = 51cm (20in) : ⅛ scale = 6.5cm (2½in)
¼ scale = 13cm (5in)

Front pattern (dia. 17(a))

A = starting point.
Square down and across from A.
B from A = 4cm (1½in) (waist line).
C from B = 19cm (7½in) (seat line).
D from A = 32cm (12½in) (rise).
E from D is ½ the inside leg minus 5cm (2in) = 35cm (13¾in) (knee position).
F from D = 80cm (31½in) (inside leg).
Square across from B, C, D, E and F.
1 is centre of B and C.
Square across from 1.
2 from D is ⅛ the scale plus 0.5cm (¼in) = 7cm (2¾in).
3 at an angle from D = half 2 from D.
Curve 2 – 3 – C for the front fly curve and to complete the centre front.
4 from E = 4cm (1½in).
5 from F = 2.5cm (1in).
Join 5 to 4 and continue the line.
6 is marked on the line from D.
Curve 2 toward 4 to join the line half-way between 6 and 4.
This completes the inside leg, 2–4–5.

Side seam

7 from B is ¼ waist = 21.5 (8½in).
8 from A = same as 7 from B plus 0.5cm (¼in) = 22cm (8¾in).
9 from 1 is ¼ seat minus 1cm (⅜in) = 24.5cm (9⅝in).
10 from C is ¼ seat = 25.5cm (10in).
11 from D is the same as 10 from C minus 0.5cm (¼in) = 25cm (9¾in).
Join 8–7–9–10–11.

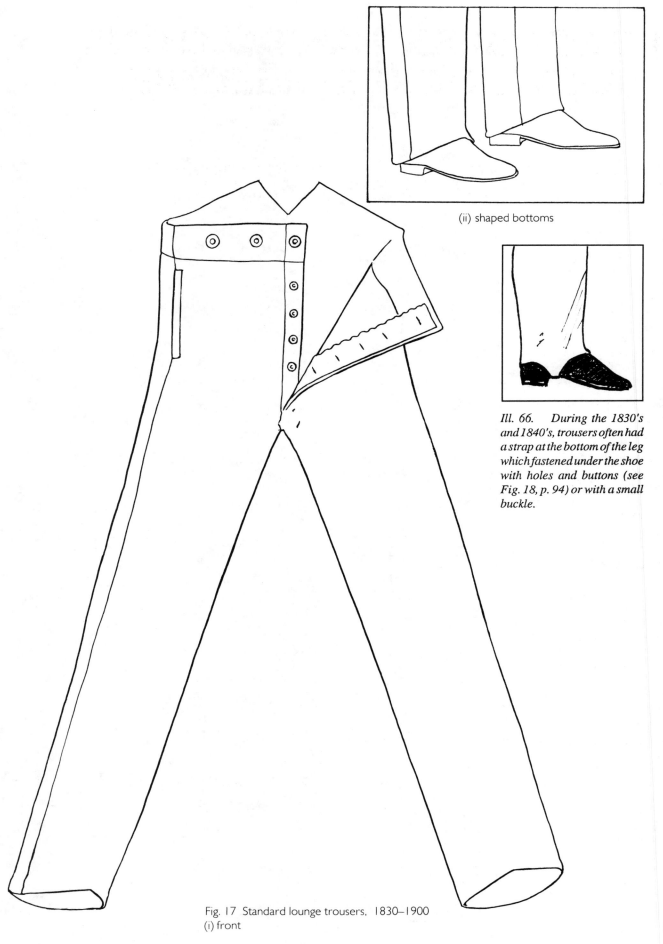

(ii) shaped bottoms

Ill. 66.   During the 1830's and 1840's, trousers often had a strap at the bottom of the leg which fastened under the shoe with holes and buttons (see Fig. 18, p. 94) or with a small buckle.

Fig. 17 Standard lounge trousers, 1830–1900
(i) front

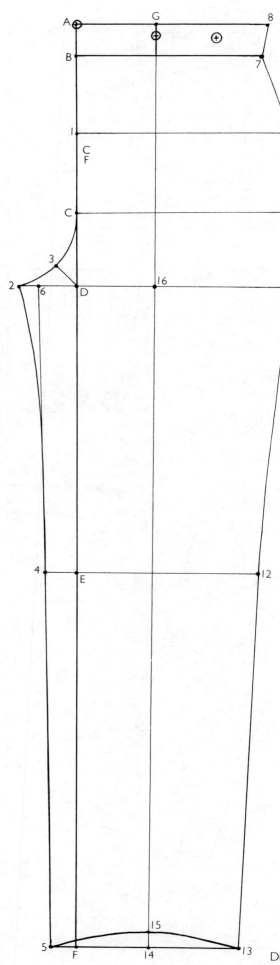

At the knee line:
12 from 4 = ½ knee measure = 25cm (9¾in).

At the bottom line:
13 from 5 = ½ bottom measure = 21.5cm (8½in).
Complete the side seam by joining 11 – 12 – 13 as in the diagram.
14 is the centre of 5 and 13.
15 squared from 14 = 2cm (¾in).
Curve 5 – 15 – 13.

Grain line

16 is the centre of 2 and 11.
Join 15 to 16 and continue to the top line and mark G.

Back pattern (dia. 17(b))

The outline of the front pattern is used as the basis for the back
    pattern.
Extend the construction lines beyond the front pattern, as in the
    diagram.
Continue the fly curve from 2.
17 from 2 = 3cm (1¼in).
Curve from 17 to join the line half-way between 2 and 4.
Continue to 4 and 5 to complete the inside leg.

Seat seam (centre back)

18 from 1 = 2cm (¾in).
19 from A = 5cm (2in).
Curve 17 – 2 – C.
Join C to 18 then 18 to 19.
Continue the line from 19.
20 from 19 = 2cm (¾in).
21 from 20 is ¼ waist plus 2cm (¾in) for the back dart = 23.5cm
(9¼in).
The measurement is applied diagonally from 20 on to the line
    extended from 7.
Join 20 to 21 for the back waist line.
22 from 21 is parallel with 7 to 8 of the front pattern.
23 from 20 = 5cm (2in).
Join 23 to 22.
24 from 23 = 4.5cm (1¾in).
25 squared from 24 = 2.5cm (1in).
Join 23 to 25 and curve 22 to 25 to complete the high back shape.
Point 23 is also the top of the seat seam, and centre back,
    23 – 20 – 18 – C – 2 – 17.

Back dart

H from 22 = 9cm (3½in).
Square a line from H.
I from H = 11.5cm (4½in).
At H mark a total of 1.3cm (½in).
At the back waist line (20 – 21) mark a total of 2cm (¾in).
Draw the back dart.
The dart is sewn together on the lines.

Dia. 17(a) Front

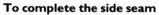

To complete the side seam

26 from 9 = 4cm (1½in).

27 from 10 = 2cm (¾in).

28 from 11 = 1.5cm (½in).

Curve 21 – 26 – 27 – 28.

Join 28 to 12 and 13.

At the bottom edge

29 below 14 = 1.3cm (½in).

Curve 5 – 29 – 13.

Trace the outline of the front pattern onto a separate sheet of paper. Then, before cutting out both patterns, add seams all round and add the turn-in at the bottom of the legs (see section on seam and turn-in allowance, p. 11).

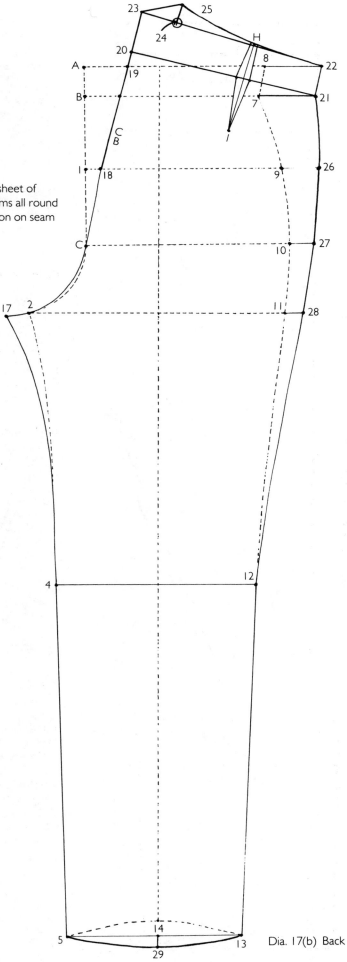

Dia. 17(b) Back

93

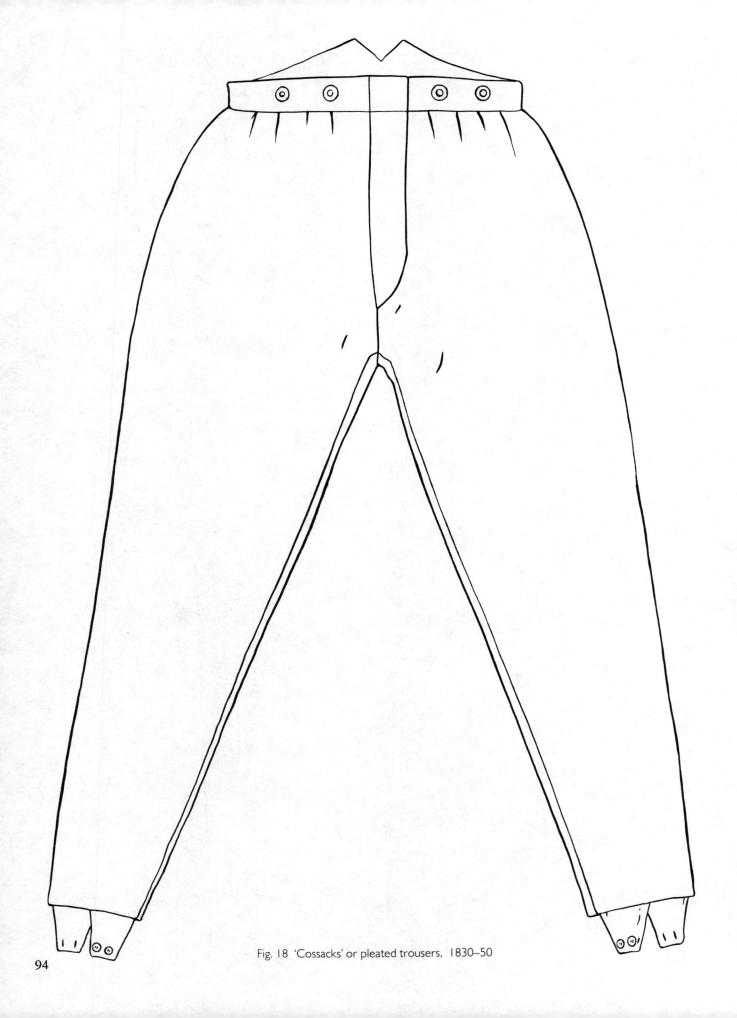

Fig. 18 'Cossacks' or pleated trousers, 1830–50

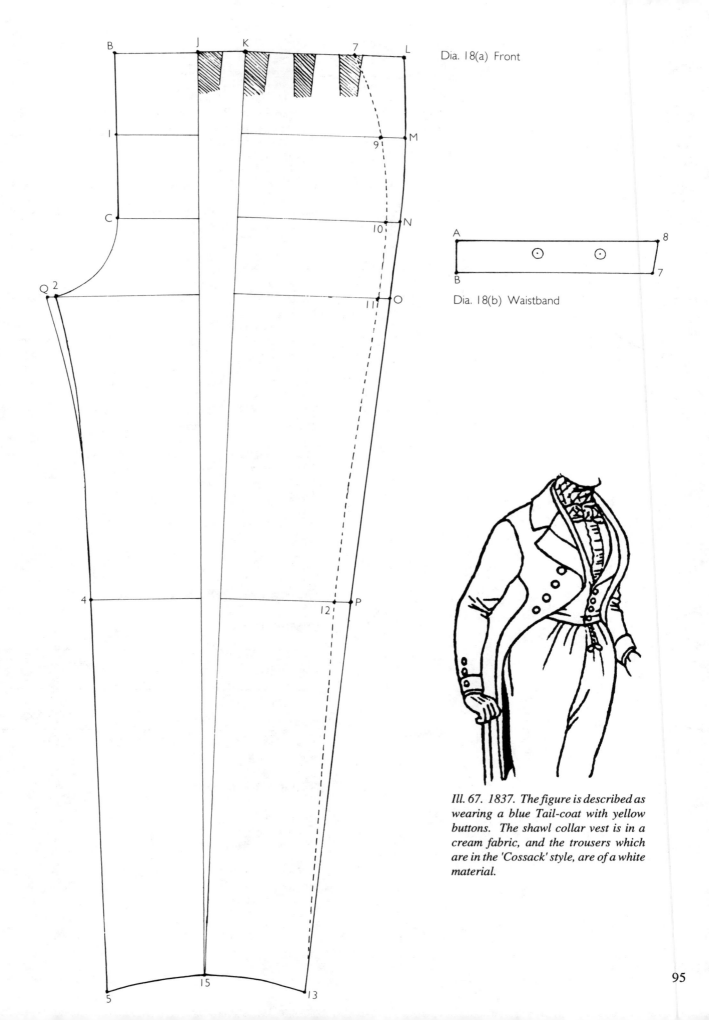

Dia. 18(a) Front

Dia. 18(b) Waistband

Ill. 67. 1837. The figure is described as wearing a blue Tail-coat with yellow buttons. The shawl collar vest is in a cream fabric, and the trousers which are in the 'Cossack' style, are of a white material.

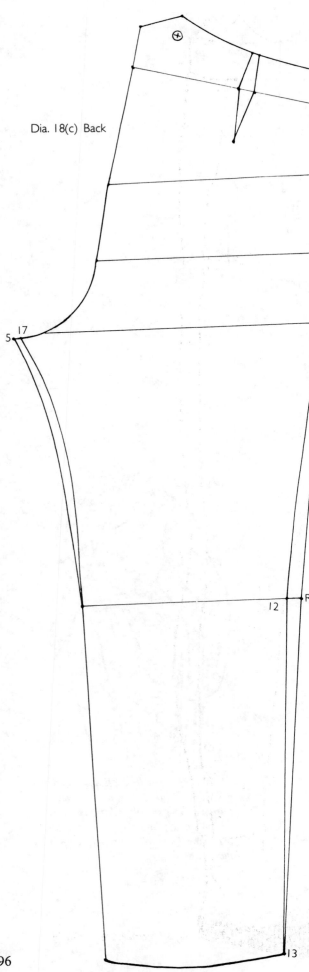

Dia. 18(c) Back

'Cossacks', 1830–50 (fig. 18; dia. 18(a)-(c))

Take the front pattern of diagram 17(a).
Fold back or cut off the waistband from B to 7.
Mark J where the grain line meets the waist line.
Retain the pattern in this position and mark the outline of the front
of the pattern, J – B – C – 2 – 4 – 5 – 15.
K from J = 5cm (2in).
Using 15 as a pivot, move J to K and locate points 7, 9, 10, 11, 12 and
13.
With the pattern remaining in that position mark the following:
L from 7 = 5cm (2in).
M from 9 = 2.5cm (1in).
N from 10 = 1.5cm (⅝in).
O from 11 = 1.3cm (½in).
P from 12 = 2cm (¾in).
Join L – M – N – O – P – 13 for the side seam.
Curve 13 to 15.
The waist has now been increased 10cm (4in).
Starting at J, mark 4 pleats. Each pleat is 2.5cm (1in) deep and
2.5cm (1in) apart.
The four pleats are folded toward the front of the trousers.
Q from 2 = 1cm (⅜in). Join Q with a moderate curve to 4.

Diagram 18(b) shows the waistband to be sewn on to the top of the
trousers after the pleats are folded out.

Diagram 18(c) shows the back pattern, which is the same as diagram
17(b), except for the following:
R from 12 = 2cm (¾in).
Join 27 – R – 13.
S from 17 = 1cm (⅜in).
Join S to 4 with a moderate curve.

Pantaloons, 1830–50 (fig. 19; dia. 19(a)-(b))

Measurements

	Outside leg	Inside leg	Waist	Seat	Knee	'Small'	Calf
cm	112	80	86	102	39	34	38
in	44	31½	34	40	15½	13½	15

Scale is half the seat measure = 51cm (20in) : ⅛ scale = 6.5cm (2½in)
⅟₄ scale = 13cm (5in)

Front pattern (dia. 19(a))

A = starting point.
Square down and across from A.
B from A = 4cm (1½in) (waist line).
C from B = 19cm (7½in) (seat line).
D from A = 32cm (12½in) (rise point).
E from D is half the inside leg minus 5cm (2in) = 35cm (13¾in)
(knee position).

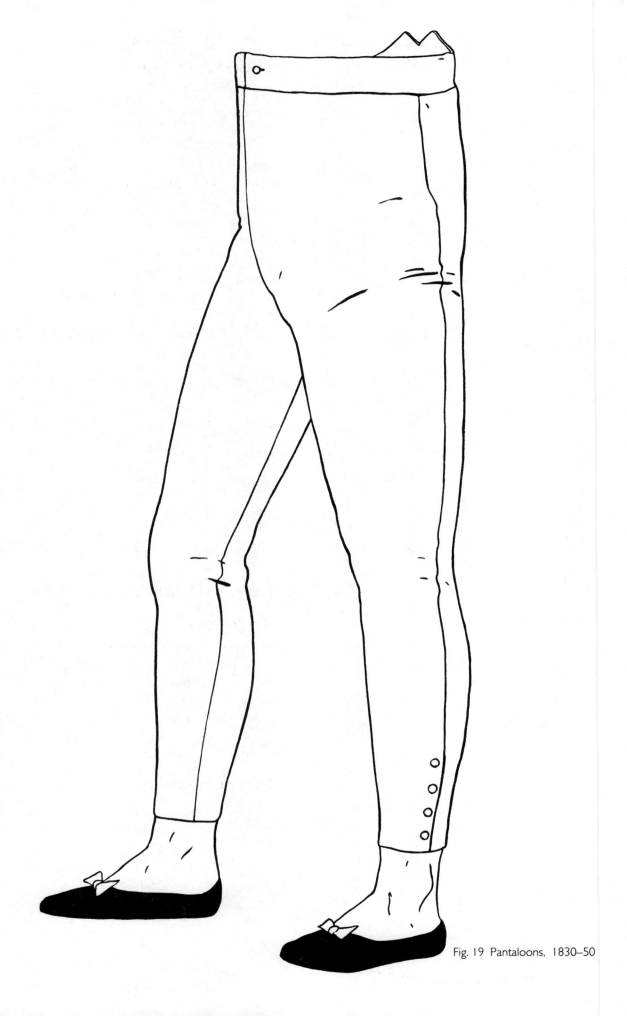

Fig. 19 Pantaloons, 1830–50

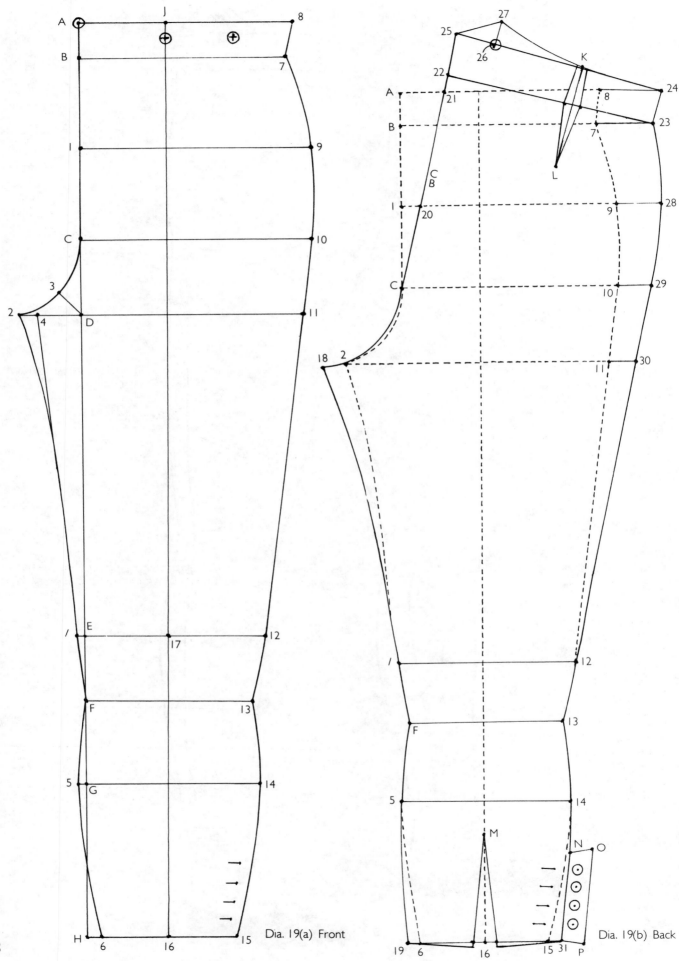

Dia. 19(a) Front

Dia. 19(b) Back

Square across from B, C, D and E.

F from E = 7cm (2¾in) ('small' position i.e. the hollow below the knee).

G from F = 9cm (3½in) (calf position).

H from G = 16.5cm (6½in) (ankle position).

Square across from F, G and H.

1 is half-way between B and C.

Square across from 1.

2 from D is ⅛ scale 6.5cm (2½in).

3 at an angle from D = half 2 from D.

Curve 2 – 3 – C.

4 from 2 = 1.3cm (½in).

Join 4 to F with a straight line and mark 1 on the knee line.

5 outside G = 1cm (⅜in).

6 inside H = 1.3cm (½in).

Curve 2 to join the line 4 – 1.

Continue from 1 to F – 5 – 6 – as in the diagram.

The inside leg is 2 – 1 – F – 5 – 6

Side seam

7 from B is ¼ waist = 21.5 (8½in).

8 from A = same as 7 from B plus 0.5cm (¼in) = 22cm (8¾in).

9 from 1 is ¼ seat minus 1.5cm (½in) = 24cm (9½in).

10 from C is the same as 9 from 1.

11 from D is ¼ seat minus 2.5cm (1in) = 23cm (9in).

Join 8–7–9–10–11.

12 from 1 is ½ knee = 19.5cm (7¾in).

13 from F is ½ 'small' = 17cm (6¾in).

14 from 5 is ½ calf = 19cm (7½in).

15 from 6 = 14cm (5½in).

Join 11–12–13–14–15 to complete the side seam.

16 is centre of 6 and 15.

17 is centre of 1 and 12.

Join 16 to 17 and continue the line to the top.

Mark J on the top line.

16 to J = grain line.

Mark the buttonholes 1cm (⅜in) inside the side seam and 2cm (¾in) apart, as in the diagram.

Back pattern (dia. 19(b))

The front pattern is used as a basis for the back pattern.

18 continued from 2 = 3cm (1¼in).

Curve 18 toward 1 and continue to F and 5.

19 from 6 = 1.3cm (½in).

Join 5 to 19 to complete the inside leg.

Seat seam (centre back)

20 from 1 = 2cm (¾in).

21 from A = 5cm (2in).

Curve 18 – 2 – C.

Join C to 20 and 20 – 21.

Continue the line from 21.

22 from 21 = 2cm (¾in).

23 from 22 is ¼ waist plus 2cm (¾in) = 23.5cm (9¼in).

The measurement is applied diagonally from 22 onto the line extended from 7.

Join 22 to 23 for the back waist line.

24 from 23 is parallel with 7 to 8.

25 continued from 22 = 5cm (2in). Join 25 to 24.

26 squared from 25 = 4.5cm (1¾in).

27 squared from 26 = 2.5cm (1in).

Join 25 to 27 and curve 24 to 27.

24 – 27 – 25 is the high back for trousers worn with braces.

Back dart

K from 24 is ⅛ scale plus 2.5cm (1in) = 9cm (3½in).

The line from K to L is squared from 24 – 25.

L from K = 11.5cm (4½in).

At K take out 1.5cm (½in).

At the waist line (28 to 30) take out a total of 2cm (¾in).

Draw the dart as in the diagram.

Side seam

28 from 9 = 5cm (2in).

29 from 10 = 4cm (1½in).

30 from 11 = 3cm (1¼in).

Join 23 – 28 – 29 – 30.

Join 30 to 12 – 13 – 14.

31 from 15 = 1.3cm (½in).

Join 14 to 31.

To create shape over the back calf, a dart is taken out below the calf as follows:

M from 16 = 13cm (5in).

Mark 1.3cm (½in) each side of 16 and join these points to M.

The dart is sewn on the lines.

Button stand

At the side seam:

N from 31 = 10cm (4in).

O from N = 2.5cm (1in).

P from 31 = 2.5cm (1in).

Join O to P.

The buttons are placed 1cm (⅜in) from the side seam.

Trace the outline of the front pattern on to a separate sheet of paper. Then, before cutting out both patterns, add seams all round.

Knickerbreeches, 1860–1900
(fig. 20; dia. 20(a)-(c))

Measurements

	Outside leg	Inside leg	Waist	Seat	'Small'	Calf
cm	112	80	86	102	34	38
in	44	31½	34	40	13½	15

Scale is half the seat measure = 51cm (20in) : ⅛ scale = 6.5cm (2½in)

¼ scale = 13cm (5in)

NOTE:
Refer to Illustration G50, as a style statement, some men wore their hose over the buttons while others wore the hose under.

Fig. 20 Knickerbreeches, 1860–1900

Front pattern (dia. 20(a))

A = starting point.

Square down and across from A.

B from A = 4cm (1½in).

C from B = 19cm (7½in).

D from A = 32cm (12½in).

E from D is ½ inside leg minus 5cm (2in) = 35cm (13¾in).
    F from E = 13cm (5in).

Square across from B, C, D, E and F.

1 is half-way between B and C.

Square across from 1.

2 from D is ⅛ scale plus 1cm (⅜in) = 7.5cm (2⅞in).

3 at an angle from D = 4cm (1½in).

Curve the fly 2 to 3 and continue the curve to the centre front at C.

4 inside 2= 1.5m (⅝in).

5 from E = 3cm (1¼in).

Join 4 to 5 with a straight line.

6 from F = 1cm (⅜in).

Curve from 2 to join the line 4 – 5.

Curve from 5 to 6. Inside leg is 2 – 5 – 6.

Side seam

7 on the line from B is ¼ waist = 21.5 (8½in).

8 from A = is the same as 7 from B plus 0.5cm (¼in) =
    22cm (8¾in).

9 from 1 is ¼ seat minus 1cm (⅜in) = 24.5cm (9⅝in).

10 from C is ¼ seat = 25.5cm (10in).

11 from D is the same.

Join 7 to 8 with a straight line.

Curve 7 – 9 – 10 – 11.

12 from 5 = 26cm (10¼in).

13 from 6 is half the 'small' plus 3 cm (1¼in) = 20cm (8in).

Join 11 – 12 – 13.

14 is half way between 6 and 13.

15 below 14 = 1cm (⅜in).

Curve 6 – 15 – 13 for the bottom edge.

Note: There is an allowance of 3cm (1¼in) included in the pattern at the bottom edge. This amount is 'gathered' on to the leg band from 6 – 15 – 13. This also applies to the back pattern.

Grain line

16 is half-way between 2 and 11.

Join 15 to 16 and continue to the top of the pattern and mark G.

Back pattern (dia. 20(b))

The outline of the front pattern (dia. 20(a)) is used as a basis for the
    back pattern.

Extend the construction lines beyond the front pattern, as in dia.
    20(b).

Continue the fly curve from 2.

17 from 2 = 3cm (1¼in).

Curve from 17 to 5 and continue to 6 to complete the inside leg.

Seat seam (centre back)

18 from 1 = 2cm (¾in).

19 from A = 5cm (2in).

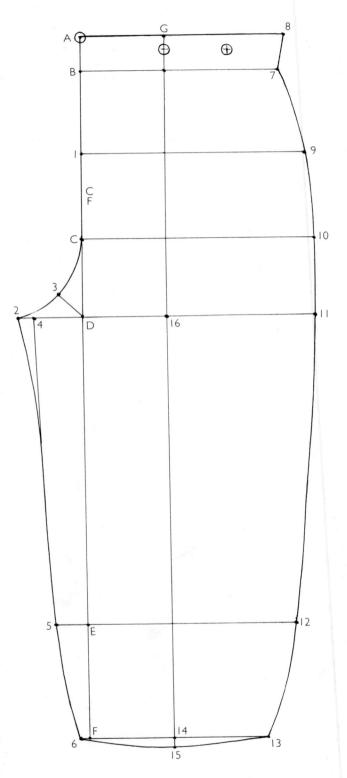

Dia. 20(a) Front

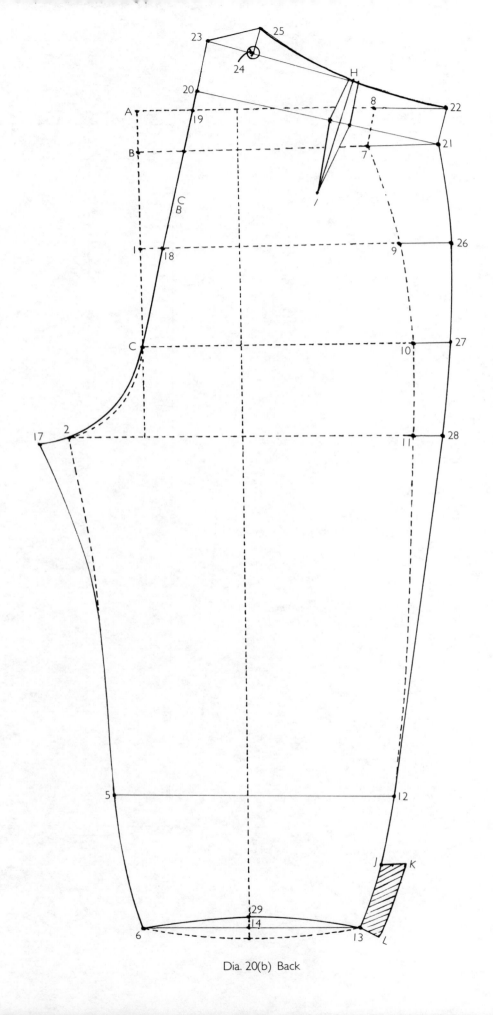

Dia. 20(b) Back

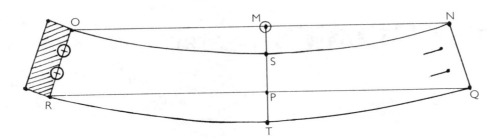

Dia. 20(c) Leg band

Curve 17 – 2 – C. Join C – 18 and 18 – 19.
Continue the line from 19.
20 from 19 = 2cm (¾in).
21 from 20 is ¼ waist plus 2cm (¾in) = 23.5cm (9¼in).
This measurement is applied diagonally from 20 on to the
  line extended from 7.
Join 20 to 21.
22 from 21 is parallel with 7 to 8 of the front pattern.
23 from 22 = 5cm (2in).
Join 23 to 22.
24 from 23 = 4.5cm (1¾in).
25 squared from 24 = 2.5cm (1in).
Join 23 to 25. Curve 22 to 25.

Back dart
H from 22 = 9cm (3½in).
Square a line from H.
I from H = 11.5cm (4½in).
At H mark a total of 1.3cm (½in).
At the back waist line (20–21) mark 2cm.
Draw the back dart.

Complete the side seam
26 from 9 = 5cm (2in).
27 from 10 = 4cm (1½in).
28 from 11 = 2.5cm (1in).
Curve 21 – 26 – 27 – 28.
Continue the curve from 28 to 12 and 13.

At the bottom edge
29 from 14 = 1cm (⅜in).
Curve 6 – 29 – 13.
There is a small opening or 'vent' at the side seam.
J from 13 = 6.5cm (2½in).
Add a small underwrap for the vent as follows:
K from J = 2.5cm (1in).
L from 13 = 2.5cm (1in).
Join K to L.

Trace the outline of the front pattern on to a separate sheet of
paper. Then, before cutting out both patterns, add seams all round.

Leg band (dia. 20(c))
(also referred to as the 'garter')

M = starting point.
Draw a line across from M.
N from M is half the 'small' = 17cm (6¾in).
O from M is half the 'small' plus 1.3cm (½in) = 18.3cm (7¼in).
P squared down from M = 6cm (2½in).
Square across from P.
Q from P is half the calf = 19cm (7½in).
R from P is half the calf plus 1.3cm (½in) = 20.3cm (8in).
Join N – Q and O – R.
S from M = 2.5cm (1in).
Curve N – S – O.
T from P = 2.5cm (1in).
Curve Q – T – R.
Mark the buttonholes 1.3cm (½in) inside N and Q.
Mark the buttons on the line O – R.
Add 2.5cm (1in) beyond O and R (shaded section).

Front view

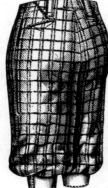

Back view

*Ill. 68. Knickerbreeches, also known as knickerbockers, leg band fastened
at the side with 2 holes and buttons. The front has a button fly. Back has two
hip pockets with flaps and button fastening. Wide belt loops on the waist.
The Delineator, January 1896.*

5 WAISTCOATS (VESTS)

During the period 1830–50, the waistcoat was a very individual garment. Although it was the smallest of a man's outer garments, it achieved prominence by the attractive materials from which it was made. The choice of fabric was both rich in texture and colour and flamboyant in pattern and design. These materials were very expensive and used only for the fronts, while the back was usually made of an inferior material. The tailoring practice of using a different material for the back has continued up to the present time.

A roll collar was favoured during this period and though both single-breasted and double-breasted styles were worn, it would seem that the single-breasted style was more popular.

Between 1850 and 1860 the waistcoat tended to match the trousers, with the more outstanding fabrics of the previous decade being replaced by checks and stripes, etc., in a material more suited to both waistcoat and trousers.

Both single- and double-breasted styles were popular and in addition to the roll collar there was also the separate lapel with collar design – known as a 'step' collar. These styles continued to the end of the nineteenth century.

After 1860, the waistcoat became even less individual as a garment and merged with the coat and trousers to form the three-piece suit all in the same material. However, waistcoats worn with the evening dress coat and the double-breasted frock coat continued to be made in a contrasting fabric.

NOTE:

Ill. G10, shows a Shawl collar vest. The bottom edge of the front is cut straight, but in Fig. 21 the fronts come to a small point.

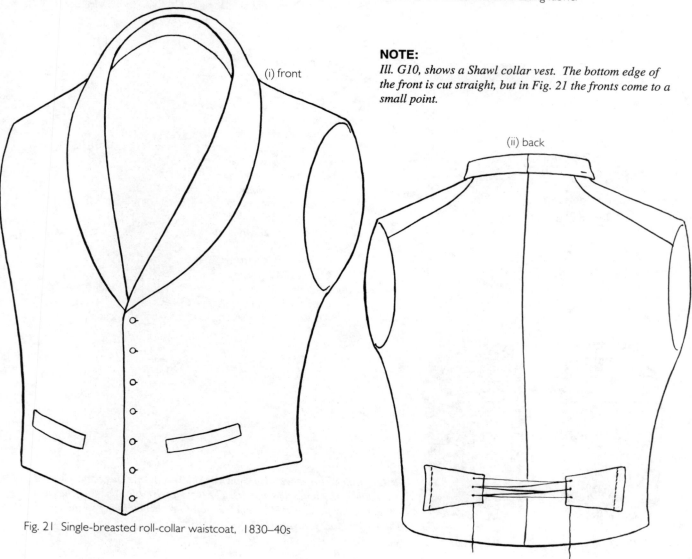

(i) front

(ii) back

Fig. 21 Single-breasted roll-collar waistcoat, 1830–40s

PLATE 19.   *The figure conveys an air of casual elegance with Tail-Coat thrown to the back of shoulders. Waistcoat, page 104, Figure 21, has a pointed front. Trousers are close fitting in the style of Pantaloons.*

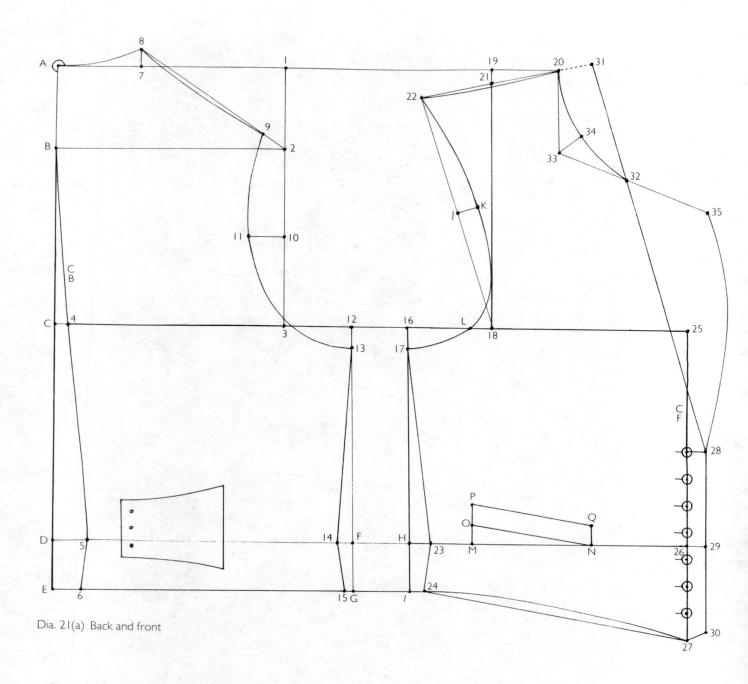

Dia. 21(a) Back and front

Single-breasted roll-collar waistcoat, 1830s–1840s (fig. 21; dia 21(a)–(c))

Measurements

	Nape to waist	Chest	Waist
cm	44.5	96	86
in	17½	38	34

Scale is half the chest = 48cm (19in) : ⅛ scale = 6cm (2⅜in)
¼ scale = 12cm (4¾in)

Back pattern

A = starting point.
Square across and down from A.
B from A = 7.5cm (3in).
C from A is ½ scale = 24cm (9½in).
D from A = 44.5cm (17½in) (nape to waist).
E from D = 4.5cm (1¾in).
Square a short line across from B and E.
Square a long line across from C and D.
1 from A = 20.5cm (8⅛in).
Square down from 1 to the chest line (line from C).
Mark 2 and 3.
4 inside C = 1.3cm (½in).
5 inside D = 3cm (1¼in).

PLATE 20. 1864. (L) Knee length Frock coat. The Vest and Trousers are in a matching fabric. The High-buttoned Vest has a narrow braiding on the edges with a similar braid on the edge of the slanted trousers pocket. (C) Single-breasted Chesterfield Topcoat with a fly front fastening. The collar is in velvet and the coat edges, flaps and cuffs are bound with a narrow braid. The striped trousers are wide at the knee then narrowing toward the bottom. Tall Top hat. (R) Long Single-breasted Jacket with a high-buttoning front. Typical of the 1860's are the wide sleeves and trousers which gives an impression of bulkiness. Low crown hat with a curved brim.

6 inside E = 2.5cm (1in).
Join A to 4 with a moderate curve and then join 4 – 5 – 6.
A – 4 – 5 – 6 = centre back seam (CB).
7 from A is ⅛ scale plus 1.5cm (⅝in) = 7.5cm (3in).
8 squared up from 7 = 1.5cm (⅝in).
Curve 8 to A for the back neck.
Join 8 to 2.
9 from 2 = 2.5cm (1in).
Slightly hollow the back shoulder from 8 to 9.
10 is half-way between 2 and 3.
11 from 10 = 3cm (1¼in).
12 from 3 is ⅛ scale = 6cm (2⅜in).
Square down from 12.
Mark F at the waist line.
Mark G at the bottom line.
13 down from 12 = 2cm (¾in).
Curve the back armhole from 13 to just above 3, then continue
    through 11 to 9.
14 from F = 1.3cm (½in).
15 from G = 0.5cm (¼in).
Join 12 – 14 – 15 to complete the side seam.

Front pattern

16 from 12 = 5cm (2in) to separate the patterns.
Square down from 16.
Mark H at the waist line and I at the bottom line.
17 down from 16 = 2cm (¾in).
18 from 16 is ⅛ scale plus 1.5cm (⅝in) = 7.5cm (3in).
19 on the top line is squared from 18.
20 from 19 is ⅛ scale = 6cm (2⅜in).
21 below 19 = 1.3cm (½in).
Join 20 to 21 and continue the line.
22 from 20 is 8 to 9 minus 1cm (⅜in) = 12.5cm (5in).
Hollow the shoulder 20 to 22.
Join 18 to 22 with a straight line.
J is centre of 18 and 22.
K squared from J = 2cm (¾in).
L from 18 = 2cm (¾in).
Curve the front armhole 22–K–L–17.
23 from H = 2cm (¾in).
24 from I = 1.3cm (½in).
Join 17–23–24 to complete the side seam.

On the chest line:
25 from 18 is ½ scale minus 6cm (2½in) = 18cm (7in).
Square down from 25 for the centre front (CF).
Mark 26 on the waist line.
27 continued from 26 = 9cm (3½in).
Mark the top button and hole 9cm (3½in) above 26.
28 from the top button and hole position = 1.5cm (⅝in).
29 from 26 = 1.5cm (⅝in).
Join 28 and 29 and continue the line.
30 from 29 = 8.5cm (3¼in).
Join 30 to 27.
Note: 28–29–30 is the front edge.
On the centre front mark the buttons and holes 2.5cm (1in) apart.
Join 24 to 27 with a moderate curve to complete the bottom edge.

At the top:
31 from 20 = 3cm (1¼in).
Join 31 to 28.
32 from 31 = 11.5cm (4½in).
33 squared down from 20 = 7.5cm (3in).
Join 33 to 32 and continue the line.
34 at an angle to 33 = 2.5cm (1in).
Curve 32 – 34 – 20.
35 from 32 = 7.5cm (3in).
Curve 35 to 28 for the front edge of the roll collar.

Welt pockets

M from 23 = 4cm (1½in).
N from M = 11cm (4¼in).
O squared up from M = 2cm (¾in).
Join O to N for the pocket position.
P from O and Q from N = 2cm (¾in) for the pocket welt.
Join P to Q.

Back tabs for lacing

The tabs are made from the same fabric as the back and are designed
to take three eyelet holes. The dimensions of the tabs are:
    5cm (2in) at the front (narrow end);
    7.5cm (3in) at the back (faces towards side seam);
    9cm (3½in) long (front to back).
The tab is positioned on to the back in the region of the waist-hollow
(see diagram) and the front of the tab is approx. 3cm (1¼in) from
the centre back seam.

Roll collar (dia. 21(b))

This diagram shows the front pattern with the relevant points
    (20–32–35–28) marked from diagram 21(a).
Join 32 to 20 and continue the line.
R from 20 is the measurement of the back neck (A – 8 of diagram
    21(a)) = 7.5cm (3in).
Draw a moderate curve from R to 32.
Square across from R.
S from R = 3cm (1¼in).
T from R = 4.5cm (1¾in).
U above T = 1cm (⅜in).
Join U to R and curve from U to 35 for collar edge.
V from 20 = 2.5cm (1in).
Join S to V and curve to 32.
Follow the neck line to 35.
The shading shows the shape of the undercollar pattern, which can
be made from the same fabric as the front. In the separate diagram,
the front facing is shown continuing round to the centre of the back
neck and using the undercollar pattern as a guide.

Chest dart for padding (dia. 21(c))

A feature of the waistcoat of the 1830s and 1840s was the padded
chest. A ply of wadding, with the edges thinned out, or similar
padding can be used. To accommodate the padding, it is necessary
to create a contour in the fronts, by taking a dart out from the
armhole towards the chest area.

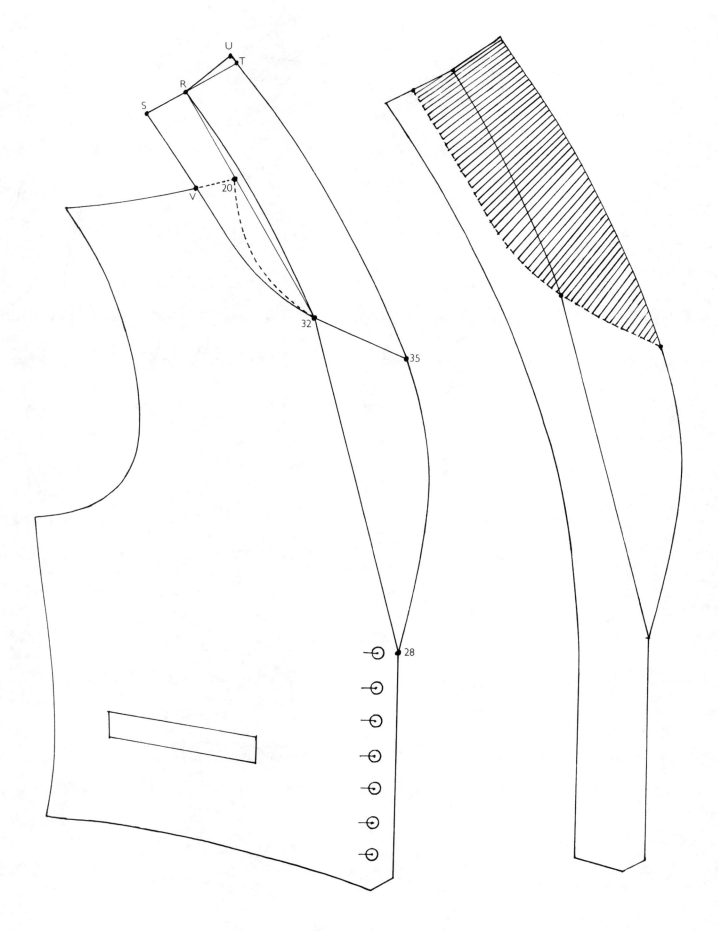

Dia. 21(b) Roll collar

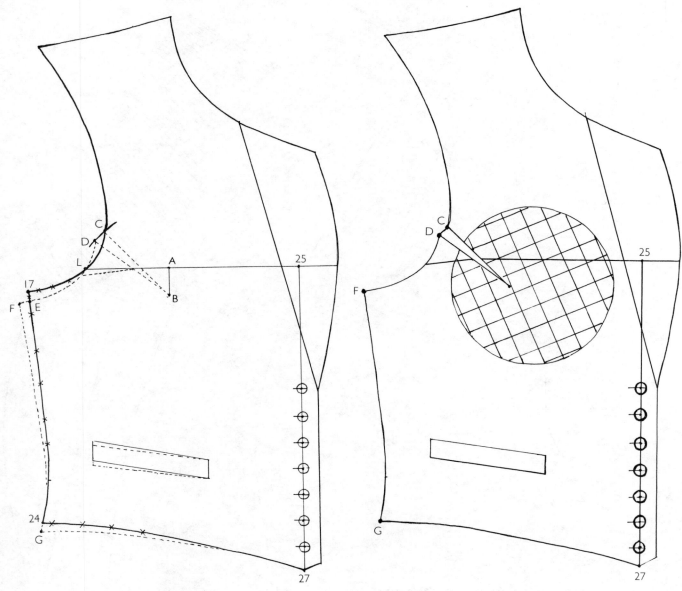

Dia. 21(c) Chest dart padding

The method is as follows:

Mark round the front pattern of dia. 21(a), and transfer the relevant
    points L, 17, 24, 25 and 27.

A from L on the chest line = 7.5cm (3in).

B squared down from A = 2.5cm (1in).

C from L on the armhole = 4cm (1½in).

Using B as a pivot draw an arc from C.

D from C = 1.3cm (½in).

Join C and D to B, forming the dart.

E below 17 = 1cm (⅜in).

Curve D – L – E.

F continued from E = 1cm (⅜in).

Place the side seam of the pattern (17–24) at F and re-draw the side
    seam as shown by the dash lines.

G continued from 24 = 1cm (⅜in).

Re-mark the bottom edge from G toward 27.

Adjust the pocket level accordingly.

The right-hand figure in dia. 21(c) shows the position of the padding.

Single-breasted waistcoat with 'step' collar, 1850–1900 (fig. 22; dia 22(a)-(b))

Measurements

	Nape to waist	Chest	Waist	Nape to opening	Nape to front length
cm	44.5	96	86	27	65
in	17½	38	34	10½	25½

Scale is half the chest = 48cm (19in) : ⅛ scale = 6cm (2⅜in)
¼ scale = 12cm (4¾in)

Back pattern

A = starting point.
Square across and down from A.
B from A = 7.5cm (3in).
C from A is ½ scale = 24cm (9½in).
D from A is the nape to waist = 44.5cm (17½in).
E from D = 6.5cm (2½in).
Square a short line across from B and E.
Square a long line across from C and D.
I from A = 20.5cm (8⅛in).
Square down from I to the chest line (line across from C).
Mark 2 and 3.
4 inside C = 1.3cm (½in).
5 inside D = 3cm (1¼in).
6 inside E = 2.5cm (1in).
Join A to 4 with a moderate curve and then join 4 – 5 – 6.
A – 4 – 5 – 6 = centre back seam (CB).
7 from A is ⅛ scale plus 1.5cm (⅝in) = 7.5cm (3in).
8 squared up from 7 = 1.5cm (⅝in).
Curve 8 to A for the back neck.
Join 8 to 2.
9 from 2 = 2.5cm (1in).
Raise the back neck as follows:
F from A = 1cm (⅜in).
G from 8 = 1cm (⅜in).
Curve F to G parallel with A to 8.
Join G to the back shoulder half-way between 8 and 9.
10 is half-way between 2 and 3.
11 squared from 10 = 3cm (1¼in).
12 from 3 is ⅛ scale = 6cm (2⅜in).
Square a line down from 12.
Mark H at the waist line.
Mark I at the bottom line from E.
13 below 12 = 2cm (¾in).
Curve the back armhole from 13 to just above 3, then continue
   through 11 to 9.
14 from H = 1.3cm (½in).
15 from I = 0.5cm (¼in).
Join 13 – 14 – 15 for the side seam.

Note: The diagram shows the back strap and buckle that has remained in use from this period up to the present time.

Front pattern

16 from 12 = 5cm (2in) to separate the patterns.
Square down from 16.
Mark J at the waist line and K at the bottom line.
17 below 16 = 2cm (¾in).
18 from 16 is ⅛ scale plus 1.5cm (⅝in) = 7.5cm (3in).
Square up from 18 and mark 19 on the top line.
20 from 19 is ⅛ scale = 6cm (2⅜in).
21 below 19 = 1.3cm (½in).
Join 20 to 21 and continue the line.
22 from 20 is 8 to 9 minus 1cm (⅜in) = 12.5cm (5in).
Hollow the front shoulder from 20 to 22.
Join 18 to 22 with a straight line.
L is the centre of 18 and 22.
M squared from L = 2cm (¾in).
N from 18 = 2cm (¾in).
Curve the front armhole 22 – M – N – 17.
23 from J = 2cm (¾in).
24 from K = 1.3cm (½in).
Join 17 – 23 – 24 to complete the side seam.

On the chest line:
25 from 18 = ½ scale minus 6cm (2½in) = 18cm (7in).
Square down from 25 and mark 26 on the waist line.
27 continued from 26 = 11.5cm (4½in).
At the top line
28 from 20 = 9cm (3½in)
Join 28 to 25.
Mark the top hole and button 5cm (2in) above 25.
The other fastenings are 5cm (2in) apart.
29 from the top button = 1.5cm (⅝in).
30 from 20 = 1cm (⅜in).
Join 30 to 29 for the 'opening'.
31 from 25 = 1.5cm (⅝in).
32 from 26 = 1.5cm (⅝in).
Join 29–31–32 and continue the line.
33 is on the front edge opposite the bottom button and hole.
34 squared from 27 = 2cm (¾in).
Join 33 to 34 for the waistcoat 'point'.
Curve slightly to 'round' the front edge from 29 to 34.
To complete the bottom edge join 24 to 34 with a moderate curve.

Check the 'opening' and front length measurements

The 'nape to opening' and 'nape to front length' measurements as listed in the table of measurements above are included in the method of drafting the front pattern of diagram 26.

Alternatively, these two measurements can be applied direct to the pattern as follows:

Front opening

Measure the neck of the back pattern F to G = 7.5cm (3in). Deduct this from the 'nape to opening' measurement:

cm	in
27	10½
7.5	3
19.5	7½

Fig. 22 Single-breasted step-collar waistcoat,
1850–1900

Fig. 23 Double-breasted waistcoat,
1850–1900

(ii) backview of Figs. 22 and 23

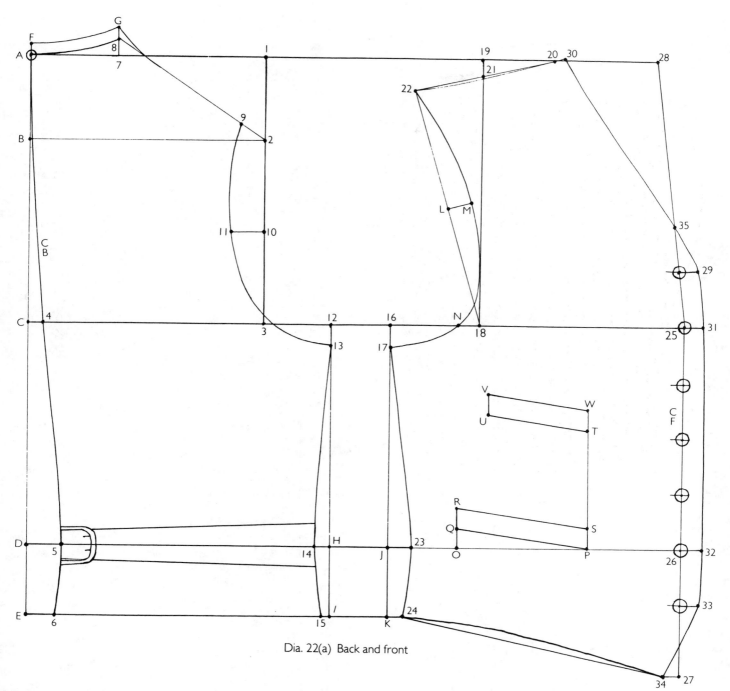

Dia. 22(a) Back and front

Measure 19.5cm (7½in) from 20 to locate 35 on the centre line. Join the advanced point 30 to 35 and continue to the front edge at point 29.

Front length
Measure the neck of the back pattern F to G = 7.5cm (3in). Deduct this from the 'nape to front length' measurement:

cm	in
65	25½
7.5	3
57.5	22½

Therefore, 27 from 20 on the front pattern = 57.5cm (22½in).

Welt pockets
There are two bottom pockets (one on either side), and one top pocket on the left front which serves as a watch pocket.
O from 23 = 4cm (1½in).
P from O = 11.5cm (4½in).
Square up from O.
Q above O = 2cm (¾in).
Join Q to P for pocket position.
R from Q and S from P = 2cm (¾in).
Join R to S for the welt.

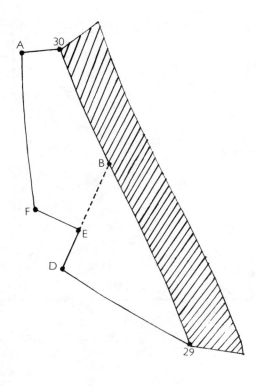

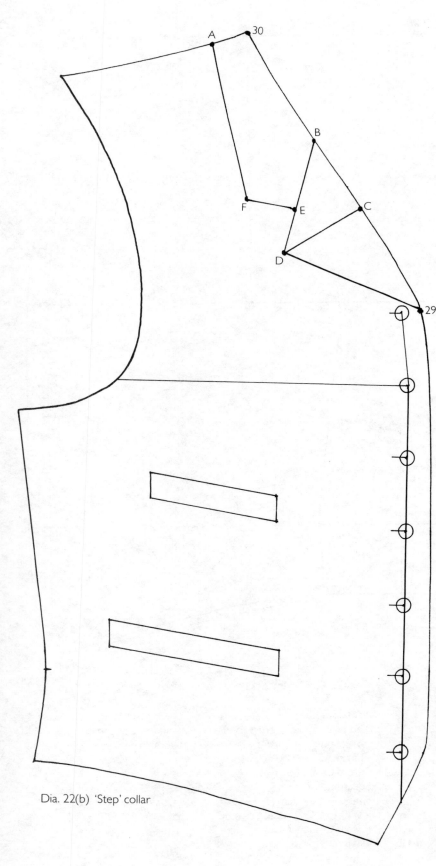

Watch pocket

T from S = 9cm (3 1/2in).
Draw a line from T, parallel with R and S.
U from T = 9cm (3 1/2in).
V above U and W from T are 2cm (3/4in).
Join V to W for the welt.

'Step' collar (dia. 22(b))

Left The combined collar and lapel is known as a 'step' collar. It is made from a separate piece of material and is laid on to the front at the opening 30 to 29. The 'collar' does not continue round the back neck but is sewn into the shoulder seam. A suitable matching lining is sewn to the back of the step collar.
Draw the shape required on to the front pattern.
A from 30 = 2.5cm (1in).
B from 30 = 9cm (3 1/2in).
C from B = 5cm (2in).
D squared from C = 5.5cm (2 1/4in).
Join D to B.
Join D to 29.
E from D = 3cm (1 1/4in).
F squared from E = 3cm (1 1/4in).
Join A to F.

Right Trace the outline of the step collar separately and add 3cm (1 1/4in) as shaded section. This amount is to be turned in over the front 'opening' and joined to the inside lining. Elsewhere, a seam allowance of 1cm (3/8in) must be added. As an added feature, a seam can be included from E to B (see diagram) by cutting the collar and lapel separately.

Dia. 22(b) 'Step' collar

Double-breasted waistcoat, 1850–1900

(fig. 23; dia 23(a)–(b))

Measurements

	Nape to waist	Chest	Waist	Nape to opening	Nape to front length
cm	44.5	96	86	28	62
in	17½	38	34	11	24½

Scale is half the chest = 48cm (19in) : ⅛ scale = 6cm (2⅜in)
¼ scale = 12cm (4¾in)

Back pattern

Follow the instructions for dia. 22(a).
A – 1 and 1 – 15.

Front pattern

Follow the instructions for dia. 22(a).
J – N and 16 – 24.
For the double-breasted front continue as follows (dia. 23(a)):
25 from 18 = ½ scale minus 6cm (2½in) = 18cm (7in).
Square down from 25.
Mark 26 on the waist line and continue the line.
27 from 26 = 9cm (3½in).
Point 27 can also be found by measuring the front length from 20, i.e.
    62cm (24½in) minus 7.5cm (3in) (back neck) = 54.5cm (21½in).
28 from 20 = 9cm (3½in).
Join 28 to 25.
To locate point 29, calculate as follows:

	cm	in
Nape to opening measurement =	28	11
Deduct the width of back neck F to G =	7.5	3
	20.5	8

Measure from 20 on to the centre line (28 to 25) this length 20.5 cm
    (8in) and mark 29.
30 from 20 = 1cm (⅜in).
Join 30 to 29 first with a straight line then a moderate hollow.
Slightly hollow 29 to 25.
Complete the bottom edge by joining 24 to 27 then curve as in
    diagram.

Double-breasted front panel

On the chest line, 31 from 25 = 4cm (1½in) to separate the
    patterns.
At the bottom edge, 32 from 27 = 4cm (1½in).
Join 31 to 32 and mark 33 at the waist line.

34 from 29 = 5.5cm (2⅛in).
Curve 34 to 31.
35 below 31 = 6cm (2⅜in).
36 squared across from 35 = 7.5cm (3in).
37 from 33 = 6.5cm (2½in).
Join 36 to 37 and continue the line.
38 from 37 = 8.5cm (3¼in).
Join 32 to 38.
39 above 36 = 1.5cm (⅝in).
Join 34 to 39 with a slight hollow.

Note: 27–29 and 32–34 should be slightly curved. The top
buttonhole is opposite point 36 and the other holes are 5cm (2in)
apart. The holes are placed 1.5cm (⅝in) from the front edge.
The buttons are placed on a level with each button hole. The buttons
are the same distance from the centre front of the main pattern as
the buttonholes are from the centre front of the panel. For example,
the top hole is 6cm (2⅜in) from 35. Therefore, the top button is
6cm (2⅜in) from the centre front line 29–27.

Welt pockets

O from 23 = 2.5cm (1in).
P from O = 11cm (4¼in).
Q squared up from O = 1.3cm (½in).
Join Q to P for the pocket position.
R from Q and S from P = 2cm (¾in).
Join R to S for the welt.

Top pocket

Draw a line 9cm (3½in) above and parallel to R and S.
T is 5cm (2in) from the line of the buttons.
U from T = 9.5cm (3¾in).
V from U and W from T = 2cm (¾in).
Join V to W for the welt.

Double-breasted lapel and collar (dia. 23(b))

Close the two centre fronts together (29–34 and 25–31).
Mark points 30 and 39.
A from 30 = 3cm (1¼in).
B from 30 = 9cm (3½in).
C from B = 4cm (1½in).
D squared from C = 9cm (3½in).
E is half-way between C and D.
Curve 39 to D and continue the line.
F from D = 3cm (1¼in).
Join F to E and E to B.
G from E = 4cm (1½in).
Join A to G.
Trace the outline of the collar and lapel onto a separate sheet of
paper and add 3cm (1¼in) for turning in at the opening. This is a 'laid
on' shape that finishes at the shoulder seam – as shown in dia. 22(b).
A seam can be included in the design from E to B by cutting the
pattern from E along the dash line so that the collar and lapel are
separate patterns.

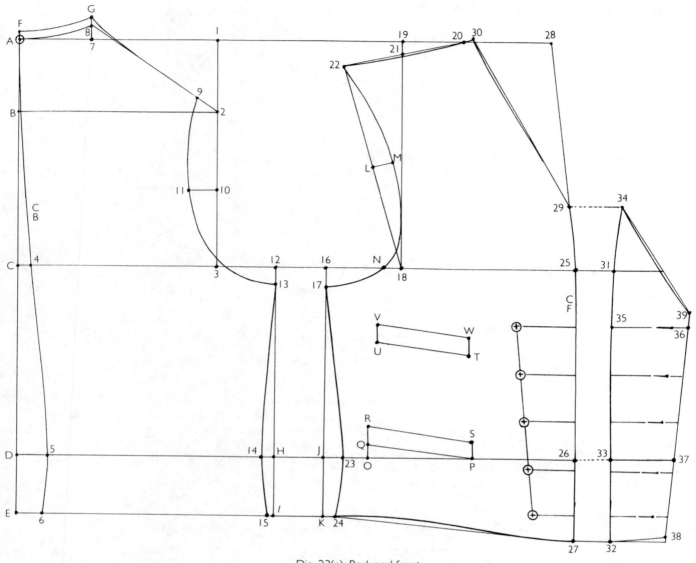

Dia. 23(a) Back and front

*Ill. 69. 1890's Double-breasted vest with 4 buttons to
fasten and 4 to 'show.' Note the shape of the collar and
revers. (Montgomery Wards catalogue, 1895.) Also refer
to G33.*

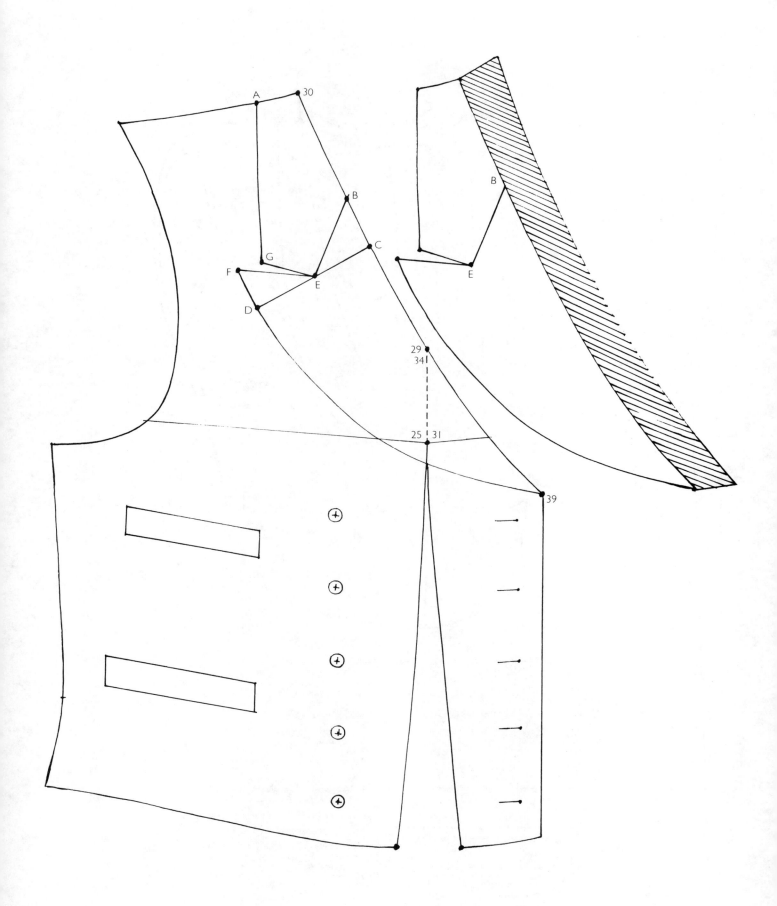

Dia. 23(b) Double-breasted collar and lapel

Fig. 24 Single-breasted evening dress waistcoat with roll collar, 1850–1900

Single-breasted evening dress waistcoat with roll collar, 1850–1900 (fig. 24; dia. 24)

Measurements

	Nape to waist	Chest	Waist
cm	44.5	96	86
in	17½	38	34

Scale is half the chest = 48cm (19in) : ⅛ scale = 6cm (2⅜in)
¼ scale = 12cm (4¾in)

Back pattern

A = starting point.
Square across and down from A.
B from A = 7.5cm (3in).
C from A is ½ scale = 24cm (9½in).
D from A = 44.5cm (17½in).
E from D = 4.5cm (1¾in).
Square across a short line from B and E.
Square across a long line from C and D.

1 from A = 20.5cm (8⅛in).
Square down from 1 to the chest line from C.
Mark 2 and 3.

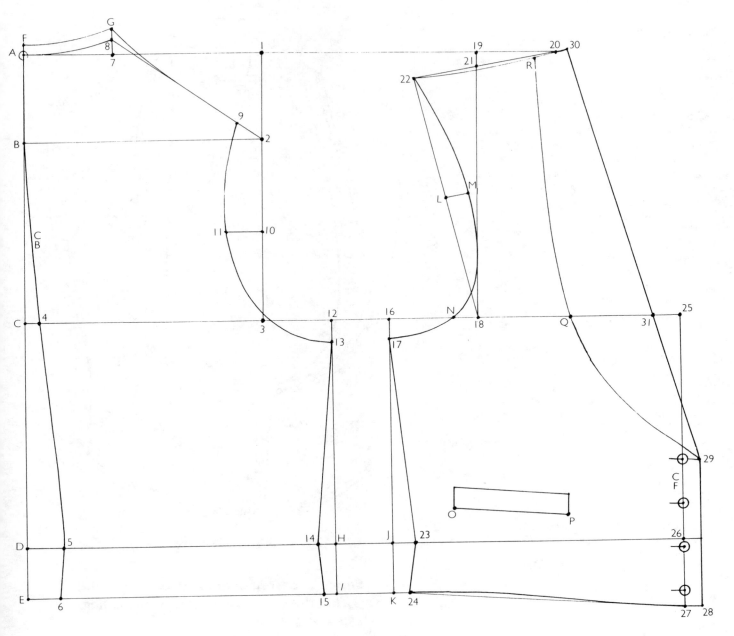

Dia. 24 Back and front

4 inside C = 1.3cm (½in).
5 inside D = 3cm (1¼in).
6 inside E = 2.5cm (1in).
Curve A to 4 and continue to 5 and 6.
A – 4 – 5 – 6 is the centre back seam (CB).
7 from A is ⅛ scale plus 1.5cm (⅝in) = 7.5cm (3in).
8 squared up from 7 = 1.5cm (⅝in).
Curve 8 to A for the back neck.
Join 8 to 2.
9 from 2 = 2.5cm (1in).

Raise the back neck as follows:
F from A = 1cm (⅜in).
G from 8 = 1cm (⅜in).

Curve F to G parallel with A to 8.
Join G to the back shoulder half-way between 8 and 9.
10 is half-way between 2 and 3.
11 squared from 10 = 3cm (1¼in).
12 from 3 is ⅛ scale = 6cm (2⅜in).
Square a line down from 12.
Mark H at the waist line from D.
Mark I at the bottom line from E.
13 below 12 = 2cm (¾in).
Curve the back armhole from 13 to just above 3, then continue
    through 11 to 9.
14 from H = 1.3cm (½in).
15 from I = 0.5cm (¼in).
Join 13–14–15 for the side seam.

119

Front pattern

16 from 12 = 5cm (2in) to separate the patterns.
Square down from 16.
Mark J at the waist line and K at the bottom line.
17 below 16 = 2cm (¾in).
18 from 16 is ⅛ scale plus 1.5cm (⅝in) = 7.5cm (3in).
Square up from 18 and mark 19 on the top line.
20 from 19 is ⅛ scale plus 1cm (⅜in) = 7cm (2¾in).
21 below 19 = 1.3cm (½in).
Join 20 to 21 and continue the line.
22 from 20 is 8 to 9 minus 1cm (⅜in) = 12.5cm (5in).
Hollow the front shoulder 20 – 22.
Join 18 to 22 with a straight line.
L is the centre of 18 and 22.
M squared from L = 2cm (¾in).
N from 18 = 2cm (¾in).
Curve the front armhole 22 – M – N – 17.
23 from J = 2cm (¾in).
24 from K = 1.3cm (½in).
Join 17 – 23 – 24 to complete the side seam.
25 from 18 on chest line is half the scale minus 6cm (2½in) = 18cm (7in).
Square down from 25 and mark 26 at the waist line.
27 continued from 26 = 6cm (2⅜in).
Join 24 to 27 and continue the line.
28 from 27 = 1.5cm (⅝in).
Draw a line from 28 parallel with the centre front.
29 from 28 = 13.5cm (5¼in).
Mark the top button and hole on the centre front opposite point 29.
The other fastenings are 4cm (1½in) apart.
30 continued from 20 = 1cm (⅜in).
Join 30 to 29 for the 'opening'.
Mark 31 on the chest line.

Welt pockets (bottom pockets only)

Draw a line 7.5cm (3in) up from, and parallel to the bottom edge of, the front pattern.
O from the side seam = 4cm (1½in).
P from O = 10cm (4in).
Add 2cm (¾in) above O and P for the welt.

Roll collar

The collar is of the 'laid on' type (see dia. 22(b)).
The dimensions are: Q from 31 = 7.5cm (3in); R from 30 = 2.5cm (1in).
Curve R – Q – 29 as in diagram.

Note: As this is a short style of waistcoat, the trousers should be cut at least 2.5cm (1in) higher in the rise, to prevent a gap between the bottom edge of the waistcoat and the top of the trousers. This also applies to dia. 25.

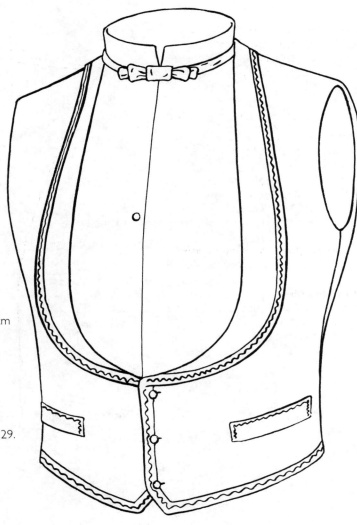

Fig. 25 Single-breasted evening dress waistcoat, 1880–1900

Single-breasted evening dress waistcoat with 'U' opening and narrow roll collar, 1880-1900 (fig. 25; dia. 25)

Note: A similar waistcoat was used for the dinner jacket.

Back pattern

As for dia. 24.

Front pattern (dia. 25).

Follow the instructions for dia. 24, J to N and 16 to 25.
Square down from 25.
26 from the waist line = 7cm (2¾in).
Mark the top button and hole 11cm (4¼in) from 26.

The other fastenings are 3cm (1¼in) apart.
27 from the top button = 1.5cm (⅝in).
28 from the bottom button = 1.5cm (⅝in).
Join 27 to 28 for the front edge.
29 from 26 = 1cm (⅜in).
Join 28 to 29.
Join 24 to 29 to complete the bottom edge.

At the top:
30 continued from 20 = 1cm (⅜in).
31 above 27 = 1cm (⅜in).
Join 30 to 31 with a straight line.
32 from 31 = 11.5cm (4½in).
33 squared from 32 = 2.5cm (1in).
Join 30 to 33 and curve to 31 for the hollow or 'U' opening.

Welt pockets (bottom pockets only)
For O to P follow the instructions as in dia. 24.

Narrow roll collar
Q from 33 = 5.5cm (2¼in).
R from 30 = 2.5cm (1in).
Join R to Q and curve to 31.

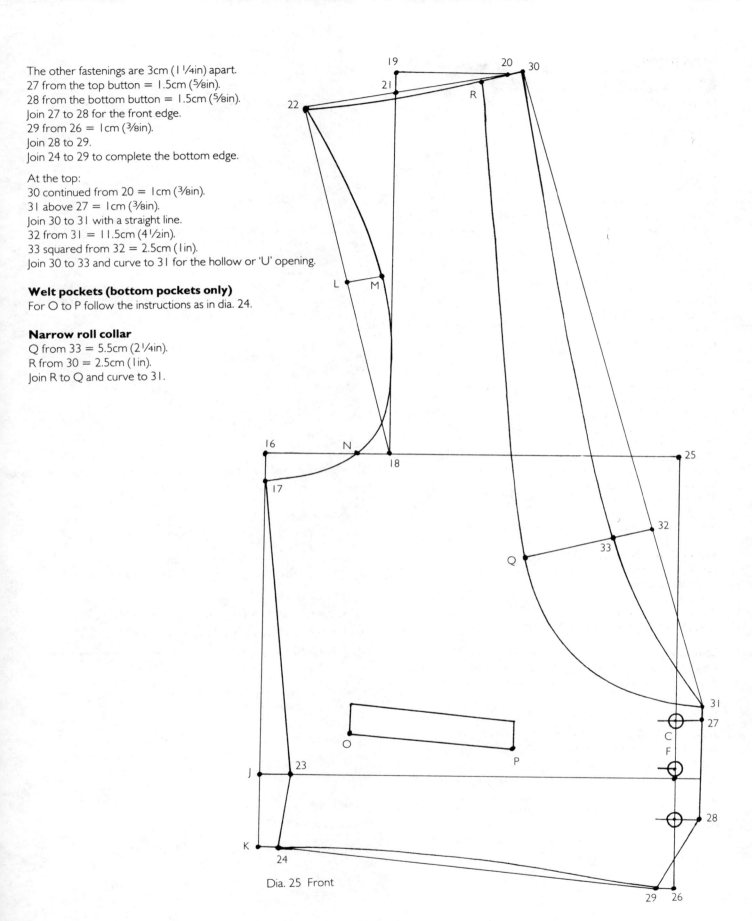

Dia. 25 Front

6 TOPCOATS

Before 1840 overgarments were generally of two types. There were various types of long cloaks with large collars, often with a shoulder cape for added protection. There were also long coats with a back similar to the frock coat. These coats had the large collar and a shoulder cape similar to those on the long cloaks.

From the 1840s new styles of overcoats appeared, which remained fashionable up to 1900. In fact, the Chesterfield and Ulster coats described below have remained standard overcoat styles to the present day.

1 Fitted style

This was the frock overcoat which was in the same style as the double-breasted frock coat but cut much longer and larger, so that it could be worn over the frock suit. It was also referred to as the 'Albert' frock topcoat.

2 Semi-fitted style (Chesterfield) (fig. 26)

This overcoat, named after the Earl of Chesterfield, was moderately shaped at the waist and could be either single- or double-breasted. On the single-breasted style, the front fastening could be either 'buttons to show' or a 'fly' front. The collar was often made of velvet.

3 Loose-fitting or 'sac' style (fig. 27)

This was similar to the single-breasted version of the Chesterfield, but without any shape in the waist. The front fastening could be either 'fly' front or 'buttons to show'.

4 Ulster topcoat (fig. 28)

This was a very long, double-breasted coat with a large collar. The waist of this style could be varied with a cloth belt all round the waist secured by a hole and button on the front ends of the belt, or with the back gathered in by means of a cloth half belt. A shoulder cape in the same fabric was worn with the coat and might be detached from the neck by means of holes and buttons.

5 Inverness caped topcoat (fig. 29)

This was originally an overcoat with a long shoulder cape extending to the length of the sleeves. By the 1870s the cape did not go round to the centre back, but was sewn in at the side seams of the coat. A further development in the 1880s was that the armhole was cut away at the front and the coat became sleeveless. In fig. 29 the fronts have a small lapel and the cape is set back from the front edge. An alternative style had the cape finishing edge to edge at the front with the coat buttoning to the neck.

Note: In the following diagrams, due to the overlap at the side seams, it is necessary to trace the outline of the back on to a separate sheet of paper. Before cutting out the patterns, add seams all round and turn-ins at the bottom edges.

Single-breasted Chesterfield topcoat (semi-fitted), 1840–1900 (fig. 26; dia. 26(a)–(c))

Measurements
With the exception of the topcoat length, all measurements are the same as those for the tail coats and jackets in the previous chapters. Additional allowances for the topcoat (depth of armhole, size of garment etc.) are incorporated in the system of pattern drafting.

	Height	Nape to waist	Full length	Half across back	Sleeve length	Chest	Waist	Seat
cm	176	44	112	20.5	82.5	96	86	102
in	69	17½	44	8⅛	32½	38	34	40

Scale is half the chest = 48cm (19in) : ⅛ scale = 6cm (2⅜in)
¼ scale = 12cm (4¾in)

Back pattern (dia. 26(a))

A = starting point.
Square across and down from A.
B from A = 7.5cm (3in).
C from A is ½ scale plus 1.5cm = 25.5cm or 9½in plus ½in = 10in.
D from A is nape to waist plus 1.5cm (½in) = 45.5cm (18in).
E from D = 20cm (8in) (seat line).
F from A = 112cm (44in) (full length).

Fig. 26 Single-breasted
semi-fitting Chesterfield topcoat,
1840–1900

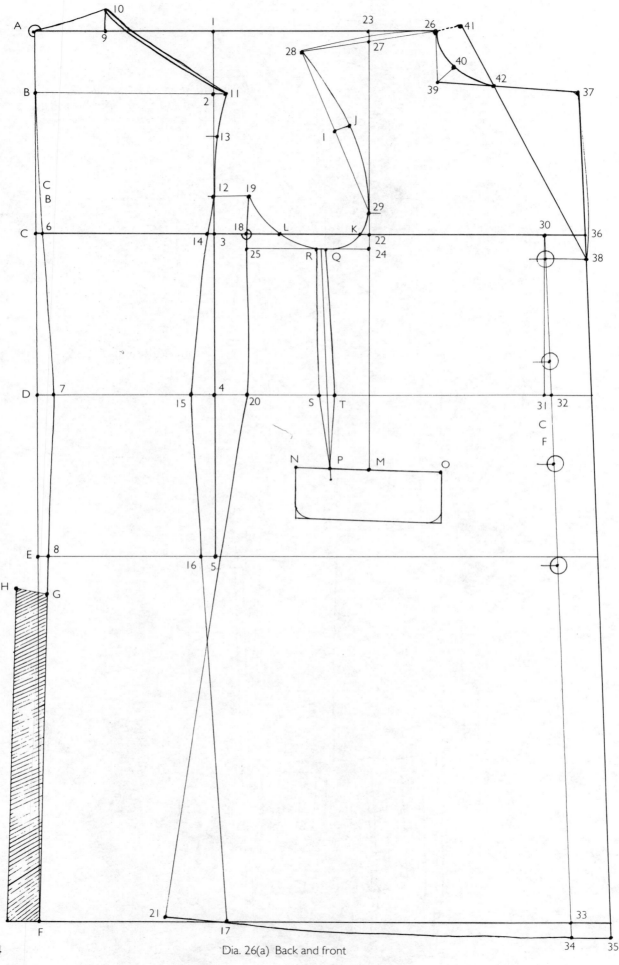

Dia. 26(a) Back and front

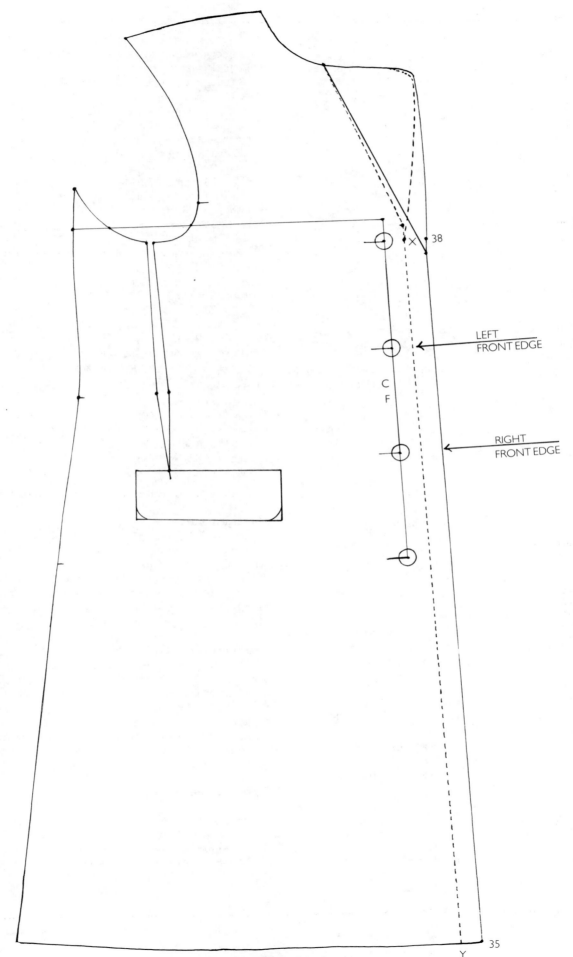

38

LEFT
FRONT EDGE

C
F

RIGHT
FRONT EDGE

35

Y

125

Dia. 26(b) 'Dressing' the fronts

Square a short line across from B.

Square long lines across from C, D, E and F.

1 from A is half across back plus 1cm (3/8in) = 21.5cm (8 1/2in).

Square down from 1 to the seat line from E.

Mark 2 – 3 – 4 – 5 as in the diagram.

6 inside C = 1cm (3/8in).

7 inside D = 2cm (3/4in).

8 inside E = 1.3cm (1/2in).

Curve B to 6 and continue the line to 7 – 8 – F.

The centre back (CB) = A – B – 6 – 7 – 8 – F.

G from F = 41cm (16in) for the back vent.

H from G = 4cm (1 1/2in).

Draw a line down from H parallel with G and F, and join to the bottom line.

At the top:

9 from A = 1/8 scale plus 2.5cm (1in) = 8.5cm (3 3/8in).

10 squared up from 9 = 2cm (3/4in).

Curve 10 to A for the back neck.

11 squared from 2 = 1.5cm (5/8in).

Join 10 to 11.

Slightly hollow the back shoulder between 10 and 11.

12 above 3 = 4.5cm (1 3/4in).

Curve the back armhole 11–12.

13 from 3 is 1/4 scale = 12cm (4 3/4in). 13 is the back sleeve balance point.

14 from 3 = 1cm (3/8in).

15 from 4 = 2.5cm (1in).

16 from 5 = 1.5cm (5/8in).

Curve 12 – 14 – 15.

Join 15 to 16 and continue to the bottom line.

Mark 17.

Front pattern (dia. 26(a))

18 from 3 = 4cm (1 1/2in).

19 from 12 = 4.5cm (1 3/4in).

20 from 4 = 4cm (1 1/2in).

Curve the side seam 19–18–20.

21 from 17 = 7.5cm (3in).

Join 20 to 21 to complete the side seam.

22 from 18 is 1/4 scale plus 3cm (1 1/4in) = 15cm (6in).

Square up from 22 and mark 23 on the top line.

24 squared down from 22 = 2cm (3/4in).

25 below 18 = 2cm (3/4in).

Join 24 to 25 for the base of the armhole.

26 from 23 is 1/8 scale plus 2 cm (3/4in) = 8cm (3 1/8in).

27 below 23 = 1.3cm (1/2in).

Join 26 to 27 and continue the line.

28 from 26 is 10 to 11 minus 1cm (3/8in) = 16.5cm (6 1/2in).

Curve the front shoulder from 26 to 28.

29 above 22 = 2.5cm (1in). 29 is the front sleeve balance point.

Join 28 to 29 with a straight line

I is half-way between 28 and 29.

J squared from I = 2cm (3/4in).

K from 22 = 1.3cm (1/2in).

L from 18 = 4cm (1 1/2in).

Draw the armhole 28 – J – 29 – K to the base of the armhole – then continue to L and 19.

30 from 22 is 1/2 scale minus 2.5cm (1in) = 21.5cm (8 1/2in).

Square down from 30 to the waist line and mark 31.

32 from 31 = 0.6cm (1/4in).

Join 30 to 32 and continue to the bottom line.

Mark 33 on the bottom line.

34 continued from 33 = 2cm (3/4in).

The centre front (CF) is 30 – 32 – 33 – 34.

Curve the bottom edge from 21 to 34.

35 squared from 34 = 5cm (2in).

36 from 30 = 5cm (2in).

Join 35 to 36 for the front edge.

Continue the front edge above 36.

37 from 36 = 18cm (7in).

38 below 36 = 3cm (1 1/4in).

Curve 37 to 38.

39 squared down from 26 = 6.5cm (2 1/2in).

Join 39 to 37.

40 at an angle to 39 = 2.5cm (1in).

41 from 26 = 3cm (1 1/4in).

Join 41 to 38.

Mark 42 at the neck line.

Curve 26 – 40 – 42.

On the centre front mark the top button and hole opposite 38.

The other fastenings are 13cm (5in) apart.

Flap pockets

Square down from 24.

M from 24 = 28cm (11in).

Draw a line across at M.

N from M = 8.5cm (3 3/8in).

O from M = 8.5cm (3 3/8in).

The flap is 6.5cm (2 1/2in) wide.

Note: Some versions of this style also had an outbreast welt pocket.

Underarm dart

P from N = 4cm (1 1/2in).

Q from 24 = 5cm (2in).

R from Q = 1.3cm (1/2in).

From the centre of R and Q draw a line to P.

At the waist line, mark S and T 1cm (3/8in) each side of the line.

Join Q – T – P and R – S – P.

The dart is sewn together on the lines.

Dressing the fronts (dia. 26(b))

The single-breasted topcoat requires a small underwrap on the right front (button side), which is included in the pattern draft. The left front (button hole side) is reduced by 2.5cm (1in) all through the front edge as X to Y. To maintain a similar angle of crease line for the lapel, direct the left crease to 2cm (3/4in) above X and the right crease line 2cm (3/4in) below 38. The buttons and holes remain on the centre front. This adjustment to the fronts is known as 'dressing' the fronts.

Topcoat sleeve (dia. 26(c))

The topcoat sleeve pattern is made 2.5cm (1in) longer than the garment worn underneath it i.e. tail coat or jacket.

This adjustment is included in the following instructions.

Scale is 48cm (19in) : 1/8 scale = 6cm (2 3/8in)

1/4 scale = 12cm (4 3/4in)

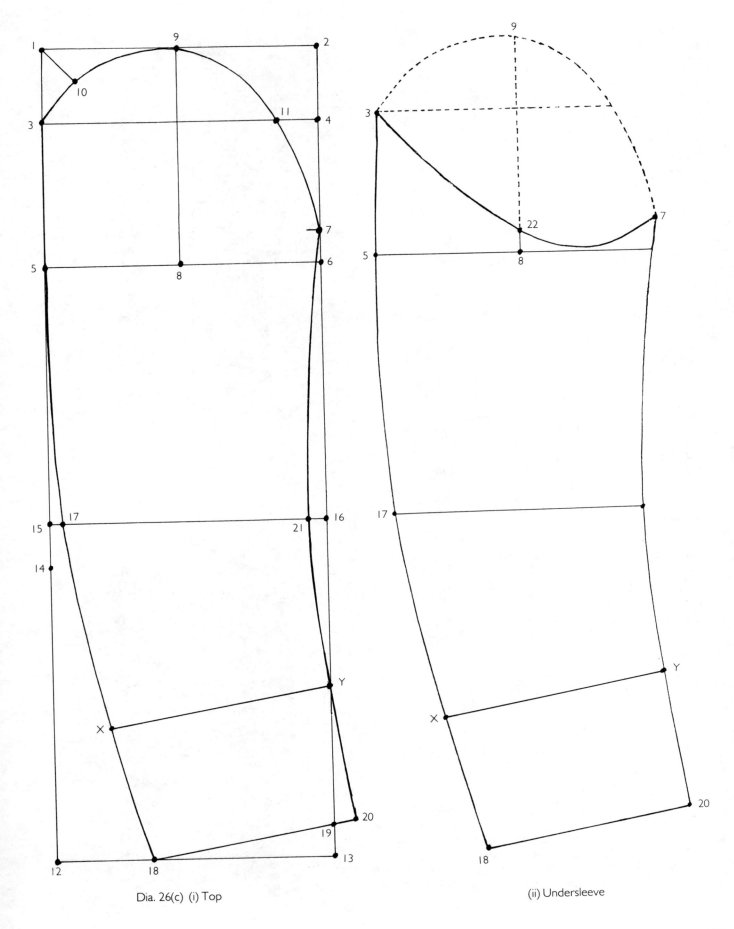

Dia. 26(c) (i) Top   (ii) Undersleeve

Top sleeve pattern

1 = starting point.

Square across and down from 1.

2 from 1 is ½ scale minus 1.5cm (⅝in) = 22.5cm (8⅞in).

Square down from 2.

3 below 1 is ⅛ scale = 6cm (2⅜in).

4 is squared from 3.

5 below 3 = 12cm (4¾in).

Square across from 5 and mark 6.

7 above 6 = 2.5cm (1in).

8 is centre of 5 and 6.

9 is squared up from 8 and located on the top line.

10 at an angle from 1 = 4cm (1½in).

11 from 4 = 3cm (1¼in).

Curve the sleeve head 3 – 10 – 9 – 11 – 7.

12 from 4 = 63.5cm (25in). This includes the increase for the topcoat sleeve length.

13 is squared across from 12.

14 is half-way between 5 and 12.

15 above 14 = 4cm (1½in) for the elbow position.

16 is squared across from 15.

17 from 15 = 1cm (⅜in).

18 inside 12 = 7cm (2¾in).

Complete the back seam 3 – 5 – 17 – 18.

19 above 13 = 2.5cm (1in).

Draw a line from 18 through 19.

20 from 19 = 2cm (¾in).

21 inside 16 = 1.3cm (½in).

Join 7 – 21 – 20 for the front seam.

Undersleeve pattern

The back seam (hindarm), front seam (forearm) and cuff are exactly the same as for the topsleeve.

To form the underside of the armhole proceed as follows:

22 above 8 = 2cm (¾in).

Curve 7 to 22 and join 22 to 3.

The false or 'formed' cuff is 11.5cm (4½in) up from the edge of the cuff (X to Y).

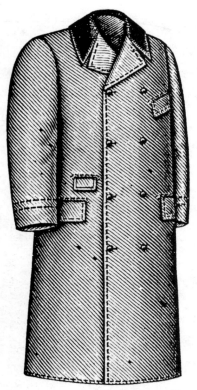

A. Front View

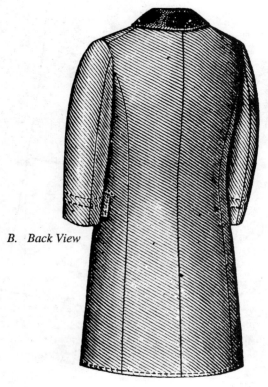

B. Back View

Plate 21. 1895. (A. Front; B. Back) Double-breasted semi-shaped Top Coat, with a velvet collar and four outside flap pockets. A single row of stitching on the edges and flaps, with two rows on the cuffs. There is usually a long slit at the centre back. (This is the double-breasted version of the Chesterfield Topcoat.) The Delineator, December, 1895.

128

The Tailor and Cutter

Summer 1888

PLATE 22. 1888. (L) *Summer Overcoat, cut on the short side, slightly shaped, short vents in sideseams. Fly front for button holes; buttons set about 2 inches (5 cm) from the edge. Made of a drab Venetian material with edges stitched. Velvet collars and silk facings continue to be popular. The coat can be worn open and turned back on the shoulders in the Yankee fashion. (R) Morning Coat with flaps at waist-seams, made of light coloured fancy Angolas and tweeds. Outbreast pocket. Trousers are slightly wider at the knee than at the bottom, and fall square across the instep. Single-breasted Vest, to match, can be seen at the coat opening. (C) The lady is stylishly dressed for a casual summer afternoon.*

Back pattern (dia. 27)

A = starting point.
Square across and down from A.
B from A = 7.5cm (3in).
C from A is ½ scale plus 1.5cm = 25.5cm or 9½in plus ½in = 10in.
D from A is nape to waist plus 1.5cm (½in) = 45.5cm (18in).
E from D = 20cm (8in).
F from A = 112cm (44in) (full length).
Square a short line across from B.
Square long lines across from C, D, E and F.
The centre back is A – F which can be cut on the fold of the fabric
    or with a seam.
1 from A is half across back plus 1cm (3/8in) = 21.5cm (8½in).
Square down from 1 to the waist line from D.
Mark 2, 3, and 4 as in the diagram.
5 from A is ⅛ scale plus 2.5cm (1in) = 8.5cm (3⅜in).
6 squared up from 5 = 2cm (¾in).
Curve 6 to A for the back neck.
7 squared from 2 = 1.5cm (⅝in).
Join 6 to 7.
Slightly hollow the back shoulder from 6 to 7.
8 above 3 = 2.5cm (1in).
9 squared from 8 = 1.3cm (½in).
Curve the back armhole 9 to 7.
10 from 3 is ¼ scale = 12cm (4¾in) for the back sleeve balance
    point.
11 from 4 = 2.5cm (1in).
Join 9 to 11 and continue to the bottom line from F.
Mark 12.
13 is located on the hip line from E.
The side seam of the back is 9 – 11 – 13 – 12.

Front pattern (dia. 27)

14 from 3 = 9cm (3½in).
Join 14 to 13 and continue the line to the bottom.
15 is 0.6cm (¼in) up from the bottom line.
Continue the line of the side seam above 14.
16 from 14 = 2.5cm (1in).
17 from 14 is ¼ scale = 12cm (4¾in).
Square up from 17 and mark 18 on the top line.
19 squared down from 17 = 2cm (¾in).
20 from 14 = 2cm (¾in).
Join 19 to 20 for the base of the armhole.
21 from 18 is ⅛ scale plus 2cm (¾in) = 8cm (3⅛in).
22 below 18 = 1.3cm (½in).
Join 21 to 22 and continue the line.
23 from 21 is 6 to 7 minus 1cm (3/8in) = 16.5cm (6½in).
Curve the front shoulder 21 to 23.
24 above 17 = 2.5cm (1in). 24 is the front sleeve balance point.
Join 23 to 24 with a straight line.
G is half-way between 23 and 24.
H squared from G = 2cm (¾in).
I from 17 = 1cm (3/8in).
J from 14 = 2.5cm (1in).
Curve the armhole 23 – H – 24 – I – J – 16 as in the diagram.
25 from 17 is ½ scale minus 2.5cm (1in) = 21.5cm (8½in).
Square down from 25 to the waist line and mark 26.
27 from 26 = 0.6cm (¼in).

Ill. 70. 1890's. Single-breasted Chesterfield Top Coat with deep flaps on the side pockets and a flap on the outbreast pocket. The coat is worn over a Single-breasted Morning Coat and Single-breasted Vest. The Trousers are a moderate width with creases pressed into the centre of the leg at the front and back. A Bowler hat finishes his attire.

Single-breasted 'sac' topcoat, 1840-1900 (fig. 27; dia. 27)

Measurements

	Height	Nape to waist	Full length	Half across back	Sleeve length	Chest	Waist	Seat
cm	176	44	112	20.5	82.5	96	86	102
in	69	17½	44	8⅛	32½	38	34	40

Scale is half the chest = 48cm (19in) : ⅛ scale = 6cm (2⅜in)
    ¼ scale = 12cm (4¾in)

Fig. 27 Single-breasted 'sac' topcoat, 1840–1900

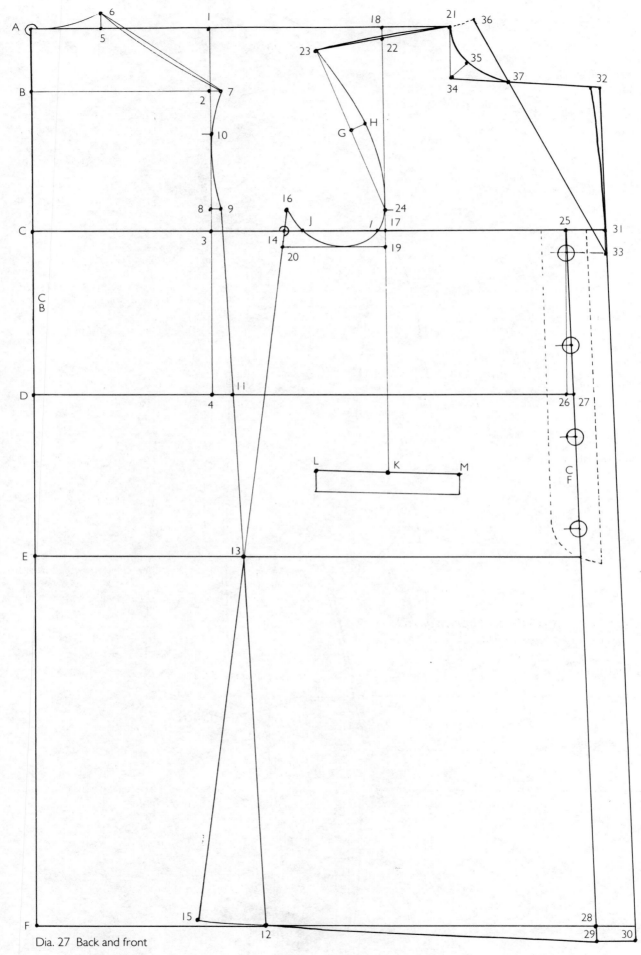

132   Dia. 27 Back and front

Join 25 to 27 and continue to the bottom line.
Mark 28.
29 continued from 28 = 2cm (¾in).
The centre front (CF) is 25–27–28–29.
Curve the bottom edge from 29 to 15 at the side seam.
30 squared from 29 = 5cm (2in).
31 from 25 = 5cm (2in).
Join 31 to 30 for the front edge.
Continue the front edge above 31.
32 from 31 = 18cm (7in).
33 below 31 = 2.5cm (1in).
34 squared from 21 = 6.5cm (2½in).
Join 32 to 34.
35 at an angle to 34 = 2.5cm (1in).
36 from 21 = 3cm (1¼in).
Join 36 to 33 and mark 37 at the neck line.
Curve the neck 21 – 35 – 37.
Mark 1cm (⅜in) inside 32 and curve the front edge of the lapel to 33.

Front fastening

Fig. 27 shows a concealed or 'fly' front as an alternative to the 'button through' style of fig. 26.
For the 'fly' front, proceed as follows:
On the centre front mark the top button and hole opposite point 33.
The other fastenings are 11.5cm (4½in) apart.
Dress the fronts as described for dia. 26(b).
The dash lines show the 'fly' stitching which is 5.5cm (2¼in) wide from the left front edge.

Side welt pockets

Square down from 19.
K from 19 = 28cm (11in).
Draw a line across at K.
L from K = 8.5cm (3⅜in).
M from K = 8.5cm (3⅜in).
The width of welt is 2.5cm (1in) and marked below L and M.
Use sleeve pattern as in dia. 26(c).

Double-breasted Ulster topcoat with shoulder cape, 1870–1900 (fig. 28; dia. 28(a)–(c))

Measurements

	Height	Nape to waist	Full length	Half across back	Sleeve length	Chest	Waist	Seat
cm	176	44	122	20.5	82.5	96	86	102
in	69	17½	48	8⅛	32½	38	34	40

Scale is half the chest = 48cm (19in) : ⅛ scale = 6cm (2⅜in)
¼ scale = 12cm (4¾in)

Back pattern (dia. 28(a))

A = starting point.
Square across and down from A.
B from A = 7.5cm (3in).
C from A is ½ scale plus 1.5cm (½in) = 25.5cm (10in).
D from A is nape to waist plus 1.5cm (½in) = 45.5cm (18in).
E from D = 20cm (8in).
F from A = 122cm (48in) (full length – can be made longer if required).
Square a short line across from B.
Square long lines across from C, D, E and F.
The centre back (CB) is A to F.
G from F is 46cm (18in) for the back vent.
H from G = 4cm (1½in).
Draw a line down from H parallel with G and F and join to the bottom line.
I from A is half across back plus 1cm (⅜in) = 21.5cm (8½in).
Square a line down from I to the waist line from D.
Mark 2, 3, and 4 as in diagram.
5 from A is ⅛ scale plus 2.5cm (1in) = 8.5cm (3⅜in).
6 squared up from 5 = 2cm (¾in).
Curve 6 to A for the back neck.
7 squared from 2 = 1.5cm (⅝in).
Join 6 to 7.
Slightly hollow the back shoulder from 6 to 7.
8 above 3 = 2.5cm (1in).
9 squared from 8 = 1.3cm (½in).
Curve the back armhole 9 to 7.
10 from 3 is ¼ scale = 12cm (4¾in). 10 is the back sleeve balance point.
11 from 4 = 2.5cm (1in).
Join 9 to 11 and continue to the bottom line from F.
Mark 12.
Point 13 is located on the seat line from E.
The half belt is 35.5cm (14in) long and 5cm (2in) wide.
The buttonholes are 2.5cm (1in) inside each end of the belt.
The buttons are placed approx. 2.5cm (1in) from the side seam (on point 4).
For extra gathers under the half belt, move the buttons to the side seam (point 11).

Front pattern (dia. 28(a))

On the chest line:
14 from 3 = 7.5cm (3in).
15 squared across from 9 = 7cm (2¾in).
Join 15 to 14.
16 from 11 = 4.5cm (1¾in).
Join 14 to 16.
Join 16 to 13 and continue to the bottom line from F.
17 is 0.6cm (¼in) up from the bottom line.
The side seam is 15–14–16–13–17.
18 from 14 is ¼ scale = 12cm (4¾in).
Square up from 18 and mark 19 on the top line.
20 below 18 = 2cm (¾in).
21 below 14 = 2cm (¾in).
Join 20 to 21 for the base of the armhole.

(i) front

(ii) back

Ill. 71. 1864. These two figures pre-date the Ulster topcoat by several years. They are very similar in style to the Ulster with wide stitching on the edges and the lapels.

Fig. 28 Double-breasted Ulster topcoat and shoulder cape, 1870–1900

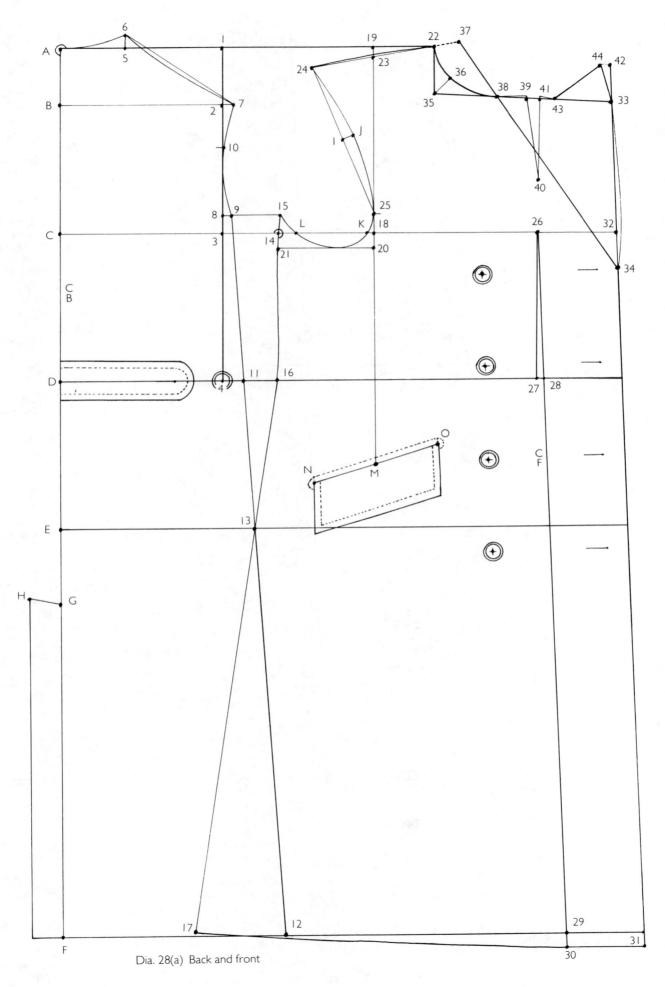

Dia. 28(a) Back and front

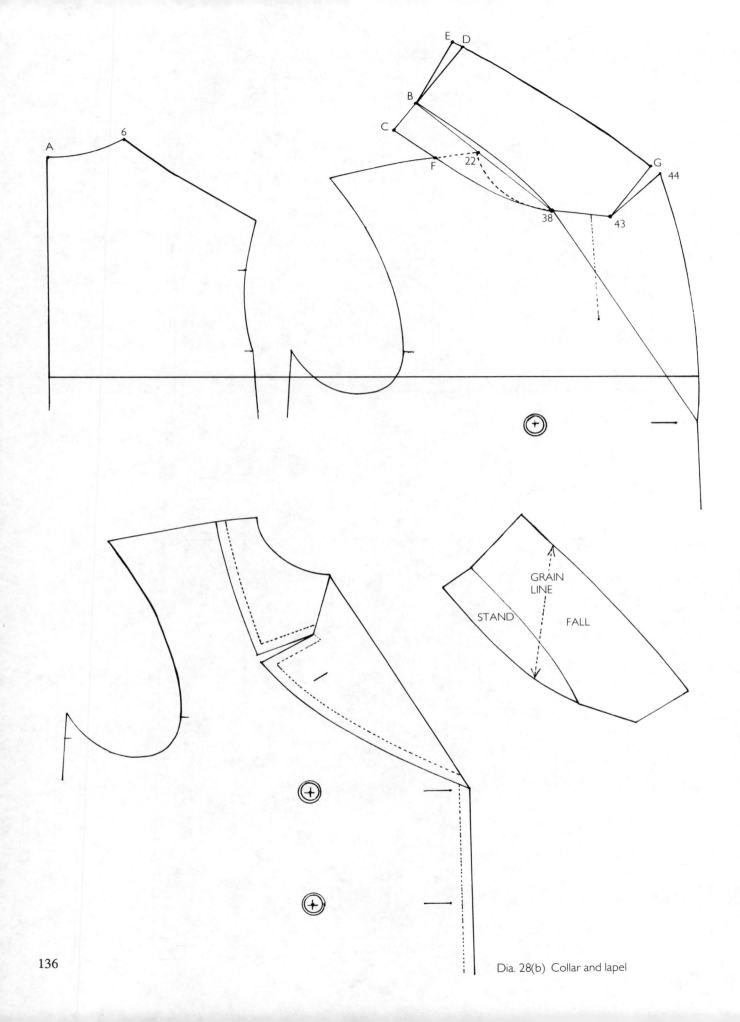

Dia. 28(b) Collar and lapel

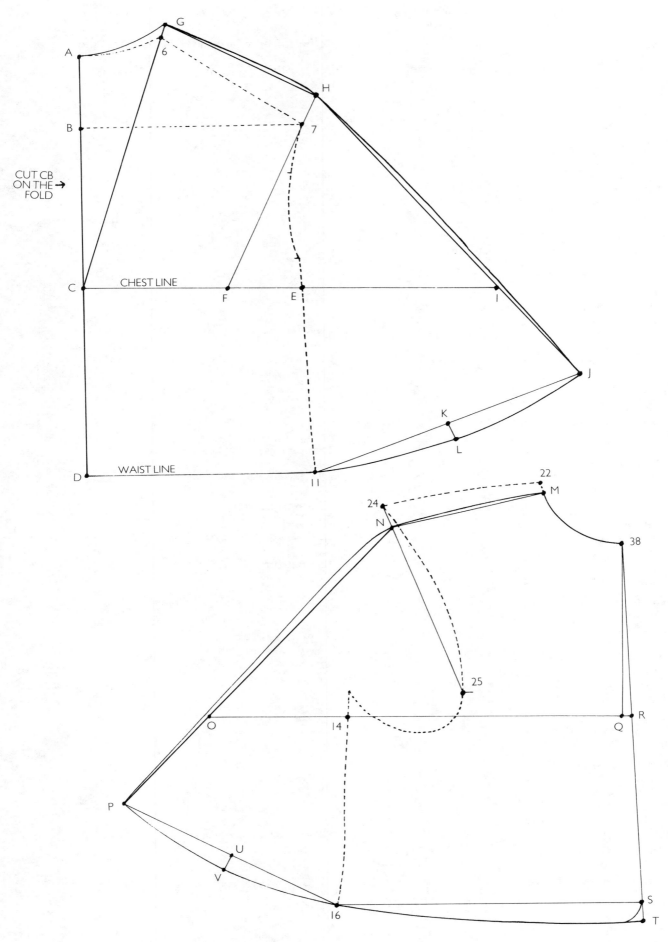

CUT CB
ON THE →
FOLD

CHEST LINE

WAIST LINE

Dia. 28(c) Shoulder cape

137

22 from 19 is ⅛ scale plus 2cm (¾in) = 8cm (3⅛in).
23 below 19 = 1.3cm (½in).
Join 22 to 23 and continue the line.
24 from 22 is 6 to 7 minus 1cm (⅜in) = 16.5cm (6½in).
Curve the front shoulder 22 to 24.
25 above 18 = 2.5cm (1in). 25 is the front sleeve balance point.
Join 24 to 25 with a straight line.
I is the centre of 24 and 25.
J squared from *I* = 2cm (¾in).
K from 18 = 1cm (⅜in).
L from 14 = 2.5cm (1in).
Curve the armhole 24 – J – 25 – K then down to the armhole base
    and curve up to L and 15.

26 from 18 is ½ scale minus 2.5cm (1in).
Square down from 26 to the waist line and mark 27.
28 from 27 = 0.6cm (¼in).
Join 26 to 28 and continue to the bottom line.
Mark 29.
30 continued from 29 = 2cm (¾in).
The centre front (CF) is 26–28–29–30.
Curve the bottom edge from 30 to 17 at the side seam.
31 squared from 30 = 10cm (4in).
32 from 26 = 10cm (4in).
Join 32 to 31 for the front edge.
33 squared up from 32 = 18cm (7in).
34 below 32 = 5cm (2in).
35 squared down from 22 = 6.5cm (2½in).
Join 35 to 33.
36 at an angle to 35 = 2.5cm (1in).
37 from 22 = 4cm (1½in).
Join 37 to 34.
Mark 38 at the neck line.
Curve 22–36–38.

Neck dart
39 from 38 = 4cm (1½in).
40 from 39 = 11.5cm (4½in).
41 from 39 = 2cm (¾in).
Join 39 and 41 to 40 to form a dart.

To complete the lapel
42 continued from 33 = 5cm (2in).
43 from 41 = 2cm (¾in).
44 from 42 = 1.3cm (½in).
Join 44 to 43.
Curve 44 to 34 for the outside edge of the lapel.
The top buttonhole is on a level with point 34.
Mark the buttonhole positions 12.5cm (5in) apart and 2.5cm (1in) in
    from the front edge.
The buttons are opposite the holes and are placed 7.5cm (3in) from
    the centre front.

Slanted flap pockets
Square down from 20.
M from 20 = 30cm (11¾in).
Draw a line at an angle across M.
N from M = 8.5cm (3⅜in).
O from M = 8.5cm (3⅜in).
The width of the flap is 7cm (2¾in).
Complete as in the diagram.

Use sleeve pattern as in dia. 26(c).

Collar for double-breasted Ulster topcoat (dia. 28(b))

Close up the dart at the front neck.
Mark points 22, 38, 43 and 44.
Join 38 to 22 and continue the line.
B from 22 is A to 6 on the back neck = 9cm (3½in).
Square across from B.
C from B = 4cm (1½in).
D from B = 8.5cm (3¼in).
E squared from D = 1.3cm (½in).
Join E to B.
Curve B to 38.
F from 22 = 4.5cm (1¾in).
Join C to F and curve to 38.
The collar follows the line of the neck from 38 to 43.
G from 44 (the lapel point) = 1cm (⅜in).
Join G to 43.
To complete the outer edge of the collar join E to G with a straight
    line then a moderate curve as the diagram.
The centre back is E – B – C.
The lower diagram (left) shows the finished collar and lapel shape
    with a stitching of 1cm (⅜in) inside the edge.
The lower right of diagram 28(b) shows the outline of the
    undercollar separated from the pattern above.
The undercollar pattern is placed on the cross or bias of the material
    and is reinforced with a layer of collar canvas cut in the same way.

Shoulder cape for Ulster topcoat (dia. 28(c))

The cape is based on the double-breasted Ulster pattern (dia. 28(a)).
The length of the cape can be varied according to design but in this
instance it ends approx. at the level of the elbow of the sleeve.
The numbered points are transferred from dia. 28(a).

Note: The centre back A to D is usually cut without a seam.

Back pattern
On a separate sheet of paper mark the outline of the Ulster back
    pattern as far as the waist line.
Draw the chest line from C and the waist line from D.
E is located where the chest line meets the side seam.
F from E is ⅓ C to E.
Draw a line from C through 6.
G from 6 = 1.3cm (½in).
Curve a line from G to join the back neck at A.
Draw a line from F through 7.
H from 7 = 3cm (1¼in).
I from E = 20cm (8in).
Join G to H.
Join H to *I* and continue the line.
J from *I* = 12.5cm (5in).
Slightly curve the lines G to H and H to J.
Join J to 11 with a straight line.
K is half-way between J and 11.
L squared from K = 2cm (¾in).
Curve the bottom edge J – L – 11 and continue straight across to D.

Front pattern

Mark round the Ulster pattern from point 38 at the front neck, then across the shoulders, round the armhole and down the side seam to 16 at the waist.

Do not mark beyond 38.

Draw the chest line across from 14 and the waist line from 16.

M from 22 on the neckline = 1.3cm (½in).

Draw a line from the shoulder end at 24 to the front balance point at 25.

N from 24= 2.5cm (1in).

Join M to N with a moderate curve.

O from 14 = 14cm (5½in).

Join N to O and continue the line.

P from O = 12.5cm (5in).

Slightly curve from N to P.

Check that H to J on the back is the same as N to P.

Square down from 38 and mark Q at the chest line.

R from Q = 1cm (⅜in).

Join 38 to R and continue the line.

Mark S at the waist line.

T continued from S = 2cm (¾in).

Join T to 16.

Draw a line from 16 to P.

U is half-way between 16 and P.

V squared from U = 1.5cm (⅝in).

Curve the bottom edge T – 16 – V – P as in the diagram.

The corner at T can be left square or rounded off.

Note: The neckline from 38 to M follows the same shape as the Ulster topcoat pattern. The cape can be sewn to the neck of the coat, or fastened on and detachable by means of holes and buttons.

Inverness (sleeveless) caped topcoat

(fig. 29; dia. 29(a)–(b))

The Inverness is based on the single-breasted 'sac' Chesterfield (dia. 27).

The centre back is cut without a seam.

A study of a made-up garment of this style would be very helpful to those who are attempting it for the first time. It is also suggested that experience can be gained by making a 'mock-up' in calico.

Back pattern

Mark round the back pattern and transfer the numbered points 6, 7, 10 and 12 from dia. 27.

Using 6 as the pivoting point, draw an arc from 7.

A from 7 = 2.5cm (1in). Check that A from 6 is the same as 7 from 6.

B from 10 = 4.5cm (1¾in).

C from the side seam on the chest line = 4cm (1½in).

At the bottom edge D from 12 = 4cm (1½in).

Join 6 to A and curve to B and C.

Join C to D with a straight line.

E from C = 18cm (7in).

F from E = 15.5cm (6in).

The outline of the Inverness back is shown by the solid lines.

Front pattern

Mark round front pattern of dia. 27 and transfer the numbered points 14, 15, 17, 21 and 23.

G from 23 = 2cm (¾in)

Join 21 to G.

H from 21 = 5cm (2in).

I from 17 = 4cm (1½in).

J from 14 = 18cm (7in) (same as E from C).

Curve H – I – J.

Continue across 2.5cm (1in) from J and mark K.

Join K to 15 at the bottom edge.

L from K = 15.5cm (6in).

Note: K and L are on the same level as E and F.

The shoulder, armhole and part of the side seam are cut away from the pattern, as shown by the shaded section.

The front neck, lapel and front edge are the same as for the 'sac' topcoat. The solid line shows the outline of the Inverness front pattern.

Side welt pockets

The top edge of the pocket is in the same position as shown in dia. 27.

The pocket opening = 18cm (7in).

Width of welt = 2.5cm (1in), added below the pocket level.

(i) front   Fig. 29 Inverness (sleeveless) caped topcoat, 1880–1900

(ii) back

140

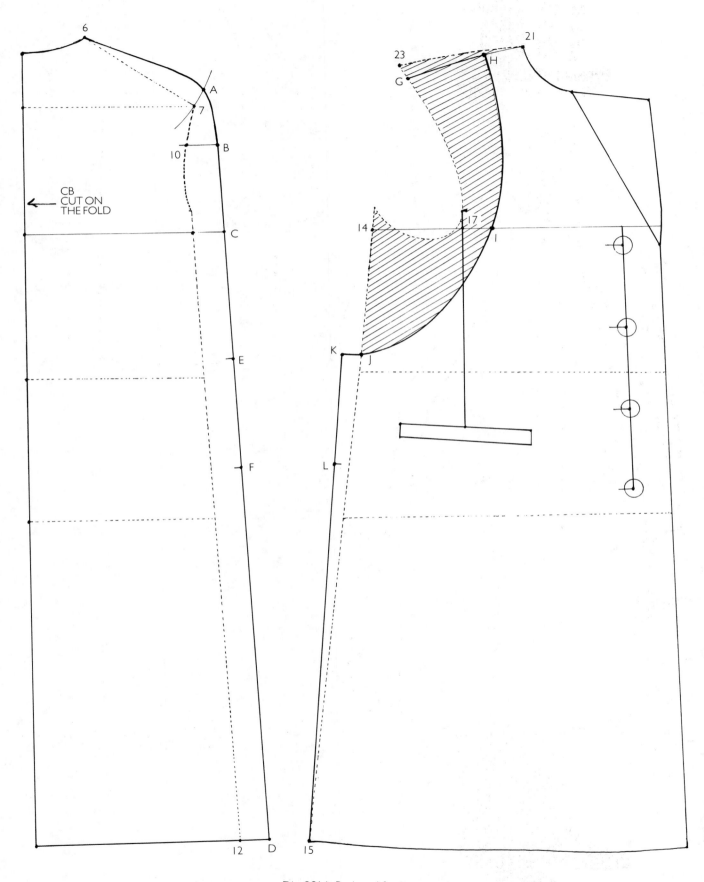

Dia. 29(a) Back and front

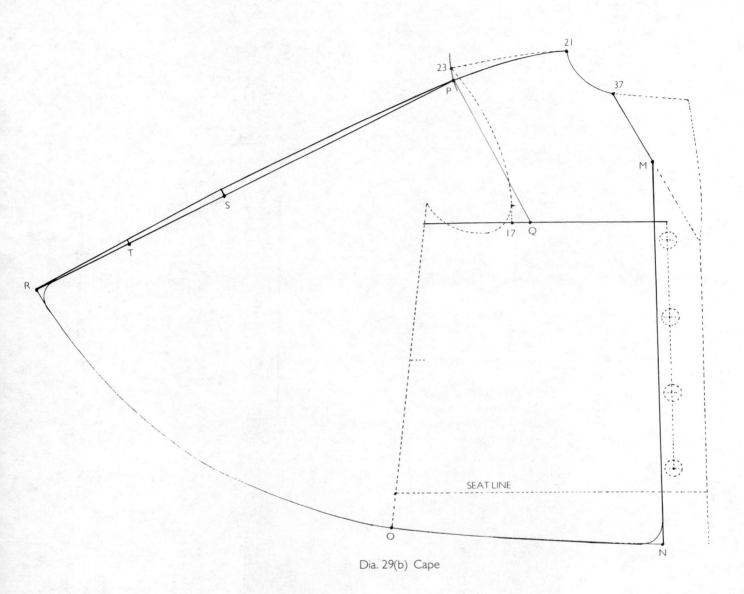

Dia. 29(b) Cape

142

Inverness cape pattern (dia. 29(b))

Draw round the outline of the front pattern (shown by broken lines) as far as the seat line only.

Mark points 17, 21, 23 and 37.

The neck 21 to 37 remains the same as in the front pattern.

M from 37 along the 'crease' line = 10cm (4in).

Draw a line down from M parallel with the centre front.

N from the seat line = 7.5cm (3in).

O at the side seam = 5cm (2in).

Join N to O with a moderate curve.

At the top:

Using 21 as the pivoting point, draw an arc from 23.

P from 23 = 2cm (¾in). Curve 21 to P.

Check that P from 21 is the same as 23 from 21.

Q from 17 = 2.5cm (1in).

Join P to Q with a straight line.

Draw a long line from P, at right angles to the line P–Q.

R from P is the same as O to P = 67cm (26½in).

Curve R to O to complete the hem of the cape.

The corners at R and N can be curved as in the diagram.

S from P is the same as A to E on the back pattern = 37.5cm (14½in).

T from S is the same as E to F = 15.5cm (6in).

Add 1cm (⅜in) seams all round the back and front patterns of dia. 29(a) and 5cm (2in) at the hems.

Add 1cm (⅜in) seams all round the cape.

After the patterns are cut out, the edges should be notched at the following points:

    Back: A, E, F and D

    Front: L and 15

    Cape: P, S and T

To place the parts together proceed as follows:

Pin the cape on to the front, so that they match on the neck line 21 – 37 and along the 'crease' line to R.

Also, secure along the shoulder 21 to H.

Pin S and T to K and L.

Sew the back shoulder 6 – A to 21 – P.

Continue sewing A – F to the cape P – T which will take in the side seam of the front from K to L.

The cape is left to hang free from T to R, but the remainder of the coat side seams F – D and L to 15 are sewn together.

Front View   *Back View*

Ill. 72. This example of the Inverness Topcoat shows a deep stand and fall collar that fastens to the front of the neck (see collar for "Tweedside," dia. 11(G) page 67). The edges of the coat and the cape have two rows of stitching by machine. The Delineator, October 1892.

MATERIALS

The development of the tailoring industry during the nineteenth century was a direct result of the changes brought about in the production of woven materials. New technology in weaving enabled the mills to produce fabrics in a greater volume and variety than before, while maintaining a high standard of quality. This meant that the tailor had a wide selection of varied materials to meet the increasing demand for tailored garments.

Many of the fabrics produced then are no longer manufactured, and in order to re-create garments of the period, it is necessary to select carefully from the materials that are available to us. The following is a list of modern fabrics suitable for the making of the garments dealt with in this book.
(Note that fashions in style and material change gradually, so the dates given can only be approximate.)

barathea and serge plain worsted cloths, each with a distinctive weave. Both are available in various weights, but the recommended weight is not less than 490 grams (16 oz) per square metre. Barathea and serge were used from 1870 onwards for dress coats and trousers (black barathea only) and for frock coats and trousers (black or dark grey barathea or serge). Around 1880 morning coats and dinner jackets and trousers were made in black, the morning coats in barathea or serge, the dinner jackets and trousers in barathea only

blazer material the cloth used in making the blazer shown in fig. 15 had narrow stripes with toned-down colours, but modern blazer material usually has a wide block stripes in bright colours. It is now therefore necessary to search among the various modern cloths to find one that has a suitable design for the blazer and waistcoat. The trousers to go with the blazer were made from a plain white or cream flannel

braids used extensively during the second half of the century as decoration on coats and waistcoats.
Trousers frequently had a row of braid down each side seam

doeskin a closely woven cloth with a smooth surface. See also *moleskin*

moleskin a cotton fabric where the surface has been processed (teazled) to give a fine 'woolly' effect.
Both doeskin and moleskin are suitable for trousers in white, fawn or cream, to be worn with the dress coat and frock coat of the period 1830–1850. For pantaloons, the doeskin is more suitable, in white, cream or black but if they are required to be close-fitting, a fabric with a 'stretch' weave should be used, e.g. cavalry twill, barathea, stretch fabric

Melton coatings plain, heavy-weight cloths which, when cut, do not fray. They are used for Chesterfield overcoats and sometimes for Ulster overcoats

serge see *barathea*

silks and brocades used for waistcoats. The 'fancy' waistcoat was worn with the dress coat and frock coat up to 1850. In the second half of the century only white or black silk was worn with the evening dress coat, and silk, brocade or contrasting cloth waistcoats were worn with the frock coat

silk facings used on both dress coats and frock coats, the silk facings covered part of the lapels

superfine often referred to as a 'faced' cloth, it has a raised surface or 'pile' which requires the paper patterns to be placed all one way on the cloth. There is a gloss finish to the surface which gives a restrained richness to the fabric. A distinct advantage of this material it that it does not fray when cut and often garments made from superfine were not seamed at the front but left as a raw edge with the facing. In addition, the hem could be left as a raw edge instead of being turned up.
Superfine is used for dress coats up to 1870, in various colours (black, blue, dark green, maroon). From 1860, mainly black is used

tweed heavy woven cloth, available in a great variety of types, including Donegal, Harris, Cheviot. These can be obtained in subdued tones or more flamboyant designs. They are used for informal outfits or sporting wear. From 1860 onwards tweeds were used for lounge jackets, waistcoats and trousers (forming the three-piece suit), 'Tweedside' jackets; caped Ulster topcoats and Inverness topcoats, Norfolk jackets and knickerbreeches.
From 1860–1880 tweeds were used for morning coats, waistcoats and trousers

velvet a material frequently used for collars on dress coats and frock coats

144

GLOSSARY

The terminology of the ancient craft of tailoring has developed over the centuries, with technical names for the various parts of garments and for the different tailoring processes. These trade names were still in daily use by cutters and tailors until the outbreak of World War II, but much of that vocabulary has now fallen into disuse. The following list is of technical terms in use at the present time, and deals mainly with the cutting of garments.

balance describes the correct relationship between the various parts of the pattern which ensures that the completed garment fits correctly on the wearer (e.g. back balance, front balance, sleeve balance etc.)

balance marks notches cut into the edges of garment pieces so that they can be sewn together correctly (also known as balance points)

crown highest point of the sleevehead curve of the topsleeve pattern

dart fold of fabric sewn to a point, used to shape a garment. A 'fish' dart can be used in the underarm seams of a jacket or in the back pattern of the trousers. A 'V' dart is used in the neck of a jacket or coat

draft a pattern which has been drawn up for a garment; the phrase 'drafting a garment' is commonly used

figuration describes the shape of the figure for which the garment is intended (e.g. 'square shoulders', 'full chest', 'head forward' etc.)

fitting (a) a garment which has been prepared for trying on the wearer is described as a *fitting*. The methods used for trying on the garment are known as the *fitting procedure*
(b) the additional pieces of material required apart from the main garment parts are called *fittings* or sometimes the *fit-up*. For a three-piece suit the fittings required are (for the jacket) front facings, topcollar, flaps and pocket facings, welt pocket piece; (for the waistcoat) facings for the fronts, pieces for the welted pockets, backstraps (made from the back lining); and (for the trousers) fly pieces and pocket facings

fly line the curved centre front of the trousers

forearm front seam of the sleeve (see also *hindarm*)

forepart front pattern of the jacket, coat and waistcoat

fork the point at which the legs of the trousers join together (crotch point). See dia. 17(a), point 2, and dia. 17(b), point 17

gorge front neck curve on jackets and coats. See dia. 12, points 27–42–41

heel curved edge of the collar that is sewn into the neck of the coat

hindarm back seam of the sleeve (see also *forearm*)

inlays extra amounts of material which can be added (in addition to the seam allowances) to certain parts of a garment when cutting from the material. Inlays give scope for letting out or for modification in styling after the garment has been cut and fitted. They should not exceed 2.5cm (1 in) in width, and they remain inside the garment when it is sewn together. The most useful places to leave the inlays are (for coats) along the centre back seam, side seam and shoulders of the fronts (foreparts) and back seam of the undersleeve; (for waistcoats) along the centre back seam and the side seam of the back; and (for trousers) along the centre back seam (seat seam) and down the inside leg of the back (underside)

leaf edge outside edge of the collar

pattern lay method of laying the pattern parts on to the material prior to cutting, in order to effect the most economical use of the material

rock of eye drawing the outline of a pattern or part of a pattern without use of a system or guide lines. This requires judgement and experience to obtain the correct shape

scye old tailoring term for the armhole. Thought to be a contraction of the word arms-eye, a term still in use in the United States

seat angle slope or angle of the seat line on the back pattern of the trousers

topside front pattern of the trousers (see also *underside*)

trimmings additional features required to finish the various garments – linings, interlinings, buttons, braids, silk facings and velvet collars

underside back pattern of the trousers (see also *topside*)

underwrap the right front of a double-breasted garment, where the left front fastens over the right front

vent an opening in the garment from the hem to a specified point above. Whereas a slit would be an edge-to-edge opening, one side of the vent opening overlaps the other (usually left over right) e.g. centre vent, cuff vent and short side vent (at the bottom of pantaloons)

ILLUSTRATION INDEX

Figures and Diagrams

The Figures (Fig.) are illustrations of a particular garment. The Diagrams (Dia.) are the patterns for the Figures.

Plates

Illustrations

Miscellaneous

Sketches

BIBLIOGRAPHY

BRUHN and TILKE, *A Pictorial History of Costume,* Praeger, 1955.

CALTHROP, D.C., *English Costume,* A & C Black, 1907.

CUNNINGTON, C.W., *Handbook of English Costume in the Nineteenth Century,* Faber and Faber, 1959.

CUNNINGTON, C.W., and P.E., *A Dictionary of English Costume,* Black, 1960.

KOHLER, C., *A History of Costume,* David McKay Company, 1928.

LAVER, J., *A Concise History of Costume,* Thames and Hudson, 1969.

LESTER, K.M., *Historic Costume,* Manual Arts Press, 1925.

LIBERTY, J.E., *Practical Tailoring,* Pitman, 1933.

McCLELLAN, E., *History of American Costume 1607-1870,* Tudor Publishing Co., 1942.

SICHEL, M., *The Victorians,* Batsford Costume reference Series, 6,Batsford, 1986.

THORNTON, J., *Sectional System of Gentlemen's Garments,* Thornton Institute, 1892.

THORNTON, J., *International System of Gentlemen's Garments,* Thornton Institute, 1907.

UZANNE, O., *Fashion in Paris,* Heineman, 1901

VINCENT, W.D.F., *Cutter's Practical Guide,* 1893.

WARWICK, E. and PITZ, H.C., *Early American Costume,* The Century Co., 1929

WAUGH, N., *The Cut of Men's Clothes 1600-1900,* Faber and Faber, 1964.

INDEX